365 DAY DEVOTIONAL

WHOLLY ADDICTED

God sets you totally free from addictions of your natural man's flesh and replaces them with holy spiritual addictions to be used for His Glory and His Kingdom.

JoAnn Koening

Stouthearted Publishing

This book is dedicated to my Lord and Savior,
Christ Jesus,
who breathes His breath into my lungs every morning
and causes my bones to sing praises to Him

to my beloved husband,
Mark Eugene Koening,
who has taught me that being happy is a choice

to my three children,
**Stacy Lynn Davis, Jack Alexander Davis, Jr., and Jeanna Ann Davis
Freeman,**
who are all miracles from God

to my two grandchildren,
Tarry Beck Hewitt and Trista Sunshine Hewitt,
who are blessings from God

to my **readers**,
whose hearts, spirits, and lives God plans to work the miraculous in

and In Loving Memory of my big sister,
Barbara Lynn Richardson
who taught me the importance of both telling and showing love

God graced me with the blessed opportunity to be at my sister's bedside with
her hand in mine as she took her first breath in Heaven on August 19, 2016.

HOLY: dedicated, consecrated or connected to God or a godly purpose; sacred

WHOLLY: to the full or entire extent; completely; to the exclusion of other things

ADDICTION: an insatiable appetite or thirst that cannot be quenched

ADDICTED: unable to do without something or someone without incurring adverse effects

Author's Personal Testimony

When I began experimenting with drugs and alcohol, I didn't plan to spend the next 30 years of my life doing it. With every substance I abused, it started out with me just wanting to "try it". However, it didn't turn out that way. That's the way sin is. Sin kept me much longer than I planned to stay; sin took me much farther than I planned to go; sin made me spend more money than I planned to spend.

The truth I want to make very clear is that it was always my choice, and I take full responsibility for it all. During those 30 very long years of daily abusing substances, I knew what it was to wake up with a total blackout of the previous night; not being able to remember anything I said, or did, the night before. I knew what it was to wake up every morning, and the first thought I had was taking inventory of what drugs and alcohol I had on hand for that day. I knew what it was to be in bondage and to be a prisoner of sin.

Now, I wake up with my mind stayed on Jesus and fresh praise on my lips to start the day! Now (after having been totally arrested by God's unconditional love), I am signed (in the Lamb's Book of Life), sealed (by His Holy Spirit), and delivered to the point of being totally set free! I know what it is to be not only delivered, but set totally free! Now, I am wholly addicted to Jesus and to the ministry of His saints! I am 100% 'souled' out to Jesus! I am Redeemed! I am an Overcomer! I am a Disciple of Christ Jesus!

"If you abide in My word, you are My disciples indeed. And you shall know the truth, and the truth shall make you free. Therefore if the Son makes you free, you shall be free indeed." (John 8:31,32,36)

My past is redeemed! My present makes sense! My future is secure! I am a finisher! I am a praiser and a worshiper! God saved me in spite of me. Then He filled me and baptized me with His Holy Ghost! What God has done for me, He can and will do for you, too! He's calling you right now. Do you hear Him? Will you choose to answer Him and call on the Name of Jesus today? I am an Overcomer by the Blood of the Lamb, and by the word of my testimony (Revelation 12:11). After 30 years of daily substance abuse (which included various illegal drugs as well as prescription drugs, alcohol, and cigarettes), I have been living a victorious and fruitful life in Christ Jesus for 18 years. All it took for me was JESUS (No AA, no support meetings) — ONLY JESUS! He did it for me, and He can and will do it for you!

God, because of His unconditional love for me, set me totally free from every single one of my fleshly addictions and replaced them with holy addictions to use for His Glory and His Kingdom! God does not love me any more than He loves you! God is more than able, and He is willing to do the very same for you!

Are you ready?

{ FOREWORD }

On six different occasions, I had very distinct and amazing encounters with Christ, one for each of the following Scriptures. Oh, yes, Jesus makes personal house calls! He is a big God, but also takes the time to be a personal God to those who love Him and are called according to His purpose.

Isaiah 43:25 "I, even I, am the one who wipes out your transgressions for My own sake, and I will not remember your sins."

Jeremiah 29:11 "For I know the plans I have for you," declares the LORD, "plans to prosper you and not to harm you, plans to give you hope and a future."

Jeremiah 31:16-17 "Thus says the LORD: "Refrain your voice from weeping, and your eyes from tears; for your work shall be rewarded," says the LORD, "and they shall come back from the land of the enemy. There is hope in your future," says the LORD, "that your children shall come back to their own border."

1Corinthians 16:15-16 "I beseech you, brethren, (ye know the house of Stephanas, that it is the firstfruits of Achaia, and that they have addicted themselves to the ministry of the saints,) that ye submit yourselves unto such, and to everyone that helpeth with us, and laboureth."

Hebrews 12:1-2 "Therefore we also, since we are surrounded by so great a cloud of witnesses, let us lay aside every weight, and the sin which so easily ensnares us, and let us run with endurance the race that is set before us, looking unto Jesus, the author and finisher of our faith, who for the joy that was set before Him endured the cross, despising the shame, and has sat down at the right hand of the throne of God."

2 Timothy 4:7-8 "I have fought the good fight, I have finished the race, I have kept the faith. Finally, there is laid up for me the crown of righteousness, which the Lord, the righteous Judge, will give to me on that Day, and not to me only but also to all who have loved His appearing."

As in the 1 Corinthians 16:15-16, I too have holy addictions. I am (w)hol(l)y addicted to Jesus and to the ministry of His saints, to staying in His presence, to experiencing His glory, to being a soul-winner for God's Kingdom, to praising and worshiping God, to talking to God (praying) and having a relationship with God, and to reading and studying and meditating on God's Word just to name a few. I am always hungry and thirsty for more of Jesus. Jesus and I are connected. Jesus is my Answer to living a God-filled and godly life.

Praising, worshiping, and talking to God is what I do first thing in the morning, throughout the day, and before I go to sleep at night. An example of my first morning praise goes like this, "Thank You, Lord, for waking me up on this glorious God morning and starting me on my way! Thank You, Lord, for putting Your breath in my lungs and giving me a new day to be about my Father's business! I am so happy to be at Your service! How will You use me today, Lord? Thank You, Jesus, that this is the very first day of the rest of my life! Dear Jesus, You sacrificed Your very life for me, so I CHOOSE to make every single minute of this day and every day that You gift me with count for You, all to the glory of our Heavenly Father!"

Seven years ago, I was led by God's Holy Spirit to begin sharing "Scripture of the Day". At that time, I was working full-time (outside the home) and sent this out via email first thing in the morning before any of my co-workers had arrived. It was my desire that all my co-workers see it first thing every morning, to start their workday off right. Presently, I am a full-time worker (at home). Jesus and I built a website together. I was strongly encouraged (by man) to join social media sites, for the purpose of marketing the website, so it would be found. God had another plan and purpose for me joining social media sites! At His leading, I began using the social media to post "Praise to Start Your Day".

An example of the format I use goes much like this:

"PRAISE TO START YOUR DAY:

Happy Monday, Jesus and everyone! JESUS SAVES AND SO MUCH MORE!!!

"For My thoughts are not your thoughts, nor are your ways My ways," says the Lord. "For as the heavens are higher than the earth, so are My ways higher than your ways, and My thoughts than your thoughts."

(Isaiah 55:8,9 NKJV)

There have been times when God answered my prayers and I said, "I would have never thought my prayer would be answered in that way! I never would have even imagined God working it out like that!" I learned a long time ago to stop wasting my time trying to figure out how God is going to do it. In fact, I now say to God, "I don't need to know how You're going to do it. I just know You're going to do it! I judge You "Faithful", Oh God!"

CHOOSE TO MAKE TODAY AND EVERY DAY GREAT AND BLESSED NO MATTER WHAT!

#PerpetualPraise #ContinualPrayer #WorshipInSpiritAndTruth"

God has kept me faithful and consistent in sharing "Praise to Start Your Day" every single day for the past seven years. My Bishop, Steve Fender, has always taught the vital importance of being consistent with God and the things of God, if you want your faith and your witness of Christ Jesus to be effective. From the first day the "Scripture of The Day" email was sent out to my small group of co-workers, I did not know what God's Master Plan for it was. Only God knows His Master Plan. I just knew that I had heard from the Lord, and it was my desire to be obedient.

Recently, I was again led by God's Holy Spirit to intertwine my personal testimony and "Praise to Start Your Day" into a book to be used by God. I have learned, many times the hard way, that obedience is better than sacrifice, as far as God and our spiritual leaders are concerned.

"So Samuel said: "Has the Lord as great delight in burnt offerings and sacrifices, as in obeying the voice of the Lord? Behold, to obey is better than sacrifice, and to heed than the fat of rams." (1 Samuel 15:22) "But you must remain faithful to the things you have been taught. You know they are true, for you know you can trust those who taught you." (2 Timothy 3:14 NLT)

Thus, the birth of WHOLLY ADDICTED.

Mission of WHOLLY ADDICTED

The mission and purpose of this book WHOLLY ADDICTED is manifold, as follows: to glorify God; to increase the Kingdom of God; to help others grow in their knowledge and understanding of the truths of God and God's

Word, and in their relationship with Jesus; and to encourage others and give them hope in God.

Vision of WHOLLY ADDICTED

The vision of this book WHOLLY ADDICTED is threefold, as follows: Bringing its readers face to face in Heaven; seeing its readers in Heaven as Jesus sees you even now today, which is as you will be when your life has been miraculously and gloriously transformed by Him; and praising and worshiping God together with you throughout all eternity.

Along with the personal examples already shared for starting your day with God through praise and worship, you will now have access to a Scripture reading for each day (365 days) throughout the year, plus comments for each Scripture to assist you with real-world application. This book, in its totality, contains over 400 Scriptures from God's Word. Praise and worship go hand-in-hand, yet there is a difference. Praise is you thanking God (1) for all that He has already done in your life, (2) for all that He is now even today doing in your life, and (3) for all that He will do in your life. When you praise God, He comes down to you and meets you right where you are. Worship is wholeheartedly loving God just for *who* He is, the Great I Am. Your wholehearted worship goes straight up to God.

I don't know where you are in your own personal spiritual walk and relationship with Jesus. Only Jesus and you know. Perhaps you have not yet begun your walk and relationship with Jesus. But this one thing I am sure of: you can never praise Jesus enough! If God woke you up this morning, you can praise Him for life.

My prayer is that we all will continually be drawn closer to the Lord, as we seek Him, and grow in our daily walk and relationship with Him, in the blessed name of Jesus! Amen, amen, and amen!!!

The Prayer of Salvation (see below) is for anyone who needs JESUS in your life and has a strong desire to have your life changed for the better and KNOW that you will have eternal life in Heaven with JESUS. If that is you, say this prayer out loud to Jesus (no matter where you are today).

Prayer of Salvation:

"Jesus, I confess to You that I am a sinner. I believe that You are the Son of God, born of the Virgin Mary, that You shed Your precious blood and died for every one of my sins. I believe You were buried, and that three days later You arose from the grave and are now sitting at the right hand of Father God, interceding for me. Jesus, I believe that You are here with me right now and can hear me. I invite You, Jesus, to come into my heart and live in me. I repent, Lord Jesus! Take away all my sins and change me to be like You. I need Your help, Jesus! PLEASE HELP ME, JESUS! Write my name down in the Lamb's Book of Life. Jesus, I believe in my heart and confess with my mouth that You have heard me and that I AM SAVED RIGHT NOW! I confess it, I believe it, I receive it, and I claim it! I will follow You for the rest of my days, Jesus! Thank You, Jesus, for dying for me and giving me eternal life with You, in the Blessed Name of Jesus! Amen, amen, and amen!"

Overcomer's Statement of Faith:

I am an Overcomer. I am a Christian. I believe the Word of God, the Blood of Jesus Christ, and the Power of the Holy Spirit. I am anointed by faith to speak the Word of God; to proclaim victory over all my situations and circumstances. Therefore, I am the head and not the tail; I am above only and not beneath; I am highly favored. God calls me His Child, Jesus calls me Redeemed, and men call me Blessed. I am an Overcomer!

Now, may God's Holy Spirit totally arrest you with His unconditional love.

{DAY 1}

PRAISE TO START YOUR DAY:

"And she conceived again and bore a son, and said, 'Now I will praise the LORD.' Therefore she called his name Judah..." (Genesis 29:35 NKJV)

The first time Praise is mentioned in the Bible is in Genesis, the very first book. That shows the importance of our praise to God. Thank You, Lord, for creating Your people to praise and worship You. Lord, Your word says that You inhabit the praises of Your people. That means that when you praise God, your praise brings You into God's very presence, and in His presence is fullness of joy! Your spirit is refreshed and restored in God's presence. Miracles happen in your life when you praise the Lord! Praise enables you to stay focused on Jesus rather than on your problems. Praise keeps the enemy away from you because the enemy hates praise. Lord, You alone are worthy of all praise all the time!

CHOOSE TO MAKE TODAY AND EVERY DAY GREAT AND BLESSED NO MATTER WHAT!

#PerpetualPraise #ContinualPrayer #WorshipInSpiritAndTruth

{DAY 2}

PRAISE TO START YOUR DAY:

"Thou wilt keep him in perfect peace, whose mind is stayed on Thee: because he trusteth in Thee. Trust ye in the Lord forever: for in the Lord JEHOVAH is everlasting strength:" (Isaiah 26:3-4 KJV)

I praise and worship You, my Jehovah-Shalom, for You are the Lord my Peace! Lord, help me and the reader(s) as we go through this day and every day to keep our minds fixed on You. When we keep our minds fixed on You, then You will keep us in perfect peace, even in the midst of troubled times. Lord Jesus, all my faith and trust is in You, and only You. I judge You faithful always. I pray this in the blessed Name of Jesus! Amen, amen, and amen!!!

CHOOSE TO MAKE TODAY AND EVERY DAY GREAT AND BLESSED NO MATTER WHAT!

#PerpetualPraise #ContinualPrayer #WorshipInSpiritAndTruth

{DAY 3}

PRAISE TO START YOUR DAY:

"Every good gift and every perfect gift is from above, and cometh down from the Father of lights, with whom is no variableness, neither shadow of turning. Blessed be the Lord, who daily loadeth us with benefits, even the God of our salvation. Selah." (James 1:17 & Psalm 68:19 KJV)

Thank You, oh God, that everything good which comes into our lives is from You, and You never change Your mind. You are always the same, and You cannot change. You will always complete the works that You begin in us, from the moment of our salvation when we turn our lives completely over to You. Your goodness begins each morning when You wake us up and breathe Your breath into our lungs, and then start us on our way. We praise and worship You, Lord God Almighty!

CHOOSE TO MAKE TODAY AND EVERY DAY GREAT AND BLESSED NO MATTER WHAT!

#PerpetualPraise #ContinualPrayer #WorshipInSpiritAndTruth

{DAY 4}

PRAISE TO START YOUR DAY:

"The Lord will perfect that which concerneth me: thy mercy, O Lord, endureth forever: forsake not the works of thine own hands." (Psalm 138:8 KJV)

Thank You, Lord, for waking me up on this glorious God morning with my mind stayed on You. It is well with my soul, Lord, because I believe that You will complete all Your promises and purposes for me and all of my loved ones. Lord, You fearfully and wonderfully created me and formed me with Your own hands, so I know You will not forsake me. I also understand that, in order for me to have a strong and close relationship with You, which I desire so much, I need to talk to you throughout each and every day. You are my constant companion, and I want You to consider me Your constant companion, too. I desire for our relationship to be so close that, when You hear my voice, it moves You to say, "Yes, there's my 'lil' buddy'"! I praise and worship You, Lord! I love You, Jesus!

CHOOSE TO MAKE TODAY AND EVERY DAY GREAT AND BLESSED NO MATTER WHAT!

#PerpetualPraise #ContinualPrayer #WorshipInSpiritAndTruth

{DAY 5}

"Are not five sparrows sold for two farthings, and not one of them is forgotten before God? But even the very hairs of your head are all numbered. Fear not therefore: ye are of more value than many sparrows." (Luke 12:6-7 KJV)

Lord, I love this Scripture! It reminds me of the words to the song "His Eye Is on the Sparrow": "I sing because I'm happy, I sing because I'm free, His eye is on the sparrow and I know He's watching me." Lord, you never overlook a single sparrow. The truth that You have numbered the very hairs on my head tells me how valuable I am to you! If you are reading this, do not let anybody "bully-talk" you into making you feel like you are worthless. God is letting you know through this Scripture that you are of great worth to Him! God Himself created and formed you just as He pleased, right down to every hair on your head! Then God saw what He had made, and it was good. Oh, praise God! Thank You, Jesus!

CHOOSE TO MAKE TODAY AND EVERY DAY GREAT AND BLESSED NO MATTER WHAT!

#PerpetualPraise #ContinualPrayer #WorshipInSpiritAndTruth

{DAY 6}

PRAISE TO START YOUR DAY:

"But You, O LORD, are a shield for me, my glory and the One who lifts up my head. I cried to the LORD with my voice, and He heard me from His holy hill. Selah, I lay down and slept; I awoke, for the LORD sustained me." (Psalm 3:3-5 NKJV)

Thank You, Lord, for waking me up on this glorious God morning and starting me on my way! I worship You, Jehovah-Kabodhi, for You are the Lord my Glory. When people hear my testimony, they look at me and say, "But you don't look like that!" Thank You, oh God, that I don't look like what I have been through, because You have fully restored and preserved me for Your use. You shield me from all harm, sickness, and disease. You have lifted my head because You have taken away all shame and pain from my past. I confess that I have the mind of Christ and I am healthy, wealthy, and wise with Godly wisdom! I confess only the Word of God over my life! To God be all the glory, praise, honor, power, and thanks, for He alone is Worthy!

CHOOSE TO MAKE TODAY AND EVERY DAY GREAT AND BLESSED NO MATTER WHAT!

#PerpetualPraise #ContinualPrayer #WorshipInSpiritAndTruth

{DAY 7}

PRAISE TO START YOUR DAY:

"I was glad when they said unto me, 'Let us go into the house of the LORD. And let us consider one another to provoke unto love and to good works: Not forsaking the assembling of ourselves together, as the manner of some is; but exhorting one another: and so much the more, as ye see the day approaching.'" (Psalm 122:1 & Hebrews 10:24-25 KJV)

Thank You, Lord, for waking me up on this glorious God morning and starting me on my way! It's time to rise and let our light shine! Jesus Himself tells us in Matthew 5:16 to let our light shine before men so they may see our good works and glorify our Father God. Lord, I love going to church and gathering with Your saints, for our spirits are all in one accord. Lord, your house is full of Your love and Your presence! Jesus, in these troubled and sinful times, we are seeing the day approaching for when You return. Even so, come quickly Lord Jesus!

CHOOSE TO MAKE TODAY AND EVERY DAY GREAT AND BLESSED NO MATTER WHAT!

#PerpetualPraise #ContinualPrayer #WorshipInSpiritAndTruth

{DAY 8}

PRAISE TO START YOUR DAY:

"Oh that men would praise the Lord for his goodness, and for his wonderful works to the children of men! And let them sacrifice the sacrifices of thanksgiving, and declare his works with rejoicing." (Psalm 107:21-22 KJV)

I praise You, Lord Jesus, for it is You Who saved and delivered me from a life of sin, which would have resulted in eternal separation from You. Oh, my God, that would have been horrible far beyond man's imagination! I rejoice that You put me on Your Potter's wheel and made me a brand-new creation—unrecognizable from the old me! You changed everything about me—my heart, my thoughts, my feelings, my desires, my health, my countenance, my likes and dislikes, my choices, my friends—literally everything! I give You the honor You deserve, my Jesus! I give the new, re-created me as my gift and sacrifice back to You, along with all thanksgiving, praise, and worship. To the reader(s) of this, I pray it encourages you. JESUS LOVES YOU just as much as He loves me, and HE WILL do the very same for you, too, if that is what you desire.

CHOOSE TO MAKE TODAY AND EVERY DAY GREAT AND BLESSED NO MATTER WHAT!

#PerpetualPraise #ContinualPrayer #WorshipInSpiritAndTruth

{DAY 9}

PRAISE TO START YOUR DAY:

"Because he hath set his love upon Me, therefore will I deliver him: I will set him on high, because he hath known My name. With long life will I satisfy him, and show him My salvation." (Psalm 91:14,16 KJV)

Lord, You loved me first, while I was still living a life full of sin. I had abandoned You, and ignored You for so very long. Yet You still loved me unconditionally and kept calling me to come back to You. God, You are Love! Love conquers all! Lord, when I did come back to You I placed my love in You, and that is where my love remains today. You are a good God all the time, and all the time You are good! I worship You, Jehovah-Mephalti, for You are the Lord my Deliverer! You are Lord over all, Savior of the world, and Giver of salvation. You are my Everything, my All-in-All!

CHOOSE TO MAKE TODAY AND EVERY DAY GREAT AND BLESSED NO MATTER WHAT!

#PerpetualPraise #ContinualPrayer #WorshipInSpiritAndTruth

{DAY 10}

PRAISE TO START YOUR DAY:

"Lord, You have been our dwelling place in all generations. Before the mountains were brought forth, or ever You had formed the earth and the world, even from everlasting to everlasting, You are God." (Psalm 90:1-2 NKJV)

Lord, You have always been a home for us. God has always existed. God and everything about Him is eternal and timeless—no beginning and no ending. God is Love and His love for you and me is eternal. Jesus is alive and He always will be. You, too, can build your home in Jesus. You can begin even now today. This is the very first day of the rest of your life.

CHOOSE TO MAKE TODAY AND EVERY DAY GREAT AND BLESSED NO MATTER WHAT!

#PerpetualPraise #ContinualPrayer #WorshipInSpiritAndTruth

{DAY 11}

"For the bread of God is he which cometh down from heaven, and giveth life unto the world. And Jesus said unto them, 'I am the bread of life: he that cometh to me shall never hunger; and he that believeth on me shall never thirst.'" (John 6:33,35 KJV)

Jesus Himself is the Bread of God and the Living Water. Jesus is God's Word made flesh. You may eat and drink as much and as often as you need to, want to, and choose to—in this instance, the more the better! When God saves you, delivers you, and frees you from your natural man's addictions, your spirit man needs to immediately begin feeding and filling up on God's Word and the things of God, to replace those other things you were feeding yourself. God desires for you to be dependent on Him alone for the well-being of your soul (mind, will, emotions), body, and spirit. Put all your faith and trust in Jesus. He will never disappoint you. Happy eating and drinking, everyone!

CHOOSE TO MAKE TODAY AND EVERY DAY GREAT AND BLESSED NO MATTER WHAT!

#PerpetualPraise #ContinualPrayer #WorshipInSpiritAndTruth

{DAY 12}

"How sweet are thy words unto my taste! Yea, sweeter than honey to my mouth! Thy word is very pure: therefore thy servant loveth it." (Psalm 119:103, 140 KJV)

Lord, the truth of Your Word is so delightful and pleasant to my spiritual taste. Your Word is wholesome, beneficial, and health-giving. Lord, I am wholly addicted to Your Word. I eat it, digest it, and still want more. I can never get enough of You and Your Word! May I always want more of Your Word than I am able to take in, in the blessed Name of Jesus! Amen, amen, and amen!!!

CHOOSE TO MAKE TODAY AND EVERY DAY GREAT AND BLESSED NO MATTER WHAT!

#PerpetualPraise #ContinualPrayer #WorshipInSpiritAndTruth

{DAY 13}

PRAISE TO START YOUR DAY:

"Therefore, my beloved brethren, be steadfast, immovable, always abounding in the work of the Lord, knowing that your labor is not in vain in the Lord." (1 Corinthians 15:58 NKJV)

WE CHOOSE to make our life here on earth worthwhile as we work for God and serve Him and His Kingdom, and WE KNOW that none of our labor in the Lord is wasted, neither is it done for nothing, because WE KNOW that we have a hereafter eternal life with Jesus promised to us. God is faithful and true and just! Therefore, remain firmly determined and set in carrying out all work that God gives you to do for Him. Be that person who does not yield, or give in, to worldly arguments and pressure which are opposed to God. As a result, you will have an abundance of spiritual fruit and harvest. Praise God!

CHOOSE TO MAKE TODAY AND EVERY DAY GREAT AND BLESSED NO MATTER WHAT!

#PerpetualPraise #ContinualPrayer #WorshipInSpiritAndTruth

{DAY 14}

"I pray that out of his glorious riches he may strengthen you with power through his Spirit in your inner being, so that Christ may dwell in your hearts through faith. And I pray that you, being rooted and established in love, may have power, together with all the Lord's holy people, to grasp how wide and long and high and deep is the love of Christ, and to know this love that surpasses knowledge—that you may be filled to the measure of all the fullness of God. Now to him who is able to do immeasurably more than all we ask or imagine, according to his power that is at work within us, to him be glory in the church and in Christ Jesus throughout all generations, for ever and ever! Amen." (Ephesians 3:16-21 NIV)

Jesus is rich in love, hope, faith, power to save and deliver, strength, knowledge, understanding, grace, mercy, forgiveness His unconditional love being the most important. When we, through faith, open up our hearts to Jesus, allowing Him to make His home there and sit on His throne there, God fills us up to the same measure of fullness as Christ Jesus with His Holy Spirit. Then Jesus transforms us completely into a gloriously beautiful new creation, who in turn glorifies God. I am praying this prayer for you today, in the blessed Name of Jesus. Amen, Amen, and Amen.

CHOOSE TO MAKE TODAY AND EVERY DAY GREAT AND BLESSED NO MATTER WHAT!

#PerpetualPraise #ContinualPrayer #WorshipInSpiritAndTruth

{DAY 15}

"I will extol thee, my God, O king; and I will bless thy name for ever and ever. Every day will I bless thee; and I will praise thy name forever and ever. Great is the Lord, and greatly to be praised; and his greatness is unsearchable." (Psalm 145:1-3 KJV)

I am wholly addicted to praising You, Jesus, and that's a good thing. I praise You with great enthusiasm and with a loud voice. All my praise belongs to You! I love to praise You! I could never overpraise You because You are Worthy of more praise—over the greatest amount of praise I am capable of giving You—even more than praising You so often that it seems never-ending. I praise You even before the promise has visually manifested. I praise You at all times and in everything I am going through, and then I praise You when You have brought me through victoriously. Praise is who I am and Praise is what I do!

CHOOSE TO MAKE TODAY AND EVERY DAY GREAT AND BLESSED NO MATTER WHAT!

#PerpetualPraise #ContinualPrayer #WorshipInSpiritAndTruth

{DAY 16}

PRAISE TO START YOUR DAY:

"The Lord is gracious, and full of compassion; slow to anger, and of great mercy. The Lord is good to all: and his tender mercies are over all his works. All thy works shall praise thee, O Lord; and thy saints shall bless thee. They shall speak of the glory of thy kingdom, and talk of thy power." (Psalm 145:8-11 KJV)

Thank You, Lord, for waking me up on this glorious God morning, pouring Your lovingkindness, grace, and mercy on me! Lord, we the saints are the ones who make up Your Kingdom here on earth. May we always reflect Your glory through every praise that comes out of our mouths, and may we always share with others about how powerful You are to change lives. I pray this in the blessed Name of Jesus, Name above every name! Amen, amen, and amen!!!

CHOOSE TO MAKE TODAY AND EVERY DAY GREAT AND BLESSED NO MATTER WHAT!

#PerpetualPraise #ContinualPrayer #WorshipInSpiritAndTruth

{DAY 17}

"Happy is that people, that is in such a case: yea, happy is that people, whose God is the Lord." (Psalm 144:15 KJV)

Thank You, Lord, for waking me up on this glorious God morning! I worship You, Lord. You are the one and only true and living God and Lord over all. I'm so grateful that I belong to You and You belong to me. You are my personal Lord and Savior, and You sit on the throne of my heart. You make all things well with my soul. As with all things, happiness is a choice and I am so happy that I came to myself and chose You, Jesus! You make me truly happy from the inside to the outside, and I choose to be happy.

JESUS = HAPPY!

CHOOSE TO MAKE TODAY AND EVERY DAY GREAT AND BLESSED NO MATTER WHAT!

#PerpetualPraise #ContinualPrayer #WorshipInSpiritAndTruth

{DAY 18}

PRAISE TO START YOUR DAY:

"But seek ye first the kingdom of God, and his righteousness; and all these things shall be added unto you." (Matthew 6:33 KJV)

Dear Lord, may I walk through this day and all the rest of my days always seeking You and Your righteousness first above all things. I seek You through praise and worship; I seek You through Your Word; I seek You through talking to You; I seek You all the time and everywhere. Glory be to God, I always find You because You want to be found. You are never hidden to those who have the desire in their heart to find You. I begin first thing every morning seeking You; I seek You throughout the day; and I seek You every evening. I worship You, my Jehovah-Jireh, for You are the God my Provider! You provide me with everything I need, and You know just what I need and when I need it. It is You Who gives me the power to gain wealth! I praise You and thank You in advance for a most productive day today! You are such an amazing and awesome God!

CHOOSE TO MAKE TODAY AND EVERY DAY GREAT AND BLESSED NO MATTER WHAT!

#PerpetualPraise #ContinualPrayer #WorshipInSpiritAndTruth

{DAY 19}

PRAISE TO START YOUR DAY:

"If the Son therefore shall make you free, ye shall be free indeed." (John 8:36 KJV)

Thank You, Lord, for waking me up on this glorious God morning with my mind stayed on You! Oh Lord, You have been so good to me! I just can't tell it all! I just can't praise You enough! Lord, I thank You for the freedom to be honest about where You have brought me from. You brought me out of a deep, dark hole—a hole too deep and dark to climb out of without Your Light, Strength, and Guidance—and You have made me whole. I am no longer bound. You have brought me such a mighty long way, and You have been right by my side every step of the way. I have great joy and peace in knowing where You're still going to take me! Dear reader(s) who may be in that deep, dark hole I was once in for so long—look up and see His Light and simply ask Jesus to help you today. If you don't know how to pray, that's OK. Just say, "JESUS!" Jesus knows your heart and will hear you and come to help you. He promises He will.

CHOOSE TO MAKE TODAY AND EVERY DAY GREAT AND BLESSED NO MATTER WHAT!

#PerpetualPraise #ContinualPrayer #WorshipInSpiritAndTruth

{DAY 20}

PRAISE TO START YOUR DAY:

"Jesus Christ the same yesterday, and today, and for- ever." (Hebrews 13:8 KJV)

Thank You, Lord, for waking me up on this glorious God morning with more faith and expectancy than ever before! Jesus, You have been faithful, tried, and true in my life. I have learned this not only from the Bible, but even more from experiencing You personally—when You saved me, delivered me, the times You have healed me, when You provided food for my children and me when I was a single mother with three teenagers, and the list goes on. From the moment my heart and my soul started longing to come back to You, You heard. You have been so good to me! Thank You for Your unconditional love that totally arrested me that night and saved me! You are my Rock of Salvation! You are my Bright and Morning Star! You are the only One I know Who never changes. Even Your Word says it, and Your Word is true. I love You forever and ever!

CHOOSE TO MAKE TODAY AND EVERY DAY GREAT AND BLESSED NO MATTER WHAT!

#PerpetualPraise #ContinualPrayer #WorshipInSpiritAndTruth

{DAY 21}

PRAISE TO START YOUR DAY:

"I will sing of the mercies of the Lord forever: with my mouth will I make known thy faithfulness to all generations. And the heavens shall praise thy wonders, O Lord: thy faithfulness also in the congregation of the saints." (Psalm 89:1,5 KJV)

I have had the privilege of singing praise and worship songs to the Lord with Living Praise Choir (LPC) at Livingway Church in San Antonio, Texas, for the last 17+ years. Since I have always been shy by nature, I seldom look in people's faces. I just keep my eyes looking up to Jesus, because He is Who I am singing to, while we are ushering His presence into the sanctuary. To be perfectly honest, I do not consider my voice as sounding as great as the voices of some of my LPC cohorts. However, God does know that I am singing wholeheartedly to Him, and He puts His anointing on my voice. I am happy about that because I always want my song to be sweet-sounding to Jesus! Singing praise and worship with LPC continues to take me to new dimensions in Christ Jesus. No matter what your voice sounds like to you, whether great or not so great, as long as you are singing from deep within your heart directly to Jesus He is going to show up and show out for you! Joyful singing, everyone!

CHOOSE TO MAKE TODAY AND EVERY DAY GREAT AND BLESSED NO MATTER WHAT!

#PerpetualPraise #ContinualPrayer #WorshipInSpiritAndTruth

{DAY 22}

"I will lead the blind by ways they have not known, along unfamiliar paths I will guide them; I will turn the darkness into light before them and make the rough places smooth. These are the things I will do; I will not forsake them." (Isaiah 42:16 NIV)

Dear reader(s), perhaps you grew up not having been taken to church regularly—maybe not at all. If that is your testimony, that's OK. Once you come to Jesus, He will place your hand in His and show you the right path to take to have life, and life more abundantly. He will turn the darkness of your life into a life full of His light, where you will want to stay. He will make your life smoother and easier. Perhaps you have tried reading the Bible, but cannot understand it. That's OK. Jesus will open your eyes of understanding and help you to understand what you are reading, if you ask Him to. I didn't understand the Bible when I first started reading it. So, I got a good study Bible and started with the Book of John in the New Testament. The more I asked the Lord to help me understand what I was reading, He did, and the more I began to understand! Thank You, Jesus, that no matter where we are in our life, all we have to do is let You put our hand in Yours and You will lead us. Thank You, Jesus, that in Your presence is our light.

CHOOSE TO MAKE TODAY AND EVERY DAY GREAT AND BLESSED NO MATTER WHAT!

#PerpetualPraise #ContinualPrayer #WorshipInSpiritAndTruth

{DAY 23}

"But the path of the just is as the shining light, that shineth more and more unto the perfect day." (Proverbs 4:18 KJV)

When you make Jesus your righteous path and your light, He will enable your knowledge and understanding of Him to keep growing and become ever clearer, until that day when you see Him face to face and just as He is. Jesus is the Son of Righteousness! Thank You, Jesus! I praise You and thank You for keeping me on the right path! Jesus, You are my Bright and Morning Star!

CHOOSE TO MAKE TODAY AND EVERY DAY GREAT AND BLESSED NO MATTER WHAT!

#PerpetualPraise #ContinualPrayer #WorshipInSpiritAndTruth

{DAY 24}

PRAISE TO START YOUR DAY:

"The Lord by wisdom hath founded the earth; by understanding hath he established the heavens. By his knowledge the depths are broken up, and the clouds drop down the dew." (Proverbs 3:19-20 KJV)

Oh God, You are Jehovah-Bara, the Creator of all, and I praise and worship You always in the firmament of Your power! By His wisdom, God created all. God perfected wisdom in Himself. God's wisdom caused everything to be that is, and God's wisdom has preserved it all. By God's knowledge, He broke up the deepest parts of the earth to make water available for us. He caused the clouds in the sky to drop down the dew, so we would have rain. We should always seek the wisdom, knowledge, and understanding of God, and not of man.

CHOOSE TO MAKE TODAY AND EVERY DAY GREAT AND BLESSED NO MATTER WHAT!

#PerpetualPraise #ContinualPrayer #WorshipInSpiritAndTruth

{DAY 25}

"But Jesus answered them, 'My Father worketh hitherto, and I work.'"
(John 5:17 KJV)

Thank You, Lord, for waking us up on this glorious God morning and starting us on our way! Our Heavenly Daddy and our Lord and Savior Christ Jesus are always working on our behalf, 24/7/365! We should also be working for God and His Kingdom, and always have a grateful heart for the opportunity to serve our Lord. God's desire for our best is in His heart, and He will never stop working to see that His plans and promises for us are brought to completion.

CHOOSE TO MAKE TODAY AND EVERY DAY GREAT AND BLESSED NO MATTER WHAT!

#PerpetualPraise #ContinualPrayer #WorshipInSpiritAndTruth

{DAY 26}

PRAISE TO START YOUR DAY:

"I waited patiently for the Lord; and he inclined unto me, and heard my cry. He brought me up also out of a horrible pit, out of the miry clay, and set my feet upon a rock, and established my goings. And he hath put a new song in my mouth, even praise unto our God: many shall see it, and fear, and shall trust in the Lord. Blessed is that man that maketh the Lord his trust..." (Psalm 40:1-4 KJV)

You may be in the pit of destruction and bogged down with seemingly no human way to escape or to be set free. If that is you today, cry out to Jesus and wait patiently for Him. He will hear you and, until He brings you out (rest assured that He will), He will use your time in the pit to turn your heart to Him as you begin to hope and trust in Him alone. Put all your faith and trust in God, and you will be blessed! He can and will do it. He will set you up on a permanent basis upon Jesus, the Rock. As you begin telling others of God's goodness and they can see the changes He is making in your life, you will begin winning souls for God and His Kingdom! Imagine the excitement of that!

CHOOSE TO MAKE TODAY AND EVERY DAY GREAT AND BLESSED NO MATTER WHAT!

#PerpetualPraise #ContinualPrayer #WorshipInSpiritAndTruth

{DAY 27}

"The preparations of the heart in man, and the answer of the tongue, is from the Lord." (Proverbs 16:1 KJV)

The righteous man prepares and lays out his plans, but it is man's acknowledgment of God's help and blessing that causes those plans to prosper. The answer of the righteous man's tongue is God-inspired. He will give you the words to say and will speak through you. God has many divine appointments for you. If you are willing, God will position you right where He needs you to be in order to use you to speak on His behalf. God wins every time. Your part is to be obedient to God and trust that He will equip you. God will never send you without equipping you first. Even if you are feeling "out of your comfort zone", do what God's Holy Spirit is leading you to do and say what He tells you to say. Do this and God will make sure that you are always a winner, too.

CHOOSE TO MAKE TODAY AND EVERY DAY GREAT AND BLESSED NO MATTER WHAT!

#PerpetualPraise#ContinualPrayer#WorshipInSpiritAndTruth

{DAY 28}

PRAISE TO START YOUR DAY:

"I, Jesus, have sent My angel to testify to you these things in the churches. I am the Root and the Offspring of David, the Bright and Morning Star." (Revelation 22:16 NKJV)

Jesus Himself testifies to us and to the churches that Jesus "the Messiah" was a descendant of David. Jesus is also the Savior of the world. Jesus, You are the brightness of our Heavenly Father's glory—brilliantly and radiantly shining. There is no darkness in You, Jesus. You are a very solid Light! I praise and worship You, my Jesus, for You are my Bright and Morning Star. Thank You, Lord, for waking me up on this glorious God morning and starting me on my way! I get to attend church today, and I am glad about it! I praise and worship You! I love You forever and ever!

CHOOSE TO MAKE TODAY AND EVERY DAY GREAT AND BLESSED NO MATTER WHAT!

#PerpetualPraise #ContinualPrayer #WorshipInSpiritAndTruth

{DAY 29}

PRAISE TO START YOUR DAY:

"I delight to do Your will, O my God, and Your law is within my heart."
(Psalm 40:8 NKJV)

I love Your commandments, Oh God, for I know that with every commandment there is a blessing attached to it, if I am obedient. I keep Your commandments in my heart so that I will not forget them and so that I will not sin against You. Not my will, Lord, but may Your Will always be done in my life. Lord God, may everything I think, say, and do today and everyday be right in line with Your Will and glorifying to You, in the blessed Name of Jesus! Amen, amen, and amen!!!

CHOOSE TO MAKE TODAY AND EVERY DAY GREAT AND BLESSED NO MATTER WHAT!

#PerpetualPraise #ContinualPrayer #WorshipInSpiritAndTruth

{DAY 30}

PRAISE TO START YOUR DAY:

"But let me run loose and free, celebrating GOD's great work, every bone in my body laughing, singing, "GOD, there's no one like you. You put the down-and-out on their feet and protect the unprotected from bullies!" (Psalm 35:9-10 MSG)

Lord, You have delivered me and set me free from terrible situations and dangers of all kinds. You have brought me through the meanness and cruelty of evil-hearted men. Only You, oh God, have kept me alive to see this day. I am forever grateful and joyful, and I choose to no longer do those things I used to do, or put myself in dangerous situations. Instead, now I have a responsibility towards You, and I choose to serve You and Your Kingdom. I love You, Jesus, and my soul cries out, "Hallelujah! It is well with my soul!"

CHOOSE TO MAKE TODAY AND EVERY DAY GREAT AND BLESSED NO MATTER WHAT!

#PerpetualPraise #ContinualPrayer #WorshipInSpiritAndTruth

{DAY 31}

"Keep me safe, my God, for in you I take refuge. I say to the LORD, 'You are my Lord; apart from you I have no good thing.' I will praise the LORD, who counsels me; even at night my heart instructs me. I keep my eyes always on the LORD. With him at my right hand, I will not be shaken. You make known to me the path of life; you will fill me with joy in your presence, with eternal pleasures at your right hand." (Psalm 16:1-2,7-8,11 NIV)

I praise You, Lord, because I can be confident that You guard and protect me as I seek refuge in You. You are my safe-haven. I do not wait for an impending disaster, but take refuge in You daily. Nothing good is found outside of or apart from You. I praise You, Lord, for through Your counseling You show me how much You care for me. Even while I am sleeping, my heart meditates on You, Lord. As I stay in Your presence, You keep me from wavering so that my choice is to keep going in the right direction with You at my side. Thus, I remain joy-filled.

CHOOSE TO MAKE TODAY AND EVERY DAY GREAT AND BLESSED NO MATTER WHAT!

#PerpetualPraise #ContinualPrayer #WorshipInSpiritAndTruth

{DAY 32}

Let the word of Christ dwell in you richly in all wisdom, teaching and admonishing one another in psalms and hymns and spiritual songs, singing with grace in your hearts to the Lord. And whatever you do in word or deed, do all in the name of the Lord Jesus, giving thanks to God the Father through Him." (Colossians 3:16-17 NKJV)

Memorize Scripture until you have them in your heart and spirit so that nobody can ever take them from you, and then you may be able to minister to others. Sing from your heart to the Lord inside and outside of His house. If you enjoy singing, join the choir in the church you attend. It is a very blessed ministry to be a part of! Thank Jesus that this is the very first day of the rest of your life. CHOOSE to make every single minute of this day count to the glory of our Heavenly Father! May all your thoughts, words, and actions be a reflection of our Lord Jesus Christ. May God's grace abound in your life. This I pray for the reader(s), in the blessed Name of Jesus! Amen, amen, and amen!!!

CHOOSE TO MAKE TODAY AND EVERY DAY GREAT AND BLESSED NO MATTER WHAT!

#PerpetualPraise #ContinualPrayer #WorshipInSpiritAndTruth

{DAY 33}

"For God has not given us a spirit of fear, but of power and of love and of a sound mind." (2 Timothy 1:7 NKJV)

God's Holy Spirit is real. There is also a real spirit of fear, which works through our natural senses (sight, hearing, taste, smell, touch) and in our minds trying to deceive us in order to bring fear into us. God knows this and that's why He has given us His Holy Spirit Who gives us power over fear, perfect love that casts out all fear, and the soundness of mind of Christ Jesus. Yes, we see and hear about much evil and danger in the world today. However, we cannot allow this to turn us into fearful hermits who never want to leave our homes for fear of danger. We must not retreat from doing God's work for fear of displeasing man. Instead, get up every morning with courage and boldness to face the world and fight for God through the power of His Holy Spirit, saying, "I'm fired up and I'm ready to go!", and then put a praise on it! Thank You, Jesus, for giving us Your Holy Spirit! We praise You, Lord!

CHOOSE TO MAKE TODAY AND EVERY DAY GREAT AND BLESSED NO MATTER WHAT!

#PerpetualPraise #ContinualPrayer #WorshipInSpiritAndTruth

{DAY 34}

PRAISE TO START YOUR DAY:

"Rejoice in the Lord always: and again I say, Rejoice. And the peace of God, which passeth all understanding, shall keep your hearts and minds through Christ Jesus. Those things, which ye have both learned, and received, and heard, and seen in me, do: and the God of peace shall be with you." (Philippians 4:4,7,9 KJV)

I worship You, my Jehovah-Shalom, for You are my God of Peace! You can still have peace in your spirit, even when it seems your world is falling apart, even when danger is closing in on every side of you. Do you have that kind of peace today? Have you asked God for it? If not, just wholeheartedly say the name "Jesus", and He will come to your rescue. Ask your Heavenly Father to fill you with His Holy Spirit and with His Peace that goes beyond what you can understand. He will do it for you even right now today. Lord Jesus, we rejoice in You today!

CHOOSE TO MAKE TODAY AND EVERY DAY GREAT AND BLESSED NO MATTER WHAT!

#PerpetualPraise #ContinualPrayer #WorshipInSpiritAndTruth

{DAY 35}

PRAISE TO START YOUR DAY:

"Who may worship in your sanctuary, Lord? Who may enter your presence on your holy hill? Those who lead blameless lives and do what is right, speaking the truth from sincere hearts." (Psalm 15:1-2 NLT)

Jesus is the Way—the only Way! We, whose sins have been washed clean by the precious Blood of Christ Jesus—we are the church. The church is the kingdom of heaven on earth, which leads to the Kingdom of Heaven. It is His Holy Spirit Who lives in us and enables us to live our lives in a way that is acceptable and pleasing to God by: loving and obeying God; loving others (even showing our enemies the love of God); being sincere in our hearts; always acknowledging and seeking God and putting Him first; staying free from sin and guilt as we stay right with God; and, when we do fall short, going immediately to God to confess so that we may receive God's forgiveness and get right back up again.

CHOOSE TO MAKE TODAY AND EVERY DAY GREAT AND BLESSED NO MATTER WHAT!

#PerpetualPraise #ContinualPrayer #WorshipInSpiritAndTruth

{DAY 36}

PRAISE TO START YOUR DAY:

"Be ye therefore followers of God, as dear children; and walk in love, as Christ also hath loved us, and hath given himself for us an offering and a sacrifice to God for a sweet-smelling savour." (Ephesians 5:1-2 KJV)

Jesus loves you so much that He thought you were to die for. In return, and because you love Jesus, follow Him. To follow Jesus means that something is required of you. You are no longer self-serving, but you are now serving God. Offer your life a living sacrifice to the Lord, always praising and worshiping Him, and being obedient (doing what is right according to what God's Word says). Just as you desire for your children to be obedient, God also desires His children to be obedient so He can reward and bless them. Your life's offering and sacrifice will go up to God and be a sweet-smelling fragrance, which will draw Him and keep Him ever closer to you.

CHOOSE TO MAKE TODAY AND EVERY DAY GREAT AND BLESSED NO MATTER WHAT!

#PerpetualPraise #ContinualPrayer #WorshipInSpiritAndTruth

{DAY 37}

"Now faith is the substance of things hoped for, the evidence of things not seen. By faith we understand that the worlds were framed by the word of God, so that the things which are seen were not made of things which are visible. But without faith it is impossible to please Him, for he who comes to God must believe that He is, and that He is a rewarder of those who diligently seek Him." (Hebrews 11:1,3,6 NKJV)

Thank You, Lord, for the faith You have given me. I believe that You are the one and only true and living God. You are my God. I belong to You and You belong to me. I understand by faith and fully believe that the worlds were created by Your spoken word with no visible materials to work with. You are God all by Yourself. You alone are Jehovah-Bara, the Lord Creator, and I worship You. I fully believe Your Word, oh God. Because I diligently seek You, You have rewarded me by performing miracles in my life. You have taken me from little faith to great faith. I know that as I continue seeking You, You will take me from great faith to greater faith. I pray the same for the reader(s), in the blessed Name of Jesus! Amen, amen, and amen!!!

CHOOSE TO MAKE TODAY AND EVERY DAY GREAT AND BLESSED NO MATTER WHAT!

#PerpetualPraise #ContinualPrayer #WorshipInSpiritAndTruth

{DAY 38}

"Delight yourself also in the LORD, and He shall give you the desires of your heart. Commit your way to the LORD, trust also in Him, and He shall bring it to pass." (Psalm 37:4-5 NKJV)

Aim to be completely dependent upon God for your pleasure. Do not fall into the trap of delighting yourself more in the blessings (things) God has given you than you do in God. Your best means of delighting yourself in the Lord is by spending as much time as possible in His Word, praying (talking/communing with God), praising, and worshiping God who has given you eternal salvation through Christ Jesus. The more time you spend with God, the more of Him you will want. You, too, will be wholly addicted to Jesus. As you walk in right-standing with God, He will fill your heart with right desires that line up with His Will, and He will bring them all to pass. You can know God's Will by meditating on His Word both day and night. Abide in Jesus, as He abides in you. Trust God, and judge Him Faithful always!

CHOOSE TO MAKE TODAY AND EVERY DAY GREAT AND BLESSED NO MATTER WHAT!

#PerpetualPraise #ContinualPrayer #WorshipInSpiritAndTruth

{DAY 39}

"Will You not revive us again, that Your people may rejoice in You? Show us Your mercy, LORD, and grant us Your salvation." (Psalm 85:6-7 NKJV)

You will never forget that overwhelming moment of rejoicing when you believed in your spirit that God had forgiven you and saved you from your sins and from eternal separation from Him, and when you were totally arrested by His Love. You felt so deeply loved and relieved and revived. God shows up to revive us over and over again, as He favors us with renewed hope for promises we have been patiently waiting for, and He lets us know that He has not forgotten. As the world gets worse, God's Church will get greater and grow ever stronger. People (our loved ones included) will be flocking to church houses in great numbers for salvation, help, refuge, comfort, and peace. Get ready, get ready, get ready, because the greatest revival of all times is on the way, and it begins in you and in me! Are you revived? Are you ready?

CHOOSE TO MAKE TODAY AND EVERY DAY GREAT AND BLESSED NO MATTER WHAT!

#PerpetualPraise #ContinualPrayer #WorshipInSpiritAndTruth

{DAY 40}

PRAISE TO START YOUR DAY:

"You are the salt of the earth; but if the salt loses its flavor, how shall it be seasoned? It is then good for nothing but to be thrown out and trampled underfoot by men. You are the light of the world. A city that is set on a hill cannot be hidden. Nor do they light a lamp and put it under a basket, but on a lampstand, and it gives light to all who are in the house. Let your light so shine before men, that they may see your good works and glorify your Father in heaven." (Matthew 5:13-16 NKJV)

As Christians, we are to be the salt and the light of the earth. Salt because our lives enhance, give meaning to, and add flavor to life. Light because the presence of Christians in the world must be like a light in the darkness, which is unmistakable. The truth of God's Word brings light to the darkened hearts of sinful man. Don't hide it—share it. God is depending on you.

CHOOSE TO MAKE TODAY AND EVERY DAY GREAT AND BLESSED NO MATTER WHAT!

#PerpetualPraise #ContinualPrayer #WorshipInSpiritAndTruth

{DAY 41}

"Who is this King of glory? The Lord strong and mighty, the Lord mighty in battle. Who is this King of glory? The Lord of hosts, he is the King of glory. Selah." (Psalm 24:8,10 KJV)

We worship You, Jehovah-Kabodhi, for You are the Lord our Glory. You love to shine your glory on Your peoples that we may establish Your covenant on the earth. We worship You, Jehovah-Gador Milchamah, for You're Mighty in Battle. Lord, You fight all our battles for us as we stand and see Your salvation, and we want to see You move in our lives today! We rejoice in You! Selah (we lift You up and exalt You). Hallelujah to the King of Glory!!!

CHOOSE TO MAKE TODAY AND EVERY DAY GREAT AND BLESSED NO MATTER WHAT!

#PerpetualPraise #ContinualPrayer #WorshipInSpiritAndTruth

{DAY 42}

PRAISE TO START YOUR DAY:

"Your way, O God, is in the sanctuary; who is so great a God as our God? You are the God who does wonders; You have declared Your strength among the peoples." (Psalm 77:13-14 NKJV)

I am so joyful and thankful for the privilege of being able to go into the house of the Lord today! Lord God, Your holiness is in the sanctuary. Your presence is in the sanctuary. Your love is in the sanctuary. I am reminded of all Your true and wondrous works towards Your people in the sanctuary! Thank You, Lord, for all the wonders You have performed in my life! I pray and praise You in advance for all the wonders You will perform in the lives of the reader(s) even now today, in the blessed Name of Jesus! Amen, amen, and amen!!!

CHOOSE TO MAKE TODAY AND EVERY DAY GREAT AND BLESSED NO MATTER WHAT!

#PerpetualPraise #ContinualPrayer #WorshipInSpiritAndTruth

{DAY 43}

"They that trust in the Lord shall be as mount Zion, which cannot be removed, but abideth forever. Do good, O Lord, unto those that be good, and to them that are upright in their hearts." (Psalm 125:1,4 KJV)

Trust in the Lord, stay in right- standing with God, devote yourself to giving all glory and honor to God wholeheartedly, and you will be like Mount Zion. The Church in general is called Mount Zion. The Church is built upon Jesus, the Rock, and therefore is very stable. The Church is made up of individual believers like you and me, who have put our trust in the Lord Jesus Christ. The Church cannot be removed, but is forever established for all eternity by God's Grace. Lord, Your Grace is Amazing, and we do not ever want to abuse it.

CHOOSE TO MAKE TODAY AND EVERY DAY GREAT AND BLESSED NO MATTER WHAT!

#PerpetualPraise #ContinualPrayer #WorshipInSpiritAndTruth

{DAY 44}

PRAISE TO START YOUR DAY:

"'Is not My word like a fire?' says the LORD, 'And like a hammer that breaks the rock in pieces?'" (Jeremiah 23:29 NKJV)

We praise You, Oh God, for Your Word is Truth and destroys all that is false! Your Word is like a fire shut up in our bones, which we must share and give to others. Your Word gives light and warmth. Your Word is so full of Your Power and Life that it causes the reader/hearer to feel the importance and value of it, as it pertains to their very life. Your Word is our only means of surviving this world. We would be eternally lost without Your Word, oh God! We praise You and thank You for Your Word!

CHOOSE TO MAKE TODAY AND EVERY DAY GREAT AND BLESSED NO MATTER WHAT!

#PerpetualPraise #ContinualPrayer #WorshipInSpiritAndTruth

{DAY 45}

PRAISE TO START YOUR DAY:

"Then the LORD appeared to Solomon by night, and said to him: 'I have heard your prayer, and have chosen this place for Myself as a house of sacrifice. When I shut up heaven and there is no rain, or command the locusts to devour the land, or send pestilence among My people, if My people who are called by My name will humble themselves, and pray and seek My face, and turn from their wicked ways, then I will hear from heaven, and will forgive their sin and heal their land. Now My eyes will be open and My ears attentive to prayer made in this place. For now I have chosen and sanctified this house, that My name may be there forever; and My eyes and My heart will be there perpetually.'" (2 Chronicles 7:12-16 NKJV)

Lord, Your Word is most straightforward, showing the vital importance You place on prayer by Christians, as well as the blessings from You which are attached to prayer. The church I attend is a sanctified house of prayer. My personal home is a sanctified house of prayer. My office is a sanctified house of prayer. My body, which is the temple of Your Holy Spirit, is a sanctified house of prayer. My car is a sanctified house of prayer. God's eyes and His heart are on me and with me perpetually. I pray this is your testimony, too, in the blessed Name of Jesus! Amen, amen, and amen!!!

CHOOSE TO MAKE TODAY AND EVERY DAY GREAT AND BLESSED NO MATTER WHAT!

#PerpetualPraise #ContinualPrayer #WorshipInSpiritAndTruth

{DAY 46}

"By faith, Noah, when warned about things not yet seen, in holy fear built an ark to save his family. By his faith he condemned the world and became heir of the righteousness that is in keeping with faith." (Hebrews 11:7 NIV)

It had not yet rained upon the face of the earth when God warned Noah and told him to build an ark to save his family. Can you imagine?! What great faith in God Noah must have had to endure all the ridicule from everyone watching him, all while he was building the ark. It is estimated that it took Noah 75 years to build the ark. Noah was 600 years of age when the floodwaters came on the earth. Yet, because of Noah's faith in God and what God told him, he was obedient. As a result of Noah's obedience, he and his family were saved. ALWAYS believe and listen to God instead of your feelings and doubts. You and your family will be saved as a result of that choice. To God be all praise and glory!

CHOOSE TO MAKE TODAY AND EVERY DAY GREAT AND BLESSED NO MATTER WHAT!

#PerpetualPraise #ContinualPrayer #WorshipInSpiritAndTruth

{DAY 47}

PRAISE TO START YOUR DAY:

"But you are a chosen generation, a royal priesthood, a holy nation, His own special people, that you may proclaim the praises of Him who called you out of darkness into His marvelous light; who once were not a people but are now the people of God, who had not obtained mercy but now have obtained mercy." (1 Peter 2:9-10 NKJV)

You were created by God to praise Him for all He does, and to worship Him for who He is—the Great I AM! You are chosen by God Himself to a royal priesthood and holiness. God brought you out of the darkness of sin, and brought you into His marvelous light of holiness and righteousness through His Son Christ Jesus. Now God Himself calls you, not just "a" people but, "the" special people of God, who are blessed with His mercy daily. Be a praiser and a worshiper, and stay in the flow of Your Living River—JESUS!

CHOOSE TO MAKE TODAY AND EVERY DAY GREAT AND BLESSED NO MATTER WHAT!

#PerpetualPraise #ContinualPrayer #WorshipInSpiritAndTruth

{DAY 48}

PRAISE TO START YOUR DAY:

"Shout for joy to God, all the earth! Sing the glory of his name; make his praise glorious. Say to God, 'How awesome are your deeds! So great is your power that your enemies cringe before you. All the earth bows down to you; they sing praise to you, they sing the praises of your name.'" (Psalm 66:1-4 NIV)

All people upon the face of the earth are to praise God. He is Sovereign and all Powerful over all of His creation. We are to reflect a holy joy in all our praises to God with all our might. Our praises to God should reflect that we are not ashamed to praise Him. We should always glorify and honor God with our praises to the very best of our ability and with all that is within us. Let our bones sing praises to God! Let us praise God perpetually, with every breath we take! God is the very air we breathe. It is His breath in our lungs. Praise the name of the Lord forevermore!

CHOOSE TO MAKE TODAY AND EVERY DAY GREAT AND BLESSED NO MATTER WHAT!

#PerpetualPraise #ContinualPrayer #WorshipInSpiritAndTruth

{DAY 49}

"Blessed be the Lord, who daily loadeth us with benefits, even the God of our salvation. Selah." (Psalm 68:19 KJV)

JESUS SAVES AND SO MUCH MORE!!! Lord, You bear all our heavy loads, and yet You are also the God of our salvation. You are Lord over all and Creator of all, and yet you are the Supporter and Sustainer of all creation. Lord, You not only created us but You also serve us. It is an honor and a privilege to be able to give back to You, our Maker. I am truly grateful and joyful to be going to the house of the Lord today to praise and worship You, Lord!

CHOOSE TO MAKE TODAY AND EVERY DAY GREAT AND BLESSED NO MATTER WHAT!

#PerpetualPraise #ContinualPrayer #WorshipInSpiritAndTruth

{DAY 50}

PRAISE TO START YOUR DAY:

**"This people I have formed for Myself; they shall declare My praise."
(Isaiah 43:21 NKJV)**

You are chosen by God, redeemed by Christ Jesus, and made new by His Holy Spirit. It is written in Ezekiel 36:26, "A new heart also will I give you, and a new spirit will I put within you: and I will take away the stony heart out of your flesh, and I will give you a heart of flesh." God formed you while you were still in your mother's womb. God formed you for His good pleasure, and so that truth and knowledge of the one and only True and Living God will be passed on to future generations, just as it has been given to you. We should share the goodness and mercy of God with others. God has called us into His Church to give Him the glory, honor, praise, and worship that He is worthy of and to serve Him. You belong to God and God belongs to you. How amazing and awesome is that? I pray that you, the reader(s), have been formed anew, redeemed by Christ Jesus, and that you are now being transformed into the very image of Christ Jesus through His Holy Spirit and through God's Word, in the blessed Name of Jesus! Amen, amen, and amen!!!

CHOOSE TO MAKE TODAY AND EVERY DAY GREAT AND BLESSED NO MATTER WHAT!

#PerpetualPraise #ContinualPrayer #WorshipInSpiritAndTruth

{DAY 51}

"Many, Lord my God, are the wonders you have done, the things you planned for us. None can compare with you; were I to speak and tell of your deeds, they would be too many to declare." (Psalm 40:5 NIV)

The Lord's good plans for you and me go beyond our wildest dreams! The merciful things You have done for Your people cannot be numbered by man! We just cannot tell it all—not in mere words or in numbers. Some of the wonders You have performed in our lives, we are not even aware of; times You have saved us from car wrecks and other dangers. We praise and thank You, Lord, for there is nobody like You!

CHOOSE TO MAKE TODAY AND EVERY DAY GREAT AND BLESSED NO MATTER WHAT!

#PerpetualPraise #ContinualPrayer #WorshipInSpiritAndTruth

{DAY 52}

PRAISE TO START YOUR DAY:

"Give to everyone what you owe them: If you owe taxes, pay taxes; if revenue, then revenue; if respect, then respect; if honor, then honor." (Romans 13:7 NIV)

My heart overflows with gratitude towards my Heavenly Father God. He loved me so much that He gave me His only begotten Son Christ Jesus so that I should believe in Him and have eternal life with Him in Heaven. My heart overflows with gratitude towards my Lord and Savior Christ Jesus, Son of God, because He loves me so much that He thought I was to die for, and that's what He did. Then He began to change me into His very image from the inside to the outside. My heart overflows with gratitude towards God's Holy Spirit, who lives in me continuously, leading and guiding me into all truth. My heart overflows with gratitude towards my pastors Steve Fender, Becky Fender, Brandon Fender, Amanda Fender, and Sean Fender. I would not be the Woman of God and of great faith that I confess to be today except for my pastors mentioned above. Since 1998 to the present, I have heard the truth, the whole truth, and nothing but the truth of the Word of God preached. Not only have I heard, but also have seen the Word of God lived out in each of my pastors' lives. I am eternally grateful to God for all my Fender pastors and for leading me to Livingway Church, where stands my loyalty and devotion always. I love you all from here to Heaven and throughout all eternity. Dear reader(s), who would you like to give respect and honor to today?

CHOOSE TO MAKE TODAY AND EVERY DAY GREAT AND BLESSED NO MATTER WHAT!

#PerpetualPraise #ContinualPrayer #WorshipInSpiritAndTruth

{DAY 53}

PRAISE TO START YOUR DAY:

"But He said, 'More than that, blessed are those who hear the word of God and keep it!'" (Luke 11:28 NKJV)

It is a blessing to hear the Word of God because, according to God's Word, faith comes by hearing the Word of God. It is a greater blessing to hear the Word of God and commit it to your memory, and then be obedient to do it and live according to what His Word says. Those only are truly blessed of the Lord. It is much the same principle as "faith without works is dead". Keep to God's Word and allow it to become your way of life. It is God's own desire for you to receive His blessings in abundance because He loves you.

CHOOSE TO MAKE TODAY AND EVERY DAY GREAT AND BLESSED NO MATTER WHAT!

#PerpetualPraise #ContinualPrayer #WorshipInSpiritAndTruth

{DAY 54}

PRAISE TO START YOUR DAY:

"To the end that my glory may sing praise to You and not be silent. O LORD my God, I will give thanks to You forever." (Psalm 30:12 NKJV)

Lord Jesus, may my soul and my tongue be my glory, and may my voice continue to sing praises to You in the good times and bad times. May I never grow careless, which would cause me to fall into sin. May I always have a testimony of Your truth and faithfulness to fulfill Your promises. May I always celebrate and tell of Your goodness and give You the glory and praise that is due You. May I persevere to the end, singing praises to You until You come again. In the Blessed Name of Jesus I pray! Amen, amen, and amen!!!

CHOOSE TO MAKE TODAY AND EVERY DAY GREAT AND BLESSED NO MATTER WHAT!

#PerpetualPraise #ContinualPrayer #WorshipInSpiritAndTruth

{DAY 55}

"Greater love has no one than this: to lay down one's life for one's friends. Therefore, I urge you, brothers and sisters, in view of God's mercy, to offer your bodies as a living sacrifice, holy and pleasing to God—this is your true and proper worship." (John 15:13; Romans 12:1 NIV)

Have you ever received an organ donation from someone you know, perhaps a friend or relative you love? Do you remember how that made you feel and what your reaction was when that beloved person told you that he/she was going to donate one of their organs to you so that you may live? Jesus loves you so much that He thought you were to die for. Jesus donated His very life for us, you and mesa that we may live eternally with Him. Shouldn't we be moved to react and show our love to Jesus even more?

Nobody has ever, or will ever, love you like Jesus loves you. No, not ever. In return, you now have the opportunity to give your love back to Jesus by offering your body as a living sacrifice that is holy and pleasing to God, by allowing the way you live, breathe, think, walk, talk, eat, drink, dress (literally everything about you) reflect that you belong to God and that you love Him with everything in you. After God delivered me and set me totally free, He replaced all of the addictions of my natural man's flesh with healthy, holy addictions. Someone I love very much, who knew me before and after being delivered, one day said to me, "You're possessed!"

The person who said that to me did not intend the remark as a compliment at the time it was said. However, I have never forgotten because it serves as a reminder to me that I belong totally to God, and I am pleasing to God. I am wholly addicted to Jesus. He thought I was to die for, and I think that makes Jesus well worth living for every second of every day.

CHOOSE TO MAKE TODAY AND EVERY DAY GREAT AND BLESSED NO MATTER WHAT!

#PerpetualPraise #ContinualPrayer #WorshipInSpiritAndTruth

{DAY 56}

PRAISE TO START YOUR DAY:

"How precious is Your lovingkindness, O God! Therefore the children of men put their trust under the shadow of Your wings." (Psalm 36:7 NKJV)

Lord God, You have loved me when I was unlovable, even when I could not love myself. All my faith and trust is in You, Lord. You are my safe place, my refuge, where the evil one cannot see, reach, or touch me. I worship You, Jehovah-Machsi, for You are the Lord my Refuge. I love You, Lord! To the reader(s), when the storms of life come—and they will—you need a ready place of refuge to go where you know you will be safe and secure from harm until the storm passes over. You need someone you love and trust, someone you have total confidence in to love you no matter what, someone you know has the ability to keep you safe. There is only One, and His Name is JESUS. Don't wait for the perfect storm to come. Get to know Him even now today. Stay in close communication with Him daily.

CHOOSE TO MAKE TODAY AND EVERY DAY GREAT AND BLESSED NO MATTER WHAT!

#PerpetualPraise #ContinualPrayer #WorshipInSpiritAndTruth

{DAY 57}

"The Lord is my shepherd; I shall not want. He maketh me to lie down in green pastures: He leadeth me beside the still waters. He restoreth my soul: He leadeth me in the paths of righteousness for His name's sake." (Psalm 23:1-3 KJV)

I worship You, Jehovah-Rohi, for You are the Lord my Shepherd. You never leave me without having enough of everything I need—spiritually, emotionally, physically, and materially. You lead me to rest. You feed my hungry heart and quench my thirsty soul as I spend time with You and in Your Word. You refresh and restore my soul! I thank You, Jesus, that I can rest in You, knowing that You love me and intend only good for my life.

CHOOSE TO MAKE TODAY AND EVERY DAY GREAT AND BLESSED NO MATTER WHAT!

#PerpetualPraise #ContinualPrayer #WorshipInSpiritAndTruth

{DAY 58}

"Thus says the LORD: 'Refrain your voice from weeping, and your eyes from tears; for your work shall be rewarded, says the LORD, and they shall come back from the land of the enemy. There is hope in your future, says the LORD, that your children shall come back to their own border.'" (Jeremiah 31:16-17 NKJV)

Thank You, Lord, that You never stop loving us no matter how far we may run from You and Your house, even when we turn our backs on You and ignore You. Thank You, Lord, for calling and for always being willing to accept Your prodigal sons and daughters back home. You took me back when I was a prodigal, and I know You will do it again. Lord, I will continue serving You and working for You and God's Kingdom. This Scripture is full of promise from God and so encouraging! Jesus visited me at home one day and led my eyes right to this Scripture. I know and believe that the Word of God is true, settled, and established.

CHOOSE TO MAKE TODAY AND EVERY DAY GREAT AND BLESSED NO MATTER WHAT!

#PerpetualPraise #ContinualPrayer #WorshipInSpiritAndTruth

{DAY 59}

"And now, dear brothers and sisters, one final thing. Fix your thoughts on what is true, and honorable, and right, and pure, and lovely, and admirable. Think about things that are excellent and worthy of praise. Keep putting into practice all you learned and received from me— everything you heard from me and saw me doing. Then the God of peace will be with you." (Philippians 4:8-9 NLT)

All actions begin as a thought. As you take control of your own thoughts and keep them fixed on Jesus and Godly things, and as you live what God's Word has taught you, then you will most certainly have peace. We have to open our minds to be influenced by God and Godly things, rather than the world and carnal things. As I have learned from my Spiritual mother, Pastor Becky Fender, everything is a choice. Only one person is responsible for the choices made in your life, and that one person is you. Choose to fulfill this Scripture in your own life and you will surely have peace, and it will be well with your soul. Father God, I pray that You open our eyes and hearts to understand, in the blessed Name of Your Son, Christ Jesus! Amen, amen, and amen!!! Lord, we give You all the glory!

CHOOSE TO MAKE TODAY AND EVERY DAY GREAT AND BLESSED NO MATTER WHAT!

#PerpetualPraise #ContinualPrayer #WorshipInSpiritAndTruth

{DAY 60}

PRAISE TO START YOUR DAY:

"Unto Thee, O Lord, do I lift up my soul. And my soul shall be joyful in the Lord: it shall rejoice in His salvation...My soul doth magnify the Lord, and my spirit hath rejoiced in God my Savior." (Psalm 25:1; Psalm 35:9; Luke 1:46-47 KJV)

Lord, I come directly to You with all my prayers, praise, thanksgiving, and worship. I lift my heart to You. My thoughts begin with You and everything about You. I meditate on Your Word both day and night. I am grateful that You saved and delivered me, and now I am free to worship You in spirit and in truth. My spirit sees You as bigger than any problem, or trouble, that comes my way. I know You are well able and willing to take care of all that concerns me in this world. My soul rejoices in You with exceedingly great joy!

CHOOSE TO MAKE TODAY AND EVERY DAY GREAT AND BLESSED NO MATTERWHAT!

#PerpetualPraise #ContinualPrayer #WorshipInSpiritAndTruth

{DAY 61}

"Verily I say unto you, except ye be converted, and become as little children, ye shall not enter into the kingdom of heaven. Whosoever therefore shall humble himself as this little child, the same is greatest in the kingdom of heaven." (Matthew 18:3-4 KJV)

One must turn to God and turn away from sin. Spiritual growth and greatness requires humility. Childlike humility is beautiful to God and rewarded by God. Very young children are totally dependent upon their parents, not desiring the right to give orders or to make decisions, and they are teachable. They have a pure trust. In the same way, this is how God wants us to come to Him. He desires that we be willingly and totally dependent upon Him and teachable unto His Word. God wants us to trust Him. When we do, God rewards us openly and generously, and He makes us the head and not the tail—the first and not the last—above only and not beneath. Glory be to God in the Highest!

CHOOSE TO MAKE TODAY AND EVERY DAY GREAT AND BLESSED NO MATTER WHAT!

#PerpetualPraise #ContinualPrayer #WorshipInSpiritAndTruth

{DAY 62}

"You did not choose Me, but I chose you and appointed you that you should go and bear fruit, and that your fruit should remain, that whatever you ask the Father in My name He may give you. So they said, 'Believe on the Lord Jesus Christ, and you will be saved, you and your household.' For all the promises of God in Him are Yes, and in Him Amen, to the glory of God through us. Not that we have dominion over your faith, but are fellow workers for your joy; for by faith you stand." (John 15:16; Acts 16:31; 2 Corinthians 1:20,24 NKJV)

Jesus chose you to be His disciple. He equipped and furnished you with His Holy Spirit that you should show forth all the fruit thereof and all to the glory of our Heavenly Father God. You are the fruit of Christ Jesus because He died for you. When you are willing to die to yourself and live in and for Christ Jesus, you become a fruit-bearer of Him who has called and appointed you. Only then will your fruit remain. Jesus is the Savior of the world and the Giver of salvation! He is not a man that He would ever lie. All His promises are believable and real. Your faith is built upon God's Word. Stand on your faith to believe each one of God's promises and trust Him. Then stand and see God fulfill His promises in your life, and you are overflowing with true joy!

CHOOSE TO MAKE TODAY AND EVERY DAY GREAT AND BLESSED NO MATTER WHAT!

#PerpetualPraise #ContinualPrayer #WorshipInSpiritAndTruth

{DAY 63}

"Now this is the confidence that we have in Him, that if we ask anything according to His will, He hears us. And if we know that He hears us, whatever we ask, we know that we have the petitions that we have asked of Him." (1 John 5:14-15 NKJV)

I know and believe with absolute certainty that You listen to me when I pray and You answer my prayers, and that right early. I trust Your Will to be done as I pray Your Will. Thank You for giving me Your Will through Your Word. I am eternally grateful. May my eyes and heart of understanding always be open and grow as I study and meditate on Your Word. I pray this for every reader, in the blessed Name of Jesus! Amen, amen, and amen!!!

CHOOSE TO MAKE TODAY AND EVERY DAY GREAT AND BLESSED NO MATTER WHAT!

#PerpetualPraise #ContinualPrayer #WorshipInSpiritAndTruth

{DAY 64}

"As every man hath received the gift, even so minister the same one to another, as good stewards of the manifold grace of God. If any man speak, let him speak as the oracles of God; if any man minister, let him do it as of the ability which God giveth: that God in all things may be glorified through Jesus Christ, to whom be praise and dominion for ever and ever. Amen." (1 Peter 4:10-11 KJV)

We have all received a special gift, or gifts, from God which we are to use for the purpose of glorifying Him. Each one of us is a mouthpiece for communicating God's truths to one another, for the purpose of encouragement and building each other up in the Lord. God uses us in different ways to minister and glorify God, according to the gift(s) He has given us. Thank You, Jesus, for giving me the desire and gift to praise and worship You through songs, and for opening the right door (Living Praise Choir) to minister to Your saints! Thank You, Jesus, for giving me the gift and ministry of writing for You and the Kingdom of God! I know that as I lift Your Name on high, You are even now today drawing more people unto You. More of You, Jesus, and less of me—less of me and more of You, Jesus.

CHOOSE TO MAKE TODAY AND EVERY DAY GREAT AND BLESSED NO MATTER WHAT!

#PerpetualPraise #ContinualPrayer #WorshipInSpiritAndTruth

{DAY 65}

"But the hour is coming, and now is, when the true worshipers will worship the Father in spirit and truth; for the Father is seeking such to worship Him. God is Spirit, and those who worship Him must worship in spirit and truth." (John 4:23-24 NKJV)

Anybody can praise God, but not everyone can worship. Worshiping God in spirit and in truth requires worshiping from deep within one's heart. One must believe and know the true and living God (according to what the Scriptures say about Him) to be able to worship Him in spirit and in truth. One must have a relationship with Jesus and have a testimony of what the Lord has done for you and how He has changed you. Only when you have encountered Jesus personally are you then able to worship Him in spirit and in truth. What is your testimony? If your answer is "I don't have a testimony", it is never too late to make one, as long as you still have a breath in your lungs. God is gracious and merciful. God is faithful and well able to save you, no matter where you may be today. No pit is too deep for God to find you. Just call His Name, "JESUS!", with all your heart and strength, and He will come running to you.

CHOOSE TO MAKE TODAY AND EVERY DAY GREAT AND BLESSED NO MATTER WHAT!

#PerpetualPraise #ContinualPrayer #WorshipInSpiritAndTruth

{DAY 66}

PRAISE TO START YOUR DAY:

"O praise the LORD, all ye nations: praise him, all ye people. For his merciful kindness is great toward us: and the truth of the LORD endureth for- ever. Praise ye the LORD." (Psalm 117:1-2 KJV)

The truth about who God is and what He is like is found in the Bible. From Genesis through Revelation, the Bible is replete with Scriptures which show you the very nature of God; God's Lovingkindness, Holiness, Righteousness, Graciousness, Merciful, Faithfulness, Forgiveness, Truthfulness, Goodness, and the list goes on and on. All these truths are on full display in the Bible for every soul on the face of the God's created earth to see. When you see, believe, know, and understand the truth about all of God's goodness, you cannot help but praise Him. These truths of the Lord will endure forever, as God will endure forever. Let everything that has breath praise the Lord!

CHOOSE TO MAKE TODAY AND EVERY DAY GREAT AND BLESSED NO MATTER WHAT!

#PerpetualPraise #ContinualPrayer #WorshipInSpiritAndTruth

{DAY 67}

"This is the LORD's doing; it is marvelous in our eyes. This is the day which the LORD hath made; we will rejoice and be glad in it." (Psalm 118:23-24 KJV)

Thank You, Lord, for waking me up on this glorious God morning and starting me on my way! This is all Your doing! I should have already died on numerous occasions through the years, but that was not in Your Master Plan for me. I do not take this day You have given me for granted. Thank You, Lord, for putting Your breath in my lungs and giving me a brand new day to spend in You, being about my Father's business! I am so happy to be at Your service! How will You use me today, Lord? Thank You, Jesus, that this is the very first day of the rest of my life! I CHOOSE to rejoice and be glad in this day, and to make every single minute of this day count for You, to the glory of our Heavenly Father! May everything I think, say, and do be pleasing and glorifying to You always!

CHOOSE TO MAKE TODAY AND EVERY DAY GREAT AND BLESSED NO MATTER WHAT!

#PerpetualPraise #ContinualPrayer #WorshipInSpiritAndTruth

{DAY 68}

"Give unto the LORD the glory due to His name; worship the LORD in the beauty of holiness." (Psalm 29:2 NKJV)

Oh God, only You deserve all glory. Thank You, Lord, for revealing Your glory through Your Word and through all You have created. I apologize to no man for my worship and praise unto You, Lord! No one, not a single person, was there when You saved me except for You and me. No one else but You and I know just how far You have brought me. I keep my garment of praise on and never take it off, so it is perpetually activated. My praise is beautiful to You, and I wholeheartedly worship You in the beauty of holiness. To the reader(s): Did you know that your life in Jesus here on earth is like your "dressing room" for Heaven? What you do for the Lord here is getting you ready for Heaven. If you love to praise and worship God here, you will love to praise and worship God in Heaven. If you love being in God's presence here, you will love being in God's presence in Heaven.

CHOOSE TO MAKE TODAY AND EVERY DAY GREAT AND BLESSED NO MATTER WHAT!

#PerpetualPraise #ContinualPrayer #WorshipInSpiritAndTruth

{DAY 69}

"Commit your works to the LORD, and your thoughts will be established." (Proverbs 16:3 NKJV)

Praise God, saints! This is a glorious God morning! Be joyful about it and alert your face so it shows in your countenance! If you are reading this, then God woke you up to a brand new day and a brand new opportunity to stay in His presence, to lift up the Name of Jesus, to be a soul-winner, and to work with God to increase His Kingdom. Today we are honored and privileged to serve the Lord and each other in our individual ministries. We get to gather today in the house of the Lord as a church family and be in the presence of the Lord together, to hear God's life-changing word preached mightily! Our thoughts have been established. With the help of God, our plans will prosper in this day because our thoughts and plans line up with God's Will. I'm revived, I'm fired up, and I'm ready to go! C'mon, saints, let's go and put a praise on it!

CHOOSE TO MAKE TODAY AND EVERY DAY GREAT AND BLESSED NO MATTER WHAT!

#PerpetualPraise #ContinualPrayer #WorshipInSpiritAndTruth

{DAY 70}

"For as he thinks in his heart, so is he..." (Proverbs 23:7 NKJV)

What a man thinks in his heart is what he will become, good or bad. If a man hears the same thing long enough and enough times, he will come to believe it, and then act upon it. The following is my daily "Overcomer's Statement of Faith". I have been confessing it daily for years now, and it is deeply rooted in my heart and spirit. Nobody can ever take it from me. "I am an Overcomer. I am a Christian. I believe the Word of God, the Blood of Jesus Christ, and the Power of the Holy Spirit. I am anointed by faith to speak the Word of God; to proclaim victory over all my situations and circumstances. Therefore, I am the head and not the tail; I am above only and not beneath; I am highly favored. God calls me His child, Jesus calls me redeemed, and men call me blessed. I am an Overcomer!" No matter what man may say about you, always speak the Word of God over yourself. Memorize it. Get it in your heart and spirit and believe it. You can believe it because it is the Word of God, and the Word of God is true. It works for me, and I know it will work for you, too.

CHOOSE TO MAKE TODAY AND EVERY DAY GREAT AND BLESSED NO MATTER WHAT!

#PerpetualPraise #ContinualPrayer #WorshipInSpiritAndTruth

{DAY 71}

PRAISE TO START YOUR DAY:

"Blessed be the God and Father of our Lord Jesus Christ, the Father of mercies and God of all comfort, who comforts us in all our tribulation, that we may be able to comfort those who are in any trouble, with the comfort with which we ourselves are comforted by God." (2 Corinthians 1:3-4 NKJV)

Lord, make me Your mouthpiece to speak Your words of comfort and encouragement today. Let Your dear ones hear Your voice, no matter how far they have run from You. Let them know how deeply You love them. May they hear Your words of healing and grace reassuring them that You Yourself have already paid the price for their sins. Remove any obstacles that hinder them from coming to You today. Meet them in the wilderness of their fear, shame, sorrow, and regret. Arrest them with Your unconditional love. Make me Your mouthpiece to comfort those who are sick and in pain and those who have lost loved ones. Bless me today, Lord, by using me to bless others. All this I pray, in the Blessed Name of JESUS! Amen, amen, and amen!!!

CHOOSE TO MAKE TODAY AND EVERY DAY GREAT AND BLESSED NO MATTER WHAT!

#PerpetualPraise #ContinualPrayer #WorshipInSpiritAndTruth

{DAY 72}

PRAISE TO START YOUR DAY:

"Blessed be the LORD God, the God of Israel, who only does wondrous things! And blessed be His glorious name forever! And let the whole earth be filled with His glory. Amen and Amen." (Psalm 72:18-19 NKJV)

We are to bless God for all He has done for us by Christ Jesus. Our God only does things marvelously and wonderfully! We are to honor God for His wondrous works towards us. We are to spend our lives blessing God, sharing the Good News of the Gospel of Christ Jesus, and filling the whole earth with His glorious praise and worship.

CHOOSE TO MAKE TODAY AND EVERY DAY GREAT AND BLESSED NO MATTER WHAT!

#PerpetualPraise #ContinualPrayer #WorshipInSpiritAndTruth

{DAY 73}

PRAISE TO START YOUR DAY:

"Let everything that hath breath praise the LORD. Praise ye the LORD." (Psalm 150:6 KJV)

We are called by the authority of God Himself to praise Him. God is Love. God created man and desires happiness for His creation. God delights in the prosperity of His children. When we show our gratitude, respect, and admiration towards God through heartfelt praise, we are also showing God our happiness. Even the birds praise the Lord in song, and it pleases Him! Happy praising, everyone!

CHOOSE TO MAKE TODAY AND EVERY DAY GREAT AND BLESSED NO MATTER WHAT!

#PerpetualPraise #ContinualPrayer #WorshipInSpiritAndTruth

{DAY 74}

PRAISE TO START YOUR DAY:

"Enter into His gates with thanksgiving, and into His courts with praise. Be thankful to Him, and bless His name." (Psalm 100:4 NKJV)

Always enter into the house of the Lord with a heart full of thanksgiving and gratitude, and with praise in your mouth. Go to the altar to bless and worship God. Whether it be praise or a worship song, every time I sing I am singing TO GOD and FOR GOD, because I LOVE GOD! Whether it be at home, in my car, or on the platform at church, it's about God and me—and me and God. The anointing that He gives my singing voice is for a reason; that it returns back TO HIM FOR HIS GOOD PLEASURE. Then He shows up in my very praise!

CHOOSE TO MAKE TODAY AND EVERY DAY GREAT AND BLESSED NO MATTER WHAT!

#PerpetualPraise #ContinualPrayer #WorshipInSpiritAndTruth

{DAY 75}

"I have fought the good fight, I have finished the race, I have kept the faith." (2 Timothy 4:7 NKJV)

Though I have not yet finished my course and am still fighting the good fight for my faith, I have kept my faith! I refuse to let this world take that from me! My faith is built upon the Word of God. I am able to stand on my faith for all of God's promises to come to pass. I trust God completely. With Jesus as the Author and Finisher of my faith and my Coach, paired with me being a determined "finisher", my finish is looking grand and glorious. I have already won! Thank you, my Jesus! We make a great team! Jesus, You are my everything! I love You all the way to Heaven and throughout all eternity!

CHOOSE TO MAKE TODAY AND EVERY DAY GREAT AND BLESSED NO MATTER WHAT!

#PerpetualPraise #ContinualPrayer #WorshipInSpiritAndTruth

{DAY 76}

"Therefore we also, since we are surrounded by so great a cloud of witnesses, let us lay aside every weight, and the sin which so easily ensnares us, and let us run with endurance the race that is set before us, looking unto Jesus, the author and finisher of our faith, who for the joy that was set before Him endured the cross, despising the shame, and has sat down at the right hand of the throne of God." (Hebrews 12:1-2 NKJV)

In order to finish this race, while enduring trials all along the way up until the end, we must keep our eyes fixed on Jesus. Many are watching us as we are running this race. We are being watched to see if we are really committed to Jesus and to see if our faith is effective enough to get us all the way to the end, while remaining obedient to God and living life as a Christian and staying right with God. What God has delivered and freed us from, we must never become bound to again. While in this world, there will always be temptations. However, we have a means of escape. His Name is Jesus! Jesus is the beginning (Alpha) and the ending (Omega). Jesus perfects and brings to completion our faith and all promises given to us as believers.

CHOOSE TO MAKE TODAY AND EVERY DAY GREAT AND BLESSED NO MATTER WHAT!

#PerpetualPraise #ContinualPrayer #WorshipInSpiritAndTruth

{DAY 77}

"The grass withers, the flower fades, but the word of our God stands forever. So shall My word be that goes forth from My mouth; it shall not return to Me void, but it shall accomplish what I please, and it shall prosper in the thing for which I sent it." (Isaiah 40:8; Isaiah 55:11 NKJV)

Though man's flesh is as grass and flowers, which wither and fade, the Word of God is always alive and fulfilled by God. The Word of God is forever established in Heaven. God's Word is never spoken without having a prospering effect where it is sent and producing what God intends it to. God's Word is alive and has creative power. That means that when you as a believer speak God's Word over your own life, or over a loved one's life, God is in it and good effects will be produced. God's spoken Word mixed with your faith has the creative power to change your life and the lives of others. Thank You, Lord, for Your eternal and everlasting word that is truth and light and life.

CHOOSE TO MAKE TODAY AND EVERY DAY GREAT AND BLESSED NO MATTER WHAT!

#PerpetualPraise #ContinualPrayer #WorshipInSpiritAndTruth

{DAY 78}

"Let the words of my mouth and the meditation of my heart be acceptable in Your sight, O LORD, my strength and my Redeemer." (Psalm 19:14 NKJV)

Lord, I pray that You keep my words and my thoughts pure. I understand that sin begins with a thought first, and then a word being spoken, before the very act of sin occurs. Yes, Lord, may everything I think, say, and do be pleasing to You, and may my heart and motives remain pure and clean, in the blessed Name of Jesus! Amen, amen, and amen!!! I worship You, Lord, for You are my strength, through the power of Your Holy Spirit Who lives in me and enables me to overcome and triumph over sin and temptations.

CHOOSE TO MAKE TODAY AND EVERY DAY GREAT AND BLESSED NO MATTER WHAT!

#PerpetualPraise #ContinualPrayer #WorshipInSpiritAndTruth

{DAY 79}

"Beloved, I wish above all things that thou mayest prosper and be in health, even as thy soul prospereth." (3 John 1:2 KJV)

God delights in the prosperity of His sons and daughters. You are God's beloved, and He wishes above all else that you be prosperous and happy. Your overall prosperity begins with the prospering of your soul (mind, will, emotions). Your soul prospers when your mind is changed and renewed through hearing, studying, and meditating on God's Word. Your thought pattern is changed as you keep your mind stayed on Jesus. As your relationship with Jesus grows, your state of mind changes from the natural (where your mood is governed by your outward circumstances) to the spiritual (where you have an inner peace no matter what your outward circumstances may be), and it is well with your soul. When your soul is well, then your physical health prospers, and your finances grow and prosper. As you learn to give all your cares to Jesus, you are no longer carrying heavy burdens around. Your worries are replaced with faith and trust in the Lord. This is what God desires for you always. Oh, HALLELUJAH! Joyful, joyful, we adore You, Jesus!

CHOOSE TO MAKE TODAY AND EVERY DAY GREAT AND BLESSED NO MATTER WHAT!

#PerpetualPraise #ContinualPrayer #WorshipInSpiritAndTruth

{DAY 80}

PRAISE TO START YOUR DAY:

"But thou art holy, O thou that inhabitest the praises of Israel…in Your presence is fullness of joy…" (Psalm 22:3 KJV; Psalm 16:11 NKJV)

God's Word says that He inhabits the praise of His people. Worship goes up to God. However, when our audible praises go up—God comes down to us and lives in our praises. In His presence there is fullness of joy. For a moment, just think about the peaceful happiness of being with God all the time. Imagine leaning back against Jesus, so close you can hear His heartbeat, and He has His loving arms wrapped around you as the two of you sit together in peace. It is "heaven on earth", and you can have that. Oh, Hallelujah! To live in the presence of God, perpetually praise Him. Praise! Praise! Praise!

CHOOSE TO MAKE TODAY AND EVERY DAY GREAT AND BLESSED NO MATTER WHAT!

#PerpetualPraise #ContinualPrayer #WorshipInSpiritAndTruth

{DAY 81}

"In this you greatly rejoice, though now for a little while, if need be, you have been grieved by various trials, that the genuineness of your faith, being much more precious than gold that perishes, though it is tested by fire, may be found to praise, honor, and glory at the revelation of Jesus Christ, whom having not seen you love. Though now you do not see Him, yet believing, you rejoice with joy inexpressible and full of glory," (1 Peter 1:6-8 NKJV)

Just as the genuineness of gold is tested by fire, the true value of your faith in God is tested by trials in your life. You will most definitely have trials of different degrees in your life. It is how you go through them that will determine how real your faith in God is. Do you groan, moan, grumble, and complain while going through, or do you continue praising, honoring, and glorifying God? Though you have not visibly seen God yet, do you still believe that He is and that He is a Rewarder of those who diligently seek Him? Though now you do not visibly see God, do you still put all your faith and trust in Him, with all God-confidence? Is your faith alive, which is proven by your praising, honoring, and glorifying God, even when things are not going well? If your answer to these questions is "Yes", then your faith is of great value to God, and He will reward and honor your faith in ways beyond your wildest dreams. Thank You, Lord, for bringing us into a new dimension of faith in You and relationship with You, Jesus! Nothing else on earth can compare!

CHOOSE TO MAKE TODAY AND EVERY DAY GREAT AND BLESSED NO MATTER WHAT!

#PerpetualPraise #ContinualPrayer #WorshipInSpiritAndTruth

{DAY 82}

"From one man he created all the nations throughout the whole earth. He decided beforehand when they should rise and fall, and he determined their boundaries. His purpose was for the nations to seek after God and perhaps feel their way toward him and find him—though he is not far from any one of us. For in him we live and move and exist. As some of your own poets have said, 'We are his offspring.'" (Acts 17:26-28 NLT)

The first parent of all mankind was Adam. Adam had the blood of all mankind in his veins, no matter their color, nation, or language. This truth alone proves the ignorance of those who show racism. It was God's plan that mankind should dwell upon all the face of the earth and multiply. Therefore, God determined the boundaries of the different nations. God gave each nation adequate boundaries so there would be no need to invade each other's. God's plan for all mankind is to have a longing inside that cannot be satisfied by anything in this world, which will lead us to the awareness of God. When we live our life in Christ Jesus, then we are His offspring, and are promised eternal life in Heaven. Glory to God in the Highest!

CHOOSE TO MAKE TODAY AND EVERY DAY GREAT AND BLESSED NO MATTER WHAT!

#PerpetualPraise #ContinualPrayer #WorshipInSpiritAndTruth

{DAY 83}

"The LORD is the one who goes ahead of you; He will be with you. He will not fail you or forsake you. Do not fear or be dismayed." (Deuteronomy 31:8 NASB)

Jesus asks you to "follow" Him so that He will be in front and leading you. As you continually "follow" Jesus, He is always right here with you. As you "follow" Jesus, He will never abandon you, and He will never give you up. You do not need to fear, worry, or stress about your future because the Lord Himself goes before you. Thank You, Jesus, that knowing and believing this Scripture gives me God-confidence for every situation in my life today and each future day to come.

CHOOSE TO MAKE TODAY AND EVERY DAY GREAT AND BLESSED NO MATTER WHAT!

#PerpetualPraise #ContinualPrayer #WorshipInSpiritAndTruth

{DAY 84}

"In everything he did he had great success, because the LORD was with him." (1 Samuel 18:14 NIV)

I like to personalize God's Word in my own life by putting my name in it, and then speak it out loud so I can actually hear myself saying it. When I read this Scripture, I say out loud, "In everything JoAnn does she has great success, because the Lord Jesus is always with her." Then I mix what I hear with my faith. When repeated often enough, this gets in my spirit and actually begins manifesting in my life. No man can take this from me because it is now hidden in my heart and it is in my spirit. The reason I do this is because this is how, like David, we encourage ourselves in the Lord. Also, this is how we work the Word of God to apply it to our own lives to create good changes. Thank You, Lord, for Your Word's creative power!

CHOOSE TO MAKE TODAY AND EVERY DAY GREAT AND BLESSED NO MATTER WHAT!

#PerpetualPraise #ContinualPrayer #WorshipInSpiritAndTruth

{DAY 85}

PRAISE TO START YOUR DAY:

"For God is working in you, giving you the desire and the power to do what pleases him." (Philippians 2:13 NLT)

Thank You, Lord, for working in me, giving me the desire to obey You and do Your Will and the power to do what pleases You. Thank You, Lord, for filling me with Your Holy Spirit Who empowers me to live a holy and righteous Christian life in You and Who keeps me right with God. Thank You, Jesus, that You put Godly desires in my heart, desires that are lined up with Your Will, and that You fulfill those desires. I desire to be more like You every day. I desire that when people see me, they see You. More of You and less of me—less of me and more of You, Jesus. I love You, Jesus!

CHOOSE TO MAKE TODAY AND EVERY DAY GREAT AND BLESSED NO MATTER WHAT!

#PerpetualPraise #ContinualPrayer #WorshipInSpiritAndTruth

{DAY 86}

"Farmers who wait for perfect weather never plant. If they watch every cloud, they never harvest. Just as you cannot understand the path of the wind or the mystery of a tiny baby growing in its mother's womb, so you cannot understand the activity of God, who does all things. Plant your seed in the morning and keep busy all afternoon, for you don't know if profit will come from one activity or another—or maybe both."
(Ecclesiastes 11:4-6 NLT)

Do you pull the covers up over your head and stay home from church just because it's raining outside? Winds and clouds of difficulty are designed to test us, when they are in God's hands. God will never tempt you, but He will test you and your faith for the sake of our good and our growth in Christ Jesus. There is a law of sowing and reaping. We should always choose not to allow difficulty and/or doubt to prevent us from sowing good and reaping our great harvest.

CHOOSE TO MAKE TODAY AND EVERY DAY GREAT AND BLESSED NO MATTER WHAT!

#PerpetualPraise #ContinualPrayer #WorshipInSpiritAndTruth

{DAY 87}

PRAISE TO START YOUR DAY:

"I will greatly rejoice in the LORD, my soul shall be joyful in my God; for He has clothed me with the garments of salvation, He has covered me with the robe of righteousness, as a bridegroom decks himself with ornaments, and as a bride adorns herself with her jewels." (Isaiah 61:10 NKJV)

When you wholeheartedly show and tell the Lord how much you delight in Him through praise and worship and being obedient to Him, your soul is filled with joy as well, and you wear that joy in your countenance. As compared to the most costly jeweled garments, the Lord clothes you beautifully with Christ's righteousness and with salvation, and then He enhances your beauty with His grace, favor, and mercy. I adore You, Jesus, and I desire more of You than ever before! My soul cries out, "Hallelujah!"

 CHOOSE TO MAKE TODAY AND EVERY DAY GREAT AND BLESSED NO MATTER WHAT!

#PerpetualPraise #ContinualPrayer #WorshipInSpiritAndTruth

{DAY 88}

"The LORD hath done great things for us; whereof we are glad." (Psalm 126:3 KJV)

God warns us not to look back at our past, living our present today in regret. At the same time, we should never forget what God has brought us out of and freed us from, and just how far He has brought us in Christ Jesus. We need to build altars to God in our hearts so we can revisit the great things God has done for us. We should praise God that we are His own skillfully-wrought works of art. I just can't tell it all! If I had a thousand tongues, I still could not praise You enough, my Jesus!

CHOOSE TO MAKE TODAY AND EVERY DAY GREAT AND BLESSED NO MATTER WHAT!

#PerpetualPraise #ContinualPrayer #WorshipInSpiritAndTruth

{DAY 89}

"But as many as received Him, to them He gave the right to become children of God, to those who believe in His name." (John 1:12 NKJV)

I am a child of God and I belong to Him because I have received Jesus as my personal Lord and Savior. Jesus lives in my heart because I extended a personal invitation to Him. The Lord filled me with His Holy Spirit. Out of obedience to the Word of God, I was baptized in water and I now walk in newness of life. I have also been baptized with the Holy Ghost because I asked God to please give me that special gift, and He did. My mother has always told me that, from the time I was just a baby, I always woke up with a big smile on my face. I praise God that I am still happy with the joy of the Lord, and smiling each morning when He wakes me up! Well, how could I be anything else knowing that I am a child of my Heavenly Father God!

CHOOSE TO MAKE TODAY AND EVERY DAY GREAT AND BLESSED NO MATTER WHAT!

#PerpetualPraise #ContinualPrayer #WorshipInSpiritAndTruth

{DAY 90}

PRAISE TO START YOUR DAY:

"All of this is for your benefit. And as God's grace reaches more and more people, there will be great thanksgiving, and God will receive more and more glory." (2 Corinthians 4:15 NLT)

Gratitude goes a very long way with God in your favor, no matter what situation you are in or whatever the circumstance you are facing. A person with a grateful heart will always be able to thank God for something, even if it's the fact that you have breath in your body. After all, God is in control of that, too. Gratitude brings miracles from God into your life. All that you do in your service to God and the Kingdom of God is for the benefit of your overall salvation. You are to win as many souls as you can for God, thereby leading many to praise Him, offer their thanksgiving to Him, and glorify Him. God is worthy to receive all glory, praise, honor, power, and thanksgiving. Worthy is the Lamb of God to be praised!

CHOOSE TO MAKE TODAY AND EVERY DAY GREAT AND BLESSED NO MATTER WHAT!

#PerpetualPraise #ContinualPrayer #WorshipInSpiritAndTruth

{DAY 91}

"One thing I have desired of the LORD, that will I seek: that I may dwell in the house of the LORD all the days of my life, to behold the beauty of the LORD, and to inquire in His temple." (Psalm 27:4 NKJV)

I am wholly addicted to the house of the Lord. I find love, joy, and peace in the house of the Lord. God's presence is in the house of the Lord. God's angels are in the house of the Lord. God's Glory is in the house of the Lord. Jesus Himself walks up and down the aisles in the house of the Lord, with His eyes set on those who are wholeheartedly praising and worshiping Him. Miracles take place in the house of the Lord. Blessings from God are in the house of the Lord. I am full of joy and ever so grateful that I get to go to the house of the Lord today to praise and worship my Jesus, to the glory of our Heavenly Father God!

CHOOSE TO MAKE TODAY AND EVERY DAY GREAT AND BLESSED NO MATTER WHAT!

#PerpetualPraise #ContinualPrayer #WorshipInSpiritAndTruth

{DAY 92}

"Draw near to God and He will draw near to you..." (James 4:8 NKJV)

Show and tell God how much you love Him. Show Him your love by being obedient to His commandments, teachings, and instructions. Talk to God continually throughout each day. Praise and worship God always and in everything. Grab ahold of God and never let go. Cleave to Him. Never let go of God's hand. It's about walking with Jesus. When He moves, you move with Him. When you know Jesus well enough you will know when and where He will be moving, so you will always be ready to move with Him. Keep Jesus up close and personal with you at all times. Do this, and you will experience miracles that last. It is not about religion, but it is all about having a close relationship with Christ Jesus as your Lord and Savior. Make Him your Constant Companion. Jesus already knows everything there is to know about you anyway, so there is absolutely nothing that you cannot talk to Him about. Jesus will never push you away, or reject you. Jesus loves you. He is drawing you near to Him because He wants to draw near to you, too.

CHOOSE TO MAKE TODAY AND EVERY DAY GREAT AND BLESSED NO MATTER WHAT!

#PerpetualPraise #ContinualPrayer #WorshipInSpiritAndTruth

{DAY 93}

"They sing the song of Moses, the servant of God, and the song of the Lamb, saying: 'Great and marvelous are Your works, Lord God Almighty! Just and true are Your ways, O King of the saints!'" (Revelation 15:3 NKJV)

I sing the song of JoAnn, the servant of God, as a testimony of Christ Jesus, my Lord and Savior, for His miraculous intervention in my life when He saved me from a life of sin, delivered, and set me totally free indeed from the chains of drugs and alcohol in which I was bound. Each year the chains got more numerous, stronger, heavier, and tighter. They were slowly, but steadily, killing me. But God broke every one of those chains off me! He made me alive in Him because He had a plan for my life, and He had something for me to do for Him through the sharing of my testimony. Truly, how great and marvelous are Your works, Lord God Almighty! Just and true are Your ways, my soon coming King! I love and adore You, Jesus! Glory to our Heavenly Father God!

CHOOSE TO MAKE TODAY AND EVERY DAY GREAT AND BLESSED NO MATTER WHAT!

#PerpetualPraise #ContinualPrayer #WorshipInSpiritAndTruth

{DAY 94}

PRAISE TO START YOUR DAY:

"Your word is very pure; therefore Your servant loves it." (Psalm 119:140 NKJV)

Thank You, Lord, for awakening me revived and with greater faith in You on this glorious God morning, and for giving me another day to be alive in You with purpose! Lord, Your Word has been proven in my life (by many trials) to be pure. This truth has come to me as a result of having a personal and close relationship with You. There have been many times in my life that I had no one and nothing but You, Your word, and Your Holy Spirit to turn to for help and comfort. I confess that in some of those times of desperate need, I did turn to man first—just to be disappointed, rejected, and/or turned away. I ask right now, Lord, for Your forgiveness for that, in the Name of Jesus! Amen, amen, and amen!!! I have learned the hard way, Jesus, that You are all I have ever needed. I will always come to you first—and only to You. I love Your Word! I love You, my Jesus! You are mine, and I am Yours!

CHOOSE TO MAKE TODAY AND EVERY DAY GREAT AND BLESSED NO MATTER WHAT!

#PerpetualPraise #ContinualPrayer #WorshipInSpiritAndTruth

{DAY 95}

"Be thankful in all circumstances, for this is God's will for you who belong to Christ Jesus. And we know that God causes everything to work together for the good of those who love God and are called according to his purpose for them." (1 Thessalonians 5:18; Romans 8:28 NLT)

Beginning in January 2015 and continuing through the end of December 2015 was a year of "shifting" and "sifting" in every area of my life! I CHOSE to PRAISE, WORSHIP, and PRAY my way through it all! As a result, I am still here living in and for God, praising and worshiping Him, knowing that my "this" is God's "that"! I love You, JESUS, with all my heart, soul, mind, and strength! You are my Everything!!! Dear reader(s), whatever situation you may be going through right now, your "this" is exactly what God is going to work for your favor and God-glorifying testimony (God's "that"), IF you will choose to praise Him through it all. I know from personal experience that this is true.

CHOOSE TO MAKE TODAY AND EVERY DAY GREAT AND BLESSED NO MATTER WHAT!

#PerpetualPraise #ContinualPrayer #WorshipInSpiritAndTruth

{DAY 96}

PRAISE TO START YOUR DAY:

"You light a lamp for me. The Lord, my God, lights up my darkness."
(Psalm 18:28 NLT)

Oh Lord, my God, You brought me out of darkness into Your glorious light. You enlighten my spirit. You are my constant Light in a world that continues to grow darker. When my spirit begins to grow dim, You are my endless Supplier of Your fresh oil of grace and mercy. You are my Lamp that never runs out of oil. You make my countenance joyful! I rejoice in You, Jesus!

CHOOSE TO MAKE TODAY AND EVERY DAY GREAT AND BLESSED NO MATTER WHAT!

#PerpetualPraise #ContinualPrayer #WorshipInSpiritAndTruth

{DAY 97}

"Mercy and truth have met together; righteousness and peace have kissed. Truth shall spring out of the earth, and righteousness shall look down from heaven. Yes, the LORD will give what is good; and our land will yield its increase. Righteousness will go before Him, and shall make His footsteps our pathway." (Psalm 85:10-13 NKJV)

Lord, Your underserved favor and trustworthiness bring us together into the Kingdom of God and make us right with God and with each other. Your presence brings peace to us and a desire to be faithful to You, because You have been faithful to us first. Lord God, You give to us that which is good. Oh God, Your righteousness brings peace and wholeness to those whose lives are centered in relationship with Christ Jesus and in His presence. Thank You, Lord, for this message of joyful assurance! Hallelujah! Bless the Lord, oh my soul, and all that is within me! Bless His Holy Name!

CHOOSE TO MAKE TODAY AND EVERY DAY GREAT AND BLESSED NO MATTER WHAT!

#PerpetualPraise #ContinualPrayer #WorshipInSpiritAndTruth

{DAY 98}

"Then His disciples remembered that it was written, 'Zeal for Your house has eaten Me up.'" (John 2:17 NKJV)

I wrote a note in my Bible years ago during one of Bishop Steve Fender's messages that says, "Going to church should be a passion; not a pastime!" According to Webster's Dictionary, the definition of "pastime" is a way of spending spare time. One of the many reasons I love Livingway Church is because it is truly a house of zeal, always filled with brethren who are passionate about being there. Do you have a church home that stirs the zeal in you? It's important to have a church to call home. Thank You, my Jesus, that I have that same passionate zeal for Your house! Home is where the heart is, and the house of the Lord is my home.

CHOOSE TO MAKE TODAY AND EVERY DAY GREAT AND BLESSED NO MATTER WHAT!

#PerpetualPraise #ContinualPrayer #WorshipInSpiritAndTruth

{DAY 99}

"Unless the LORD builds the house, the builders labor in vain. Unless the LORD watches over the city, the guards stand watch in vain." (Psalm 127:1 NIV)

"God, who made the world and everything in it, since He is Lord of heaven and earth, does not dwell in temples made with hands. Nor is He worshiped with men's hands, as though He needed anything, since He gives to all life, breath, and all things." (Acts 17:24-25 NKJV)

God dwells in our spirit (which is the temple of God's Holy Spirit) and in our hearts. It is the Lord Who builds and keeps His own church. We should trust the Lord's house to the Lord of the house. We need God's help and guidance, and we need God's blessing. Man cannot do it alone and be successful. We must acknowledge God to be the Giver of all things. God is in control of every breath we take. Our very lives depend upon God. God is our ultimate preservation, no matter what care or precaution may be used by man. Thank You, Lord, that You allow and help us to build our home in You. When our home is built in You, only then will we be safe and comfortable in it, and be able to enjoy it. We worship You, oh God, for You are Lord above all!

CHOOSE TO MAKE TODAY AND EVERY DAY GREAT AND BLESSED NO MATTERWHAT!

#PerpetualPraise #ContinualPrayer #WorshipInSpiritAndTruth

{DAY 100}

"If then you were raised with Christ, seek those things which are above, where Christ is, sitting at the right hand of God. Set your mind on things above, not on things on the earth." (Colossians 3:1-2 NKJV)

At the beginning of your spiritual life, you passed from death, your "old life before Christ", to your "resurrected life in Christ". According to God's Word, you are still in the world, but you are not of the world. You are just passing through on your way to your eternal home with Jesus. It is now necessary to put away carnal thoughts (those thoughts relating to the physical: lustful, sexual, sensual thoughts) and stay focused on Christ Jesus, in order to have your spiritual needs met. Choose your thoughts carefully and wisely. Let Jesus and Heaven fill your thoughts today and every day. Lord Jesus, help us to keep our minds stayed on You and Heavenly things, and not on the things of the world, in the blessed Name of Jesus! Amen, amen, and amen!!!

CHOOSE TO MAKE TODAY AND EVERY DAY GREAT AND BLESSED NO MATTER WHAT!

#PerpetualPraise #ContinualPrayer #WorshipInSpiritAndTruth

{DAY 101}

PRAISE TO START YOUR DAY:

"Hallelujah! O servants of Jehovah, praise his name. Blessed is his name forever and forever. Praise him from sunrise to sunset! For he is high above the nations; his glory is far greater than the heavens. Who can be compared with God enthroned on high? Far below him are the heavens and the earth; he stoops to look, and lifts the poor from the dirt and the hungry from the garbage dump, and sets them among princes! He gives children to the childless wife, so that she becomes a happy mother. Hallelujah! Praise the Lord." (Psalm 113:1-9 TLB)

This Psalm begins and ends with "Hallelujah". "Hallel" is a Hebrew word that means "praise", or "say something or someone is very great". When that someone is the Lord God, then the word becomes "hallelujah". This means "the Lord is very great". We who serve the Lord are to bless Him with our praise. Our Lord is above all, over all, and in all, and yet He still helps people in need because He loves His creation. Hallelujah! Praise the Lord, for He alone is Worthy of all the glory, praise, honor, power, and thanksgiving!

CHOOSE TO MAKE TODAY AND EVERY DAY GREAT AND BLESSED NO MATTER WHAT!

#PerpetualPraise #ContinualPrayer #WorshipInSpiritAndTruth

{DAY 102}

PRAISE TO START YOUR DAY:

"As for God, His way is perfect; the word of the LORD is proven; He is a shield to all who trust in Him. For who is God, except the LORD? And who is a rock, except our God?" (Psalm 18:30-31 NKJV)

God is the Great Being, the Great I AM, and only His way is perfect—as good as it is possible to be, above the realm of possibility for mankind. Your Word has been tested and tried as far back as the biblical patriarchs Abraham, Isaac, Jacob, and Noah. Lord, I personally have tried and tested Your Word. Oh God, Your Word is from everlasting to everlasting, and will forever stand to be faithful and true. I trust in You, oh God, and in Your Word, and in Your Son, Christ Jesus. I worship You, Jehovah-Magen, for You are the Lord my Shield Who protects me and enables me to force back the fiery darts of the devil! I worship You, Jehovah-Sel'i, for You are the Lord my Rock! You are my solid Rock Who I have built my life and my home upon.

CHOOSE TO MAKE TODAY AND EVERY DAY GREAT AND BLESSED NO MATTER WHAT!

#PerpetualPraise #ContinualPrayer #WorshipInSpiritAndTruth

{DAY 103}

"The LORD is compassionate and merciful, slow to get angry, and filled with unfailing love. He will not constantly accuse us, nor remain angry forever. He does not punish us for all our sins; he does not deal harshly with us, as we deserve. For his unfailing love toward those who fear him is as great as the height of the heavens above the earth. He has removed our sins as far from us as the east is from the west. The LORD is like a father to his children, tender and compassionate to those who fear him. For he knows how weak we are; he remembers we are only dust." (Psalm 103:8-14 NLT)

God is not standing over His children, ready to hit us in the head every time we mess up. No, much to the contrary! God is compassionate and merciful, and He wants us to be the same way with each other. God Himself has not forgotten that He created man from mere dust. He is well aware that we are weak and that we are not perfect. When we receive His Son Christ Jesus as our Lord and Savior, God totally blots out our sins and does not remember them. They are gone forever. Then God sees us through the precious Blood of Christ Jesus which covers us, and He sees us as white as snow, clean with no spots or blemishes.

CHOOSE TO MAKE TODAY AND EVERY DAY GREAT AND BLESSED NO MATTER WHAT!

#PerpetualPraise #ContinualPrayer #WorshipInSpiritAndTruth

{DAY 104}

PRAISE TO START YOUR DAY:

"Sing to the LORD, for He has done excellent things; this is known in all the earth." (Isaiah 12:5 NKJV)

God has done majestic and wonderful things, which only He could do, not only in biblical times but also in our own lives. All these things are worthy of celebrating in all the earth. We praise You, oh God, our Creator, our Sustainer, our Lord and Savior, our Redeemer, our Deliverer, our Provider, our Protector, our Healer, our Provider, our Waymaker, our Conqueror, our soon coming King…! How excellent is Your Greatness, oh God! JESUS SAVES AND SO MUCH MORE!!!

CHOOSE TO MAKE TODAY AND EVERY DAY GREAT AND BLESSED NO MATTER WHAT!

#PerpetualPraise #ContinualPrayer #WorshipInSpiritAndTruth

{DAY 105}

PRAISE TO START YOUR DAY:

"Those who are planted in the house of the LORD shall flourish in the courts of our God. They shall still bear fruit in old age; they shall be fresh and flourishing, to declare that the LORD is upright; He is my rock, and there is no unrighteousness in Him." (Psalm 92:13-15 NKJV)

Those who get planted and stay in the house of the Lord, even in their old age will be constant and enduring in their Godliness because of the grace of God and His righteousness. Pray that God will lead you to a true "word and worship" church (according to what God's Word says), get planted there, and stay in covenant with God and with your church by acknowledging your pastor(s) as your spiritual father(s)/mother(s); serving God and your fellow brothers and sisters in your church; being loyal and faithful to your church; not leaving your church when you get your feelings hurt (only God is perfect), when you don't get your own way, or when the pastor preaches on something that causes you to feel an "Ouchy".. That is the Holy Spirit convicting your spirit about something you need to change in your life, and it is part of your spiritual growth process. You prayed to God, and He led you to your true "word and worship" church. So, in God's eyes, you are now in a covenant relationship with Him and with your church (like a bride and groom). Stay where God placed you, and stay with a right heart. God holds you in very high regard when you stay planted and faithful, and He blesses and rewards you in many ways.

CHOOSE TO MAKE TODAY AND EVERY DAY GREAT AND BLESSED NO MATTER WHAT!

#PerpetualPraise #ContinualPrayer#WorshipInSpiritAndTruth

{DAY 106}

PRAISE TO START YOUR DAY:

"I will praise the LORD according to His righteousness, and will sing praise to the name of the LORD Most High." (Psalm 7:17 NKJV)

I praise You for Your faithfulness to Your Word, Lord. I praise You, Lord, because You are not an unjust judge, but instead You are the Just Judge and Your judgments are always right and just according to Your Word. You take vengeance upon those who cause pain and suffering to Your people. Throughout Your Word, You give warning to sinners and, because You are long-suffering and patient, You give the sinner plenty of time to repent (express sincere regret and remorse about their wrongdoing) and turn to You. I praise You, Lord, for You faithfully keep Your promises to Your people. I worship You, Jehovah-Elyon, for You are the Lord Most High, and I sing praises to Your Name!

CHOOSE TO MAKE TODAY AND EVERY DAY GREAT AND BLESSED NO MATTER WHAT!

#PerpetualPraise #ContinualPrayer#WorshipInSpiritAndTruth

{DAY 107}

"Therefore, having been justified by faith, we have peace with God through our Lord Jesus Christ, through whom also we have access by faith into this grace in which we stand, and rejoice in hope of the glory of God." (Romans 5:1-2 NKJV)

We, as believers, are declared or made righteous in the sight of God by our faith. We have peace with God through our Lord Jesus Christ, Who redeemed us and Who is now sitting at the right hand of God interceding on our behalf. We are blessed to stand in God's grace by our faith. We have great joy even now because we have the hope of sharing in God's glory when we go to Heaven. In Heaven, we will be similar to Christ, freed from all sin, and therefore we will be glorified with the Lord and will get to see all of His Glory.

CHOOSE TO MAKE TODAY AND EVERY DAY GREAT AND BLESSED NO MATTER WHAT!

#PerpetualPraise #ContinualPrayer#WorshipInSpiritAndTruth

{DAY 108}

"The LORD bless you and keep you; the LORD make His face shine upon you, and be gracious to you; the LORD lift up His countenance upon you, and give you peace." (Numbers 6:24-26 NKJV)

In this Scripture, the meaning of the word "bless" is to make somebody or something holy. We become holy when we accept Jesus Christ as our Lord and Savior. We receive His righteousness. The Lord protects His people from the evil one and gives His people power over sin. The Lord keeps His people in His grace and takes care of His people. The Lord gives His people peace. Thank You, oh God, that it is Your heart's desire to bless Your people. Thank You for seeing us through Christ Jesus after we have accepted Him as our Lord and Savior. Then Your countenance is always a smile when You look at us. Praise God from whom all blessings flow! Dear reader(s), I am praying this Scripture and message over you today, in the blessed Name of Jesus! Amen, amen, and amen!

CHOOSE TO MAKE TODAY AND EVERY DAY GREAT AND BLESSED NO MATTER WHAT!

#PerpetualPraise #ContinualPrayer #WorshipInSpiritAndTruth

{DAY 109}

"Brethren, I do not count myself to have apprehended; but one thing I do, forgetting those things which are behind and reaching forward to those things which are ahead, I press toward the goal for the prize of the upward call of God in Christ Jesus." (Philippians 3:13-14 NKJV)

Though I have not yet arrived at the point of complete spiritual maturity, I keep moving forward in the growth process; never backward and never standing still like a "sitting duck" for the enemy. I do not dwell on regrets from my past; however, I will never forget just how far God has brought me. I keep growing and spiraling upward in my movement toward my goal for the prize of eternal life in the eternal presence of Christ Jesus in Heaven.

CHOOSE TO MAKE TODAY AND EVERY DAY GREAT AND BLESSED NO MATTER WHAT!

#PerpetualPraise #ContinualPrayer #WorshipInSpiritAndTruth

{DAY 110}

"The Sovereign LORD has given me a well-instructed tongue, to know the word that sustains the weary. He wakens me morning by morning, wakens my ear to listen like one being instructed." (Isaiah 50:4 NIV)

Thank You, Lord, for waking me up on this glorious God morning and starting me on my way! How will You use me today, Lord? Thank You, Jesus, that Your word teaches and instructs me what to say to those who are weary to encourage, strengthen and support them. Lord, use me today as an "encourager" for someone who is weary. Thank You, Jesus, for giving me spiritual ears to hear Your divine instructions and Your Holy Spirit to understand what I hear, and for keeping me prepared so that I am always ready and able to bring forth Your divinely instructed word in season. Today is the day; now is the time. I pray this over each and every Reader today, in the precious and blessed Name of Jesus! Amen, amen, and amen!

CHOOSE TO MAKE TODAY AND EVERY DAY GREAT AND BLESSED NO MATTER WHAT!

#PerpetualPraise #ContinualPrayer#WorshipInSpiritAndTruth

{DAY 111}

"Whom have I in heaven but You? And there is none upon earth that I desire besides You. My flesh and my heart fail; but God is the strength of my heart and my portion forever." (Psalm 73:25-26 NKJV)

I praise God that I no longer delight in worldly things on earth, but now I delight in Jesus and all things godly. Now I go to my Heavenly Daddy and talk to Him whenever I want. I eat, fill up and digest His Word daily. At times my flesh fails, but then my spirit man overcomes my flesh. When others break my heart to the point of it weakening and failing me, You come to support, strengthen, and restore my heart through my faith in You and Your promises. Jesus, You are all I need. I worship You, Lord.

CHOOSE TO MAKE TODAY AND EVERY DAY GREAT AND BLESSED NO MATTER WHAT!

#PerpetualPraise #ContinualPrayer #WorshipInSpiritAndTruth

{DAY 112}

"Praise the Lord! I will praise the Lord with my whole heart, in the assembly of the upright and in the congregation. The works of the Lord are great, studied by all who have pleasure in them. His work is honorable and glorious, and His righteousness endures forever. He has made His wonderful works to be remembered; the Lord is gracious and full of compassion." (Psalm 111:1-4 NKJV)

We are to wholeheartedly praise the Lord for the great and miraculous works He has done. We are to praise Him at church and not forsake gathering with His people. As we delight in the Lord, we will desire and have a longing to study His Word to find out all we can about Jesus and what He has done. As we grow in our knowledge of Jesus, we will never forget what He did when He walked the earth in the form of a God-man, and we will also never forget what He has done in our own lives—impossible, great, powerful and mighty things! Jesus, we will continue to praise and worship You always and forevermore!

CHOOSE TO MAKE TODAY AND EVERY DAY GREAT AND BLESSED NO MATTER WHAT!

#PerpetualPraise #ContinualPrayer#WorshipInSpiritAndTruth

{DAY 113}

PRAISE TO START YOUR DAY:

"Where can I go from Your Spirit? Or where can I flee from Your presence?" (Psalm 139:7 NKJV)

I praise and worship You, Jehovah-Shammah, for You are my ever present God! I offer thanksgiving unto You. You live in me and I live in You. You are my Lord and Savior. It is written that my body is the temple of Your Holy Spirit. Therefore, wherever I am, there Your Holy Spirit is also; and whenever You move, I move also, so Your presence is always with me. In You I live, I move, I have my being, I perpetually praise and worship You. I live in Your presence by choice. I have made the right choice. Glory to our Father God! Father God, I am praying this over each and every Reader today, in the blessed Name of Your Son Christ Jesus! Amen, amen, and amen! The biblical definition of "Amen" is "so be it".

CHOOSE TO MAKE TODAY AND EVERY DAY GREAT AND BLESSED NO MATTER WHAT!

#PerpetualPraise #ContinualPrayer #WorshipInSpiritAndTruth

{DAY 114}

PRAISE TO START YOUR DAY:

"I will bless the LORD at all times; His praise shall continually be in my mouth. My soul shall make its boast in the LORD; the humble shall hear of it and be glad. Oh, magnify the LORD with me, and let us exalt His name together." (Psalm 34:1-3 NKJV)

I will bless the Lord at all times through loving Him and others; through forgiving myself and others as He has forgiven me; through telling others about Jesus and leading others to Him; through continually praising and worshiping Him with my mouth; through having a two-way relationship with Him; through being obedient; through sharing my testimony; through sharing His goodness with others; through living my life in, through and for Him; through glorifying Him; through having faith in Him; through putting all my trust in Him; through thinking about Him all the time; and through any and all other ways I can think of to bless Him! My only boast is of the Lord and everything about Him. Others hear (read) of Jesus, and He brings joy to their spirit! Come and magnify the Lord with me—our God is BIG—BIGGER—BIGGEST—than anybody or anything! He is HIGHEST in Power over all!

CHOOSE TO MAKE TODAY AND EVERY DAY GREAT AND BLESSED NO MATTER WHAT!

#PerpetualPraise #ContinualPrayer #WorshipInSpiritAndTruth

{DAY 115}

"He who loves purity of heart and has grace on his lips, the king will be his friend. Blessed are the pure in heart, for they shall see God." (Proverbs 22:11; Matthew 5:8 NKJV)

Jesus, You are my Best Friend and my Constant Companion, and I desire for You to always call me Your friend, too. I want to see You face to face. I want to see Your Glory in the fullest. Lord Jesus, may my heart remain pure and clean, and may my conscience always be free from guilt so that what flows from my heart and comes out of my mouth is a gracious sound to You and to the other hearers (readers) of my words, in the blessed Name of Jesus! Amen, amen, and amen!

CHOOSE TO MAKE TODAY AND EVERY DAY GREAT AND BLESSED NO MATTER WHAT!

#PerpetualPraise #ContinualPrayer #WorshipInSpiritAndTruth

{DAY 116}

PRAISE TO START YOUR DAY:

"Bless the LORD, O my soul! O LORD my God, You are very great: You are clothed with honor and majesty,...O LORD, how manifold are Your works! In wisdom, You have made them all. The earth is full of Your possessions—" (Psalm 104:1,24 NKJV)

Lord, may my soul always bless You. May all my thoughts be from You and of You, and may I meditate on You both day and night. You illuminate majestic splendor, holiness, righteousness, and honor. Thank You, Lord, for the great protective care, You take with all You have created in the earth! My soul cries out "Hallelujah" to You!!! You are a very Great God!

CHOOSE TO MAKE TODAY AND EVERY DAY GREAT AND BLESSED NO MATTER WHAT!

#PerpetualPraise #ContinualPrayer #WorshipInSpiritAndTruth

{DAY 117}

"And Nehemiah continued, "Go and celebrate with a feast of rich foods and sweet drinks, and share gifts of food with people who have nothing prepared. This is a sacred day before our Lord. Don't be dejected and sad, for the joy of the LORD is your strength!" (Nehemiah 8:10 NLT)

If you are feeling sad and downhearted today, feeling like nobody cares about you, there is something you can do that will make you happy and joyful. Go help somebody else and/or encourage somebody else. When you do this, God will restore and fill your spirit with joy. Our true inner joy comes from the Lord and strengthens us so that we can encourage, help and strengthen others. The joy of our Lord Christ Jesus as He was beaten and nailed to the cross and stayed there dying for you and for me (even though Jesus had the power to save Himself) was in knowing that His death, burial, and resurrection would make it possible for sinners to be made right with God. With each soul you win to Christ, your inner joy will become more full, and your joy will also show on the outside especially in your face. This is the day that the Lord has made and we shall rejoice and be glad in it! Every day is holy unto our Lord. Glorify God by making the best of each day He gifts you with.

CHOOSE TO MAKE TODAY AND EVERY DAY GREAT AND BLESSED NO MATTER WHAT!

#PerpetualPraise #ContinualPrayer #WorshipInSpiritAndTruth

{DAY 118}

"Oh, give thanks to the Lord, for He is good! For His mercy endures forever. I called on the Lord in distress; the Lord answered me and set me in a broad place. The Lord is on my side; I will not fear. What can man do to me?" (Psalm 118:1,5,6 NKJV)

God is Good all the time, and all the time God is Good! He alone is Worthy of all our praise, glory, honor, power and thanksgiving! Out of severe heartache and/or mental torment, have you ever (either at home or in a public place such as a park, beach…) just dropped to your knees and cried out, "JESUS!", loud and clear? If you have, your prayer went straight to God's heart. Then you built an altar to God in your heart when He heard and answered you so that you would always be able to revisit that altar in your heart and never forget that the Lord was on your side that day. The Lord is still on your side even now today. There is no need to fear what man can do to you. If you are on the Lord's side, then He is on your side all the time. God is All Powerful! If you are on the Lord's side, then Jesus is in front of you, His Grace and Mercy are following you, and His angels have you surrounded with His protection! It is so good to know that the Lord is on our side! We praise You, Lord!

CHOOSE TO MAKE TODAY AND EVERY DAY GREAT AND BLESSED NO MATTER WHAT!

#PerpetualPraise #ContinualPrayer #WorshipInSpiritAndTruth

{DAY 119}

"Behold, bless the LORD, all you servants of the LORD, who by night stand in the house of the LORD! Lift up your hands in the sanctuary, and bless the LORD. The LORD who made heaven and earth bless you from Zion!" (Psalm 134:1-2 NKJV)

Believers are instructed to look around the sanctuary and everywhere and see reasons to praise God, the Creator of all, in the beauty of holiness. We are instructed to lift up our hands as a way of showing forth praise to our God. Our obedience greatly blesses God. I am always happy and grateful that I am able to go to the house of the Lord to stand praising and worshiping the Lover of my soul, Jesus, with my beloved brothers and sisters in Christ Jesus! I love Monday nights because I get to go to the house of the Lord for the EmpowHer ladies' class! I love Tuesday nights because I get to go to the house of the Lord for Living Praise Choir rehearsal to sing praise and worship songs to the Lord and learn new songs to sing to Him! I love Wednesday nights because I get to go to the house of the Lord for a midweek praise and worship service and hear the anointed word of God preached, which refreshes and quickens my spirit! I love all the other days and nights when special occasions arise, which give me another opportunity to go to the house of the Lord! One might think, or even say, "She's addicted!" Oh yes, indeed I am! I am a servant of the Lord, who is holy addicted to the house of the Lord, and God sees that as being very good.

CHOOSE TO MAKE TODAY AND EVERY DAY GREAT AND BLESSED NO MATTER WHAT!

#PerpetualPraise #ContinualPrayer #WorshipInSpiritAndTruth

{DAY 120}

"The LORD will send rain at the proper time from his rich treasury in the heavens and will bless all the work you do. You will lend to many nations, but you will never need to borrow from them." (Deuteronomy 28:12 NLT)

God knows all of His chosen people from the inside of their hearts to the outside. He has even counted the number of hairs on our heads! God knows, much better than we do, when we are ready to receive His richest blessings. He knows beforehand just what we will do with each blessing He desires to give us. Sometimes God's answer to our prayer may be, "Be patient; you are not yet ready." Instead, He will keep us close to His heart until we are ready. Be patient, for at the proper time, God will bless all the work you do unto Him and through Him. God will make you the head and not the tail. You will be above only and not beneath. Thank You, Lord, for all the many blessings You bestow upon Your chosen people. We worship You, oh God, for You have all wisdom and knowledge and power!

CHOOSE TO MAKE TODAY AND EVERY DAY GREAT AND BLESSED NO MATTER WHAT!

#PerpetualPraise #ContinualPrayer #WorshipInSpiritAndTruth

{DAY 121}

PRAISE TO START YOUR DAY:

"Now it shall come to pass, if you diligently obey the voice of the Lord your God, to observe carefully all His commandments which I command you today, that the Lord your God will set you high above all nations of the earth. And all these blessings shall come upon you and overtake you because you obey the voice of the Lord your God: Blessed shall you be in the city, and blessed shall you be in the country." (Deuteronomy 28:1-3 NKJV)

Thank You, Lord, that with every single one of Your commandments comes tremendous blessings, if only we are obedient. Though the word "if" is a tiny word, it carries with it a huge impact on the extent of the blessings we receive from God. "If" your heartfelt desire to be obedient and pleasing to God (and He will know by what you think, say and do) outweighs your desire to be ambushed and overtaken with God's richest blessings, then "look up" because they are on their way!

CHOOSE TO MAKE TODAY AND EVERY DAY GREAT AND BLESSED NO MATTER WHAT!

#PerpetualPraise #ContinualPrayer #WorshipInSpiritAndTruth

{DAY 122}

PRAISE TO START YOUR DAY:

"Praise the LORD! For it is good to sing praises to our God; for it is pleasant, and praise is beautiful." (Psalm 147:1 NKJV)

Hallelujah! Praise the Lord! Praising God is the right thing to do. God comes down and lives in our praises, so praising God blesses us as well. What better way to praise God than in singing joyfully to Him (no matter what your singing voice sounds like). When God hears our joyful songs of praise, He is pleased and blessed by them, and they always sound beautiful to God. Make God's day today! Joyful singing everybody!

CHOOSE TO MAKE TODAY AND EVERY DAY GREAT AND BLESSED NO MATTER WHAT!

#PerpetualPraise #ContinualPrayer #WorshipInSpiritAndTruth

{DAY 123}

"Praise ye the LORD. Sing unto the LORD a new song, and his praise in the congregation of saints." (Psalm 149:1 KJV)

The Lord desires to be blessed by His people through new songs of praise, not only for what He has already done, but for what He is now doing and for what we believe by faith He is about to do and will do in the future. We are all, even now today, God's work in progress. He is working in our lives daily changing us into His image. God has given us promises concerning our loved ones that we have not yet seen manifested; but, because we walk by faith and not by sight, we still believe. We have already been promised eternal life in Heaven with Jesus. By faith, we believe that it will be so. We must praise the Lord even before we see the promise come to pass, no matter how impossible it may seem due to what we are seeing and hearing. We must praise God while we are waiting on God. We must praise God after we see our promises happen. We serve a BIG GOD, who never fails! Praise God in the congregation of saints. Praise God everywhere and at all times. Praise-Praise-Praise and then praise some more! Happy praising everybody! Oh yeah, you have put a big smile on God's face and made Him a "Happy Camper" now! Hallelujah!

CHOOSE TO MAKE TODAY AND EVERY DAY GREAT AND BLESSED NO MATTER WHAT!

#PerpetualPraise #ContinualPrayer #WorshipInSpiritAndTruth

{DAY 124}

"Let all that I am praise the Lord; with my whole heart, I will praise his holy name. Let all that I am praise the Lord; may I never forget the good things he does for me. He forgives all my sins and heals all my diseases. He redeems me from death and crowns me with love and tender mercies. He fills my life with good things. My youth is renewed like the eagle's!" (Psalm 103:1-5 NLT)

JESUS SAVES AND SO MUCH MORE!!! The Lord not only saves us from eternal death, but He also forgives our sins, heals us, and blesses us with His lovingkindness and holy mercies. He fills our lives with the good things of His holy nature (such as making our hearts pure and clean and changing us into His image), which are most satisfying to our souls. These are some of His richest blessings which cause the renewing of our youthful strength and enthusiasm, as well as good health. Just think, God makes it possible for those who are in their 60's thru 90's to still have plenty of "vim and vigor"! It is well with my soul! I thank You, Jesus, that I can rest in You knowing that You love me and intend only good for my life. I choose to receive ALL of Your benefits so that my youth is renewed like the eagle's. Glory HALLELUJAH!

CHOOSE TO MAKE TODAY AND EVERY DAY GREAT AND BLESSED NO MATTER WHAT!

#PerpetualPraise #ContinualPrayer #WorshipInSpiritAndTruth

{DAY 125}

"Don't be drunk with wine, because that will ruin your life. Instead, be filled with the Holy Spirit, singing psalms and hymns and spiritual songs among yourselves, and making music to the Lord in your hearts. And give thanks for everything to God the Father in the name of our Lord Jesus Christ." (Ephesians 5:18-20 NLT)

I worship You, Jehovah-Mephalti, for You are the Lord my Deliverer! God delivered me from being addicted to manmade wine and drugs, and He set me totally free. Now I am daily filled to overflowing on the new wine of the Holy Spirit. Every day, He takes me "higher" than I have ever been before and fills me with unspeakable joy! Thanks to You, Jesus, I no longer spend each day in utter sin and recklessness. I am now alive in You, Lord. Now I am really living, singing and thanking God for every good and holy thing in my life. I give all glory to God our Heavenly Father through Christ Jesus! Dear reader(s), God loves you as much as He loves me, and He will do the same for you if that is what you wholeheartedly desire. God will recreate you and form you again into His very own image. That is why God is referred to as the Potter, and we are His clay. Lift both of your hands of clay to God right now and just ask Him. He will do it for you.

CHOOSE TO MAKE TODAY AND EVERY DAY GREAT AND BLESSED NO MATTER WHAT!

#PerpetualPraise #ContinualPrayer #WorshipInSpiritAndTruth

{DAY 126}

" Everything God does is right—the trademark on all his works is love. God's there, listening for all who pray, for all who pray and mean it. He does what's best for those who fear him—hears them call out, and saves them." (Psalm 145:17-19 MSG)

All of God's ways and works are worthy of our praise. God's ways are always right and holy, and He does everything in love. When you call upon the Lord with your whole heart and with a sincere spirit, you will find Him to be a very present help. God always does what is best for those who treat Him with deep respect. That's who God is. God is Love.

CHOOSE TO MAKE TODAY AND EVERY DAY GREAT AND BLESSED NO MATTER WHAT!

#PerpetualPraise #ContinualPrayer #WorshipInSpiritAndTruth

{DAY 127}

"Therefore humble yourselves under the mighty hand of God, that He may exalt you in due time, casting all your care upon Him, for He cares for you." (1 Peter 5:6-7 NKJV)

God is Omnipotent (all-powerful with unlimited power, almighty, able to do anything). He defends and gives grace to the humble and satisfies your soul. God frowns upon those who are full of self-pride, or in today's terms "full of themselves". Jesus wants you to cast ALL of your cares upon Him as an offering and a sacrifice. No care or concern that you have is too small in God's eyes. Big or small—He wants them all. Jesus considers it a sacrifice on your part when you share your concerns with Him because it shows that you are dependent on Him and that you trust and have faith in Him. Do this and God will honor and promote you in His perfect timing. Praise God because He cares for you!

CHOOSE TO MAKE TODAY AND EVERY DAY GREAT AND BLESSED NO MATTER WHAT!

#PerpetualPraise #ContinualPrayer #WorshipInSpiritAndTruth

{DAY 128}

"Lead me, Lord, in your righteousness because of my enemies—make your way straight before me. Not a word from their mouth can be trusted; their heart is filled with malice. Their throat is an open grave; with their tongues, they tell lies. But let all who take refuge in you be glad; let them ever sing for joy. Spread your protection over them, that those who love your name may rejoice in you. Surely, Lord, you bless the righteous; you surround them with your favor as with a shield." (Psalm 5:8-9,11-12 NIV)

I worship You, oh God, for You are my Refuge—my Safe Haven! Lord, I pray You give me spiritual direction in the path of right conduct. Make it plain for me to be able to see and understand, oh God. Help me by giving me spiritual discernment, so I will have the ability to decide what is truth and what is an error, right and wrong, and protect me from being deceived by lies. Surround me with Your favor as with a protective shield. All this I pray in the blessed Name of Jesus! Amen, amen, and amen! Dear reader(s), this is a great and much-needed prayer that you can pray for yourself or a loved one.

CHOOSE TO MAKE TODAY AND EVERY DAY GREAT AND BLESSED NO MATTER WHAT!

#PerpetualPraise #ContinualPrayer #WorshipInSpiritAndTruth

{DAY 129}

PRAISE TO START YOUR DAY:

"And they worshiped him, and returned to Jerusalem with great joy: And were continually in the temple, praising and blessing God. Amen." (Luke 24:52-53 KJV)

Thank You, Jesus, that I am always grateful and consider it a great privilege to go to Your house to praise and worship You. I always enter Your house with praise, and I always leave Your house joy filled and praising You. Your joy always follows me home, along with my praise and worship. I love blessing You, oh God! As long as I have Your breath in my lungs, I will have a praise in my mouth and on my lips for You and will worship You, in the blessed Name of Jesus! Amen, amen, and amen!

CHOOSE TO MAKE TODAY AND EVERY DAY GREAT AND BLESSED NO MATTER WHAT!

#PerpetualPraise #ContinualPrayer #WorshipInSpiritAndTruth

{DAY 130}

"But they that wait upon the LORD shall renew their strength; they shall mount up with wings as eagles; they shall run, and not be weary, and they shall walk, and not faint." (Isaiah 40:31 KJV)

Some may think that waiting upon the Lord means doing nothing and expecting that God is going to do it all, but that is not the correct assumption. The words "wait upon" makes me think of a waiter/waitress who waits on people. The waiter/waitress is serving people, with the goal being to make their dining experience as pleasant as possible. The waiter/waitress is actively serving, working and being productive until that goal is met. On another note, physically speaking, the worst thing an elderly person can do is become inactive. When that happens, his/her strength quickly weakens, muscle mass is soon diminished, and his/her health begins failing. While we are waiting upon the Lord to fulfill His promises, we should be blessing God and actively serving Him by praising and worshiping God; praying; staying focused on God and the things of God; attending church regularly; serving in ministries; reading, studying and meditating on God's Word daily; living our lives in a godly manner; sharing God's goodness with others; winning souls for God's Kingdom; volunteering; working (either outside the home or at home); taking care of our physical bodies; helping others; and the list goes on. God will continually be renewing our strength. Also, all of these holy habits will keep us in right standing with God and bring us great joy while we are waiting upon the Lord, and will also help to keep us from becoming anxious about God's promises as we keep trusting in Him.

CHOOSE TO MAKE TODAY AND EVERY DAY GREAT AND BLESSED NO MATTER WHAT!

#PerpetualPraise #ContinualPrayer #WorshipInSpiritAndTruth

{DAY 131}

"For I know the plans I have for you," declares the LORD, "plans to prosper you and not to harm you, plans to give you hope and a future." (Jeremiah 29:11 NIV)

Lord, thank You for this Your promise that we may KNOW You have only good, prosperous, holy and righteous plans for our lives. Your plans go beyond our wildest dreams, not only for even now today but also for tomorrow and our future days to come. Father God, we are so blessed that You think about us specifically, individually and dearly! Lord, we KNOW that as we live according to Your good and perfect will and not our will, You are able and willing to fulfill all of Your plans for us and our loved ones. We love You, Lord!

CHOOSE TO MAKE TODAY AND EVERY DAY GREAT AND BLESSED NO MATTER WHAT!

#PerpetualPraise #ContinualPrayer #WorshipInSpiritAndTruth

{DAY 132}

"I love the LORD because He has heard my voice and my supplications. Because He has inclined His ear to me, therefore I will call upon Him as long as I live. I will offer to You the sacrifice of thanksgiving, and will call upon the name of the LORD." (Psalm 116:1-2,17 NKJV)

I thank You, Jesus, for hearing my voice, for saving me from eternal death, for delivering me from being chained and bound to a lifestyle of sin, and for setting me totally free indeed! I am now free to praise and worship You all the days of my life! I will continue to call upon Your Name, "JESUS"! If I had a thousand tongues, I could never thank You enough! You thought I was to die for and I love You, Jesus

CHOOSE TO MAKE TODAY AND EVERY DAY GREAT AND BLESSED NO MATTER WHAT!

#PerpetualPraise #ContinualPrayer #WorshipInSpiritAndTruth

{DAY 133}

PRAISE TO START YOUR DAY:

"It is good to give thanks to the LORD, and to sing praises to Your name, O Most High; to declare Your lovingkindness in the morning, and Your faithfulness every night," (Psalm 92:1-2 NKJV)

Thank You, Lord, for waking me up on this God morning and starting me on my way! Thank You, Lord, for breathing Your breath into my lungs and giving me another day to offer praise, worship and thanksgiving unto You and to bless You. I worship You, Jehovah-Elyon, for You are the Lord Most High! My precious Jesus, may everything I think, say and do this day and every day be pleasing to You, put a big smile on Your face, and make Your countenance to shine even brighter upon me. May we both draw so close and near to each other that we may feel each other's breath and heartbeat, and may they be synchronized and in one accord. May I be an encourager and a hope-giver to others as I share Your lovingkindness and faithfulness. May my harvest for the Kingdom of God reflect that I am a "great faith-doer" as I establish Your Covenant in my life and on the earth, to the Glory of our Heavenly Father, in the blessed Name of Jesus! Amen, amen, and amen!

CHOOSE TO MAKE TODAY AND EVERY DAY GREAT AND BLESSED NO MATTER WHAT!

#PerpetualPraise #ContinualPrayer #WorshipInSpiritAndTruth

{DAY 134}

"For the LORD God is a sun and shield; the LORD will give grace and glory; no good thing will He withhold from those who walk uprightly. O LORD of hosts, blessed is the man who trusts in You!" (Psalm 84:11-12 NKJV)

It's time to rise and let the Son of Righteousness shine upon us as He rises from within us on this glorious God morning! Thank You, Jesus, for increasing our capacity to receive more of Your goodness, grace and glory, which will enable us and to give more back to You and others. Thank You, Lord, for keeping us covered with Your precious Blood today. As we trust in You, this shall be a most productive and miraculous day, in the blessed Name of Jesus! Amen, amen, and amen! If you are reading this, you have already had your first miracle today because the Lord woke you up and started you on His right way! Put a praise on it! Hallelujah!!! Praise the Lord!!!

CHOOSE TO MAKE TODAY AND EVERY DAY GREAT AND BLESSED NO MATTER WHAT!

#PerpetualPraise #ContinualPrayer #WorshipInSpiritAndTruth

{DAY 135}

PRAISE TO START YOUR DAY:

"Praise the LORD! Praise the LORD, O my soul! While I live I will praise the LORD; I will sing praises to my God while I have my being." (Psalm 146:1-2 NKJV)

I praise You, Lord, for waking me up on this glorious God morning by putting Your breath in my lungs, and I praise You for giving me spiritual life in You! When I opened my eyes this morning I was looking at the ceiling, and I praised You for providing a roof over my head and shelter from the storm, and I praised You for being my Refuge, my Protector, and my Shelter from the trials and troubles of this world. When I had to choose what to wear today, I praised You for providing me with more than one change of clothes, and I praised You for clothing me with the garment of praise, joy, holiness and righteousness. When I ate breakfast, I praised You for providing me with food to eat and water to drink, and I praised You for satisfying me for You are the Bread of Life (God's Word) and You are the Living Water (Your Holy Spirit). When I starting working today, I praised You for giving me something to do and enabling me to do it, and I praised You for allowing and equipping me to serve You and Your people and for giving me the power to gain wealth. Lord Jesus, I not only praise You in the natural physical sense, but also in the spiritual sense, and all to the Glory of our Heavenly Father. You are mine and I am Yours forevermore! I love You so much, Jesus!

CHOOSE TO MAKE TODAY AND EVERY DAY GREAT AND BLESSED NO MATTER WHAT!

#PerpetualPraise #ContinualPrayer #WorshipInSpiritAndTruth

{DAY 136}

PRAISE TO START YOUR DAY:

"He will bless those who fear the LORD, both small and great. May the LORD give you increase more and more, you and your children." (Psalm 115:13-14 NKJV)

Thank You, Oh God, that You delight in blessing all who believe that You are and that You are a rewarder of those who diligently seek You, and those who have a deep respect for You no matter our age, gender, race, color, or status in life. You bless us and our children with good things while on earth, and with eternal glory in Heaven. You give increase to us and our children in every area of our lives. For this, we bless You, oh God, and we love You, Jesus!

CHOOSE TO MAKE TODAY AND EVERY DAY GREAT AND BLESSED NO MATTER WHAT!

#PerpetualPraise #ContinualPrayer #WorshipInSpiritAndTruth

{DAY 137}

"The LORD is good to those who wait for Him, to the soul who seeks Him. It is good that one should hope and wait quietly for the salvation of the LORD." (Lamentations 3:25-26 NKJV)

God is good to those who seek Him while waiting on His promises to manifest; those who place their faith and trust in Him. Know that our God is always right on time – never early and never late. His timing is perfect. He has the Master Plan and sees all from beginning to end. He is the Alpha and the Omega. Wait patiently with endurance and know that God will save and deliver you and that He will set you totally free from any and everything that would hinder His blessings from coming to you. Keep seeking Him through His Word, through meditating on Him both day and night, through talking to Him and then taking the time to listen to Him. No matter how many times you may have left God, no matter how long it has been since you have "been on the run" from God, no matter how far you have run from God and ignored Him, He still loves you and He will take you back again and come through for you.

CHOOSE TO MAKE TODAY AND EVERY DAY GREAT AND BLESSED NO MATTER WHAT!

#PerpetualPraise #ContinualPrayer #WorshipInSpiritAndTruth

{DAY 138}

PRAISE TO START YOUR DAY:

"I love those who love me, and those who seek me diligently will find me." (Proverbs 8:17 NKJV)

God accepts your love with His lovingkindness. Seek God and He will reward you for your effort. Love God and seek Him first above everyone and everything with genuine sincerity. God is not untouchable, nor is He difficult to find. He desires for you to find Him. He is closer now than you may think. God teaches man the knowledge of Himself and shows man His will. The more you learn about God, the more you will love God and feel His love towards you, and the more you will love others through the influence of His Holy Spirit at work in you. Thus, you will continue increasing in every area of your life. Blessed be the Name of the Lord!

CHOOSE TO MAKE TODAY AND EVERY DAY GREAT AND BLESSED NO MATTER WHAT!

#PerpetualPraise #ContinualPrayer #WorshipInSpiritAndTruth

{DAY 139}

PRAISE TO START YOUR DAY:

"...Let the weak say, 'I am strong.'" (Joel 3:10 NKJV)

"Each time he said, "My grace is all you need. My power works best in weakness." So now I am glad to boast about my weaknesses so that the power of Christ can work through me. That's why I take pleasure in my weaknesses, and in the insults, hardships, persecutions, and troubles that I suffer for Christ. For when I am weak, then I am strong." (2 Corinthians 12:9-10 NLT)

Thank You, Lord, for waking me up on this glorious God morning and starting me on my way! By faith, I believe in Your word and its power to create and change my life. Therefore, even when I may not feel like it, I still speak Your very word to my soul. Your word builds me up and strengthens me in Christ Jesus, so I remain an overcomer and victorious! I praise You, Lord God Almighty, because Your strength is made perfect in my weakness! Dear reader(s), as you live your life in and for Jesus, be ready for insults and troubles to come. Those who hate God will hate the Jesus in you; therefore, they will hate on you. But rejoice and be glad because God is in you and He is greater, stronger and more powerful than he who is in the world! That means that you are too! Hallelujah Jesus!!!

CHOOSE TO MAKE TODAY AND EVERY DAY GREAT AND BLESSED NO MATTER WHAT!

#PerpetualPraise #ContinualPrayer #WorshipInSpiritAndTruth

{DAY 140}

PRAISE TO START YOUR DAY:

"Then I turned to see the voice that spoke with me…." (Revelation 1:12 NKJV)

Jesus has visited me with His presence on numerous occasions to share Scriptures He knew I was in desperate need of hearing at the very moment of each of His visits. God knew what I was feeling. I had opened up my Bible not even knowing what I was searching for, and God fixed my eyes right on the Scripture each time and spoke to my spirit through it. His presence was so real that I turned my head, ever so steadily but slowly, expecting to see Jesus standing right there beside me or behind me. It was as though my reality became like a slow-motion scene in a movie. Though I was not able to see Him in the natural, I saw Him in the spiritual. He was there, and I knew that I knew that I knew He was right there! My spirit felt Him. I cannot explain in words the overwhelming impact His presence had in my spirit. His personal visits have changed my life, my eternal destination, and my relationship with Him. "Blessed are the poor in spirit, for theirs is the kingdom of heaven." (Matthew 5:3 NIV) Turn to Christ Jesus in faith and with a humble spirit and He will personally visit you, too. Turn to Jesus when you are feeling low, and He will take you over the top.

CHOOSE TO MAKE TODAY AND EVERY DAY GREAT AND BLESSED NO MATTER WHAT!

#PerpetualPraise #ContinualPrayer #WorshipInSpiritAndTruth

{DAY 141}

"I have loved you, my people, with an everlasting love. With unfailing love, I have drawn you to myself." (Jeremiah 31:3 NLT)

Dear Jesus, I well remember when You began drawing me back to You after I had distanced myself from You for so long. You let me know that Your love for me was truly unconditional. I remember the moment when Your unconditional love totally arrested me. Thank You for taking me back on more than one occasion. I will never forget just how far You have brought me because You have brought me a mighty, mighty long way! Lord, today I not only remember how far You have brought me, but also I am reflecting on how far You are still going to take me! My best is yet to come! God, my Alpha and my Omega! Jesus, the Author and Finisher of my faith! I worship and adore You! Thank You, my Jesus, for tenderly loving me and for Your unfailing love.

CHOOSE TO MAKE TODAY AND EVERY DAY GREAT AND BLESSED NO MATTER WHAT!

#PerpetualPraise #ContinualPrayer #WorshipInSpiritAndTruth

{DAY 142}

"Let Your work appear to Your servants, and Your glory to their children. And let the beauty of the LORD our God be upon us, and establish the work of our hands for us; yes, establish the work of our hands." (Psalm 90:16-17 NKJV)

Thank You, Lord, for waking me up on this glorious God morning and starting me on my way! I will never forget the day You showed me a glimpse of Your glory; a halo of very solid light which encircled my face, brilliantly shining and illuminating, splendor with crystal and gorgeous colors. I had never seen anything so magnificent before, nor have I since. I knew with certainty that You were blessing me with Your presence in a most special way. I knew that Your splendor and beauty was upon me. Lord, I don't know why You chose me to bless in that way, but You did and I am wholeheartedly grateful that You did. Thank You, Lord, for establishing and blessing the work of my hands! Yes, Lord, may You enable me to achieve all my goals, plans, and purposes in my work is done for You, and may they all be gratifying and glorifying to You, in the blessed Name of Jesus! Amen, amen, and amen! You are so gracious, Lord, and I love You with all my heart, soul, mind and strength! My soul cries out, "HALLELUJAH"!

CHOOSE TO MAKE TODAY AND EVERY DAY GREAT AND BLESSED NO MATTER WHAT!

#PerpetualPraise #ContinualPrayer #WorshipInSpiritAndTruth

{DAY 143}

PRAISE TO START YOUR DAY:

"And I will give you shepherds according to My heart, who will feed you with knowledge and understanding." (Jeremiah 3:15 NKJV)

I praise and thank You, Lord, that You have blessed each one of Livingway Church's Pastors with a heart after Your own heart. Thank You, Lord, for giving each one of Livingway Church's Pastors the knowledge, understanding, spiritual insight into Your Word, and Your anointing that they need to feed Your people. Thank you, Lord, for placing and planting me under the shepherding of Livingway Church's Pastors. I worship You, oh God, and am grateful for each one of Livingway Church's Pastors.

CHOOSE TO MAKE TODAY AND EVERY DAY GREAT AND BLESSED NO MATTER WHAT!

#PerpetualPraise #ContinualPrayer #WorshipInSpiritAndTruth

{DAY 144}

"And you shall know the truth, and the truth shall make you free. But now having been set free from sin, and having become slaves of God, you have your fruit to holiness, and the end, everlasting life." (John 8:32 & Romans 6:22 NKJV)

It is through the truth of God's word (the Bible) that you are set free from sin and evil. After being set free, then Jesus sets you apart (sanctifies you) for God and His service. You are no longer without fruit. Your fruit is your new Christian life and your service to God which leads to holiness and then to eternal life with Christ Jesus. Thank You, Lord, for setting me free from the power of sin over my life. I now willingly choose to be Your servant and at Your beckoned call all the days of my life on earth, and to have everlasting life with You, Jesus!

CHOOSE TO MAKE TODAY AND EVERY DAY GREAT AND BLESSED NO MATTER WHAT!

#PerpetualPraise #ContinualPrayer #WorshipInSpiritAndTruth

{DAY 145}

"But he who endures to the end shall be saved." (Matthew 24:13 NKJV)

We, as believers, must continue to follow Jesus and live the Christian life. We must continue to be in right standing with God. We must continue to stand on our faith, be firm and stay strong. We are soldiers in the Army of God. We must stay on fire for God. We must do all these things until Jesus comes back, or until we die, whichever comes first. I am believing for the first one. If we do, we will spend eternity with Christ Jesus in Heaven. God is readying true Christians. The Lord is on our side, and we are on the Lord's side! We shall endure to the end, in the blessed Name of Jesus! Amen, amen, and amen! Praise the Lord!

CHOOSE TO MAKE TODAY AND EVERY DAY GREAT AND BLESSED NO MATTER WHAT!

#PerpetualPraise #ContinualPrayer #WorshipInSpiritAndTruth

{DAY 146}

"Now we ask you, brothers and sisters, to acknowledge those who work hard among you, who care for you in the Lord and who admonish you. Hold them in the highest regard in love because of their work. Live in peace with each other. For they refreshed my spirit and yours also. Such men deserve recognition. Remember your leaders, who spoke the word of God to you. Consider the outcome of their way of life and imitate their faith." (1 Thessalonians 5:12-13; 1 Corinthians 16:18; Hebrews 13:7 NIV)

Our Pastors at Livingway Church have worked hard and stayed consistent in building up a true church for the Kingdom of God for many years. They have given their whole lives to shepherding and leading. They know that one day they will have to give account to the Lord for every soul in their congregation, and they desire to be able to give a good account for each and every soul. Our Pastors set the precedent for living a godly life without wavering. We love, respect and highly esteem our faithful Pastors, and we thank them for always refreshing our spirits through their preaching of the Word of God! Oh God, may You refresh the spirits of our Pastors today and every day, and overtake them with tremendous blessings beyond their wildest dreams, in the blessed Name of Jesus! Amen, amen, and amen! We praise and thank You always, oh God, for our Pastors Steve Fender, Becky Fender, Sean Fender, Brandon Fender and Amanda Fender!

CHOOSE TO MAKE TODAY AND EVERY DAY GREAT AND BLESSED NO MATTER WHAT!

#PerpetualPraise #ContinualPrayer #WorshipInSpiritAndTruth

{DAY 147}

PRAISE TO START YOUR DAY:

"But I will sing of Your power; yes, I will sing aloud of Your mercy in the morning; for You have been my defense and refuge in the day of my trouble. To You, O my Strength, I will sing praises; for God is my defense, my God of mercy." (Psalm 59:16-17 NKJV)

Lord, I will sing of Your power. My God is Omnipotent—all-powerful, almighty, supreme, unlimited power, able to do anything! I will sing aloud of Your mercy in the morning for Your mercies are fresh and new every morning! Lord, I worship You for all of Your Names and what each of them means to me personally. I worship You, Jehovah-Chatsahi, for You are the Lord my Strength! I worship You, Jehovah-Ganan, for You are the Lord Our Defense! I worship You, Jehovah-Machsi, for You are the Lord my Refuge! I will praise and worship You forevermore!

CHOOSE TO MAKE TODAY AND EVERY DAY GREAT AND BLESSED NO MATTER WHAT!

#PerpetualPraise #ContinualPrayer #WorshipInSpiritAndTruth

{DAY 148}

"The law of Your mouth is better to me than thousands of coins of gold and silver." (Psalm 119:72 NKJV)

Your law is better for me than monetary and material riches. I delight in Your law because it leads and guides me unto everlasting life with Christ Jesus. I hold Your spoken law in the highest esteem. I love Your law, O God, because I know Your law is for my own good. My obedience to Your law shows You that I love You, Lord, plus it releases You to bless me. Thank You, Abba Father, for loving me enough to give me Your law, which enabled me to see all my wrongdoing. I love You, Lord. I will praise and worship You always!

CHOOSE TO MAKE TODAY AND EVERY DAY GREAT AND BLESSED NO MATTER WHAT!

#PerpetualPraise #ContinualPrayer #WorshipInSpiritAndTruth

{DAY 149}

"Oh come, let us worship and bow down; let us kneel before the LORD our Maker. For He is our God, and we are the people of His pasture, and the sheep of His hand." (Psalm 95:6-7 NKJV)

God's chosen people are strongly encouraged to worship God out of holy reverence and gratitude. Kneeling is a form of sacrifice to God. We belong to God. The Lord is our Shepherd our Guardian, our Defender, our Protector, our Keeper, and the list goes on. God takes care of us. God's intentions were honorable and holy and good when He created us. God created us to praise, worship, love, honor, and please Him. God created us to bless us. We worship You, Lord!

CHOOSE TO MAKE TODAY AND EVERY DAY GREAT AND BLESSED NO MATTER WHAT!

#PerpetualPraise #ContinualPrayer #WorshipInSpiritAndTruth

{DAY 150}

"But solid food is for the mature, who by constant use have trained themselves to distinguish good from evil." (Hebrews 5:14 NIV)

Everyone begins his walk with Christ Jesus as a spiritual infant. As you grow in knowledge and understanding, you become rooted and established in God's Word. The longer you live according to the Word of God, you grow in spiritual discernment with the ability to distinguish between that which is good and that which is evil. You are able to recognize the difference clearly by sight or some other sense. I am a follower of God's Word, and I pray that you are as well. I praise You, Lord, that You have given me the gift of the Holy Spirit so that I now have power and discernment. I praise and worship You, O God, forevermore!

CHOOSE TO MAKE TODAY AND EVERY DAY GREAT AND BLESSED NO MATTER WHAT!

#PerpetualPraise #ContinualPrayer #WorshipInSpiritAndTruth

{DAY 151}

"However, when He, the Spirit of truth, has come, He will guide you into all truth; for He will not speak on His own authority, but whatever He hears He will speak; and He will tell you things to come. He will glorify Me, for He will take of what is mine and declare it to you. All things that the Father has are mine. Therefore I said that He will take of mine and declare it to you." (John 16:13-15 NKJV)

Thank You, Jesus, for the work of Your Holy Spirit! The Holy Spirit speaks the eternal truth which He hears straight from God Himself. The Holy Spirit will tell you things to come before they happen, in order to help prepare you. He has done this for me on more than one occasion. He glorifies Christ Jesus. Thank You, Jesus, for giving me Your Holy Spirit, Who comforts me, leads and guides me into all of Your truth, gives me insider knowledge of things to come even before those things happen, and more!

CHOOSE TO MAKE TODAY AND EVERY DAY GREAT AND BLESSED NO MATTER WHAT!

#PerpetualPraise #ContinualPrayer #WorshipInSpiritAndTruth

{DAY 152}

PRAISE TO START YOUR DAY:

"Rejoice always, pray without ceasing, in everything give thanks; for this is the will of God in Christ Jesus for you. Do not quench the Spirit. Do not despise prophecies. Test all things; hold fast what is good. Abstain from every form of evil." (1 Thessalonians 5:16-22 NKJV)

In everything (in good times and in bad times) give thanks, rejoicing, praying and trusting that God will turn it all around in your favor, "if" you love Him and are living according to His Will and not your will. The Holy Spirit works as fire, by enlightening you, brightening up your spirit, and cleansing your soul. When you do not allow the Holy Spirit to be seen in your actions and you do what you know is wrong, you are quenching the Holy Spirit. You are not to neglect regular attendance in a church, hearing the Word of God preached. Ministers are God-appointed messengers who God has given authority to preach the gospel of Christ Jesus. Apply these commandments and make them holy habits in your life. In doing so, God will bless you, as follows: "Now may the God of peace Himself sanctify you completely; and may your whole spirit, soul, and body be preserved blameless at the coming of our Lord Jesus Christ. He who calls you is faithful, who also will do it. The grace of our Lord Jesus Christ be with you. Amen." (1 Thessalonians 5:23-24, 28 NKJV)

CHOOSE TO MAKE TODAY AND EVERY DAY GREAT AND BLESSED NO MATTER WHAT!

#PerpetualPraise #ContinualPrayer #WorshipInSpiritAndTruth

158

{DAY 153}

**"And he said to them, follow me, and I will make you fishers of men."
(Matthew 4:19 KJV)**

Winning souls to God is a high calling from God. God gives favor to those
who put forth diligent effort to win souls to Him, and it also encourages us to
live a holy life. First, we must follow Christ Jesus, and He will make us
fishers of men, not that we of ourselves can do it without God. Thank You,
Jesus, for increasing our capacity and anointing us as soul winners for God's
Kingdom, in the blessed Name of Jesus! Amen, amen, and amen!

CHOOSE TO MAKE TODAY AND EVERY DAY GREAT AND
BLESSED NO MATTER WHAT!

#PerpetualPraise #ContinualPrayer #WorshipInSpiritAndTruth

{DAY 154}

"Praise the LORD! Praise God in His sanctuary; praise Him in His mighty firmament! Praise Him for His mighty acts; praise Him according to His excellent greatness! Praise Him with the sound of the trumpet; praise Him with the lute and harp! Praise Him with the timbrel and dance; praise Him with stringed instruments and flutes! Praise Him with loud cymbals; praise Him with clashing cymbals! Let everything that has breath praise the LORD. Praise the LORD!" (Psalm 150:1-6 NKJV)

We are to follow God's own instructions for praising Him. We are to praise God in the Lord's house with our voices, with singing and dancing, and with musical instruments. We are to praise God in His mighty created universe. God created the heavens (sun, moon, stars), the earth, the seas, and everything in them according to His excellent greatness! If God woke you up this morning, then you have breath in your body. Put a praise on it to the Lord!

CHOOSE TO MAKE TODAY AND EVERY DAY GREAT AND BLESSED NO MATTER WHAT!

#PerpetualPraise #ContinualPrayer #WorshipInSpiritAndTruth

{DAY 155}

"These things I write to you, though I hope to come to you shortly; but if I am delayed, I write so that you may know how you ought to conduct yourself in the house of God, which is the church of the living God, the pillar and ground of the truth." (1 Timothy 3:14-15 NKJV)

I praise God for ordering my steps to and planting me in a "true church" comprised of people from all races and backgrounds, where all are welcomed and accepted with the love of Christ Jesus, and where church members assemble themselves for praise, worship, and fellowship! A "true church" is a dressing room in which the saints are preparing for their final journey Home to live with Jesus eternally. If you do not like passionate praise and worship here, you will not like it in Heaven either. If you have a problem with people who are of a different race, culture and color than you here, you will not like Heaven because all will be there. If you are attending a "true church" which is rooted and grounded in the whole truth of God's Word, which also has an altar call at the end of each service giving lost souls the chance to be saved and won to God, and which also has a means for water baptism and believes in Holy Ghost baptism, stay there and become deeply planted. If you are not attending a "true church", ask God to order your steps to one today. It could make the difference in where you spend your eternity.

CHOOSE TO MAKE TODAY AND EVERY DAY GREAT AND BLESSED NO MATTER WHAT!

#PerpetualPraise #ContinualPrayer #WorshipInSpiritAndTruth

{DAY 156}

"Surely goodness and mercy shall follow me all the days of my life; and I will dwell in the house of the LORD forever." (Psalm 23:6 NKJV)

Lord Jesus, the blessedness of knowing that Your goodness and mercy are always following me is greatly comforting, and it shows me that You have my best interest in Your heart. Lord, Your word says that You will never leave me, nor forsake me. You are my Constant Companion, Jesus. Your word also says that those who dwell in Your house are blessed. I love the house of the Lord because I love You, I love blessing You, I love being in Your presence, and I love Your people!

CHOOSE TO MAKE TODAY AND EVERY DAY GREAT AND BLESSED NO MATTER WHAT!

#PerpetualPraise #ContinualPrayer #WorshipInSpiritAndTruth

{DAY 157}

PRAISE TO START YOUR DAY:

"So He came to Nazareth, where He had been brought up. And as His custom was, He went into the synagogue on the Sabbath day, and stood up to read." (Luke 4:16 NKJV)

As followers and disciples of Jesus, Christians are to follow the example set by Jesus Himself and attend church worship services regularly in an assembled congregation with other Christians. God called the Sabbath a "holy convocation", which means "commanded assembly." Jesus Christ obeyed this command; therefore, so should we. Lord Jesus, we praise and thank You for teaching us the right way to live by showing Your love towards our Heavenly Father God through Your own obedience towards Him.

CHOOSE TO MAKE TODAY AND EVERY DAY GREAT AND BLESSED NO MATTER WHAT!

#PerpetualPraise #ContinualPrayer #WorshipInSpiritAndTruth

{DAY 158}

"Whether you turn to the right or to the left, your ears will hear a voice behind you, saying, "This is the way; walk in it." (Isaiah 30:21 NIV)

Thank You, Lord, that even when we are tempted to wander off the right road, You gently guide and direct us back to the right way again through the voice of Your Word and Your Holy Spirit. I am so grateful that I know and hear Your voice and that I trust and follow Your guidance! I praise and worship You, Jehovah-Rohi, for You are the Lord my Shepherd! You have never done me anything but good! That is why all my faith and trust is in You, and only in You, Jesus!

CHOOSE TO MAKE TODAY AND EVERY DAY GREAT AND BLESSED NO MATTER WHAT!

#PerpetualPraise #ContinualPrayer #WorshipInSpiritAndTruth

{DAY 159}

"And the LORD God formed man of the dust of the ground, and breathed into his nostrils the breath of life; and man became a living soul. The spirit of God hath made me, and the breath of the Almighty hath given me life." (Genesis 2:7; Job 33:4 KJV)

We praise and worship You, Lord, for creating and forming us, and for breathing Your breath of life into our lungs. You are the very air we breathe. Lord God, You chose to cover our souls from the dirt of the ground. You are the Potter and we are Your molded clay. We lift up our hands of clay in praise to You, and we worship You because You give us life morning by morning. Every breath we take is from You and for You! Glory be to God in the Highest!

CHOOSE TO MAKE TODAY AND EVERY DAY GREAT AND BLESSED NO MATTER WHAT!

#PerpetualPraise #ContinualPrayer #WorshipInSpiritAndTruth

{DAY 160}

"But friends, that's exactly who we are: children of God. And that's only the beginning. Who knows how we'll end up! What we know is that when Christ is openly revealed, we'll see him—and in seeing him, become like him. All of us who look forward to his Coming stay ready, with the glistening purity of Jesus' life as a model for our own." (1 John 3:2-3 MSG)

We are now sons and daughters of the Most High God because we believe in God's Son Christ Jesus, which gives us assurance and His promise for our future. Even with that assurance, we know not yet just how pure, holy, intelligent and well informed, and wise we shall be in our souls; or exactly how our glorified heavenly bodies will look; or to the extent of the joy, we will experience. What we do know is that when we see Jesus, we will become like Him, with respect to our souls, our bodies, and all the riches of inheritance that we will share with Jesus forevermore. This is why we need to be ready and stay ready for when Jesus comes. If we continue following Jesus and use His pure and holy life as a model for our own lives until that day, we will be ready. My precious Jesus, I am looking forward to Your Coming, always looking toward the eastern sky with the greatest of expectation!

CHOOSE TO MAKE TODAY AND EVERY DAY GREAT AND BLESSED NO MATTER WHAT!

#PerpetualPraise #ContinualPrayer #WorshipInSpiritAndTruth

{DAY 161}

"Blessed are the pure in heart: for they shall see God." (Matthew 5:8 KJV)

Jesus Himself said this to show us that He is concerned about our hearts. Only God knows all that is within our hearts. Our purity begins in our hearts. Scriptures tell us that everything we say comes directly from within our hearts, and that from the heart are all the issues of life. So, it is not enough for us to get cleaned up on the outside only. Only Jesus can create in us a pure, clean heart; and only Jesus can renew a right spirit within us. Just ask Him with a wholehearted desire, and He will do it for you. Lord Jesus, may all the desires, affections and motives of my heart be found by You to be pure because I desire to see You, in the blessed name of Jesus! Amen, amen, and amen!

CHOOSE TO MAKE TODAY AND EVERY DAY GREAT AND BLESSED NO MATTER WHAT!

#PerpetualPraise #ContinualPrayer #WorshipInSpiritAndTruth

{DAY 162}

"And I am certain that God, who began the good work within you, will continue his work until it is finally finished on the day when Christ Jesus returns." (Philippians 1:6 NLT)

We can be fully God-confident (not self-confident) that the goodness, holiness, and righteousness which God has begun in us will also be completed by God until that day when Jesus comes to receive us to Himself. God will never abandon any work He has started. God will not forsake the works of His hands. God started it, and God will surely finish it. He's the Alpha and the Omega, the Beginning and the End, the Author and Finisher of our faith. God has the Master Plan. God's promises are fresh and new every morning!

CHOOSE TO MAKE TODAY AND EVERY DAY GREAT AND BLESSED NO MATTER WHAT!

#PerpetualPraise #ContinualPrayer #WorshipInSpiritAndTruth

{DAY 163}

PRAISE TO START YOUR DAY:

"For whoever is ashamed of Me and My words, of him the Son of Man will be ashamed when He comes in His own glory, and in His Father's, and of the holy angels." (Luke 9:26 NKJV)

The Word did not become a philosophy, a theory, or a concept to be discussed, debated or pondered. The Word became a person to be followed, enjoyed and loved. His Name is JESUS. In this sinful world we live in, we must never be ashamed of Christ Jesus and His Gospel of salvation. If you really love Jesus, you will not be ashamed to show and tell it everywhere you go. People can tell by both your actions and your words whether you are a true Christian. Most importantly, God knows because nothing is hidden from Him. God really knows you. Lord Jesus, I love You and I am not ashamed to show forth my praise towards You no matter where I am. Blessed be Your Holy Name! Praise JESUS

CHOOSE TO MAKE TODAY AND EVERY DAY GREAT AND BLESSED NO MATTER WHAT!

#PerpetualPraise #ContinualPrayer #WorshipInSpiritAndTruth

{DAY 164}

PRAISE TO START YOUR DAY:

"Therefore God also has highly exalted Him and given Him the name which is above every name, that at the name of Jesus every knee should bow, of those in heaven, and of those on earth, and of those under the earth, and that every tongue should confess that Jesus Christ is Lord, to the glory of God the Father." (Philippians 2:9-11 NKJV)

Jesus, Who gained the pardoning and final salvation of the whole world through His total humiliation and death on the cross, is now in a state of extreme joy and has been placed in the supreme and highest-ranking level at the right hand of Father God. Not one of God's creatures is so highly exalted and so glorious as Christ Jesus. The angel Gabriel stated that His name should be called Jesus because He would save the world from their sins. The qualifications of the Savior of the world were so extraordinary, the redeeming acts so stupendous, and the result of all so glorious both to God and man, that it is impossible to conceive a higher name or title than that of Jesus, our Savior of the world. We praise and worship You, Jesus, for You alone are Worthy!

CHOOSE TO MAKE TODAY AND EVERY DAY GREAT AND BLESSED NO MATTER WHAT!

#PerpetualPraise #ContinualPrayer #WorshipInSpiritAndTruth

{DAY 165}

"While Jesus was here on earth, he offered prayers and pleadings, with a loud cry and tears, to the one who could rescue him from death. And God heard his prayers because of his deep reverence for God. Even though Jesus was God's Son, he learned obedience from the things he suffered. In this way, God qualified him as a perfect High Priest, and he became the source of eternal salvation for all those who obey him." (Hebrews 5:7-9 NLT)

Jesus knew what He was about to have to endure for the sake of the eternal salvation of the world. He cried out to Father God for help, and at the same time crying out that His Father's Will be done. Jesus loved His Father God and was obedient always to the point of His very death. Jesus is our Perfect Example. Like Jesus, we also have to suffer pain, heartache, and all kinds and degrees of trials and troubles. Like Jesus obeyed His Father God out of a deep and holy respect, we are also to obey Jesus and receive our eternal salvation. We worship You, Jesus—Lamb of God, Lord, and Savior of the world!

CHOOSE TO MAKE TODAY AND EVERY DAY GREAT AND BLESSED NO MATTER WHAT!

#PerpetualPraise #ContinualPrayer #WorshipInSpiritAndTruth

{DAY 166}

"I have no greater joy than to hear that my children walk in truth." (3 John 1:4 NKJV)

If you are a Christian mother (whether in the natural or spiritual sense, or both), you know this Scripture to be truth. Soul prosperity is the richest blessing on this side of Heaven. The highest possible blessing of joy a child can give his/her parents is choosing to become a Christian and follow Jesus. There is nothing that would give more peace to a Christian parent than to be able to leave this world with the assurance that his/her children will always walk in God's truth. Dear Lord, as a Christian praying mother and grandmother, may I never fail to pray for my children and grandchildren and seek Your Will for them. May I always lift them up to You in faith and trust, in love, and in the power of the Holy Spirit. May this and future generations be blessed because of my prayers. I pray this in the blessed Name of Jesus! Amen, Amen and Amen!

CHOOSE TO MAKE TODAY AND EVERY DAY GREAT AND BLESSED NO MATTER WHAT!

#PerpetualPraise #ContinualPrayer #WorshipInSpiritAndTruth

{DAY 167}

PRAISE TO START YOUR DAY: **"Then they rose early in the morning and worshiped before the LORD," (1 Samuel 1:19 NKJV)**

God remembers His early morning frequent and regular visitors who start their day with praise and worship. This is how I begin each of my mornings as well. "Lord God, thank You for waking me up early on this glorious God morning! It is Your breath in my lungs, so I pour out my praise to You only. Lord, You didn't have to wake me up this morning, but You did. Why? I know why. The reason You woke me up is because You have work for me to do for You and for Your Kingdom, and I rejoice in You always for that! I am happy to be at Your service! What would You have me do for You today? Again I say, "Rejoice in the Lord always!"

CHOOSE TO MAKE TODAY AND EVERY DAY GREAT AND BLESSED NO MATTER WHAT!

#PerpetualPraise #ContinualPrayer #WorshipInSpiritAndTruth

{DAY 168}

"The LORD is my strength and my shield; my heart trusted in Him, and I am helped; therefore my heart greatly rejoices, and with my song I will praise Him." (Psalm 28:7 NKJV)

Blessed be the Name of the Lord! Thank You, Lord, that You are both my natural and spiritual strength. You strengthen my body and my heart so that I am able to endure in troubling times and so that I am able to continue serving You and Your Kingdom. You give me the spiritual strength of mind, the strength of godly character, Christ-mindedness, steadfastness, and courage in pain and adversity. At times when I become weak, You carry me until I am again strong enough to walk. You help me because I wholeheartedly trust and have faith in You. Therefore, my heart is full of joy! Every song I sing is unto you Lord, my Great God, and I praise You!

CHOOSE TO MAKE TODAY AND EVERY DAY GREAT AND BLESSED NO MATTER WHAT!

#PerpetualPraise #ContinualPrayer #WorshipInSpiritAndTruth

{DAY 169}

"He who dwells in the secret place of the Most High shall abide under the shadow of the Almighty. I will say of the LORD, "He is my refuge and my fortress; my God, in Him I will trust. But I will sing of Your power; yes, I will sing aloud of Your mercy in the morning; for You have been my defense and refuge in the day of my trouble." (Psalm 91:1-2; Psalm 59:16 NKJV)

When you make God your home and place of shelter to live in, you will have a peaceful, joyful, comfortable and safe place of rest. God's divine care will be your protective covering. You will praise the Lord for His Almighty Power to rescue you from danger. When your trouble is over and the light of day has come, you will praise God for saving and delivering you unharmed. What a great and mighty God we serve! Oh Hallelujah! Blessed be the Name of the Lord our God!

CHOOSE TO MAKE TODAY AND EVERY DAY GREAT AND BLESSED NO MATTER WHAT!

#PerpetualPraise #ContinualPrayer #WorshipInSpiritAndTruth

{DAY 170}

"You shall tread upon the lion and the cobra, the young lion and the serpent you shall trample underfoot. Behold, I give you the authority to trample on serpents and scorpions, and over all the power of the enemy, and nothing shall by any means hurt you." (Psalm 91:13; Luke 10:19 NKJV)

It is a good thing to know who you are in Christ Jesus. When you are living in Jesus and Jesus is living in you, you need not fear the devil. God has given you greater power than the enemy has. No weapon that the enemy uses against you will prosper because the Greater and most Powerful One lives in you. His name is JESUS. Your name is Conqueror, Overcomer, and Finisher. That is my confession, and my profession is faith. Go ahead and make it yours, too.

CHOOSE TO MAKE TODAY AND EVERY DAY GREAT AND BLESSED NO MATTER WHAT!

#PerpetualPraise #ContinualPrayer #WorshipInSpiritAndTruth

{DAY 171}

"But He answered and said, "It is written, 'Man shall not live by bread alone, but by every word that proceeds from the mouth of God.'" (Matthew 4:4 NKJV)

Jesus said, "every word". That means not just some of His Word and not just the parts of His Word that we would pick and choose to receive and act upon. Don't be a "cafeteria Christian". We are to eat all of His Word, digest it and do it so that we may live, thrive and be victorious Christians. Jesus is our spiritual Bread of Life. We are what we eat. It is vitally important that we know God's Word and have it hidden in our hearts so that, when the tempter comes, we will be able to tell him, "It is written…". The tempter will flee from us as we resist him and take a firm stand upon the Word of God. The Word of God works when we work it. Blessed be the Name of the Lord both now and forevermore!

CHOOSE TO MAKE TODAY AND EVERY DAY GREAT AND BLESSED NO MATTER WHAT!

#PerpetualPraise #ContinualPrayer #WorshipInSpiritAndTruth

{DAY 172}

"May your unfailing love come to me, LORD, your salvation, according to your promise; then I can answer anyone who taunts me, for I trust in your word. Never take your word of truth from my mouth, for I have put my hope in your laws. I will always obey your law, for ever and ever. I will walk about in freedom, for I have sought out your precepts. I will speak of your statutes before kings and will not be put to shame, for I delight in your commands because I love them. I reach out for your commands, which I love, that I may meditate on your decrees." (Psalm 119:41-48 NIV)

Thank You, oh God, that You grant unconditional love and mercy that leads to salvation. When Jesus spent 40 days fasting and praying in the wilderness just before His Ministry began, the tempter taunted Him. Jesus replied to the tempter with portions of Scripture and began His replies with, "It is written…" Like Jesus, we must have a ready answer for when reproaches and temptations come against us. The only weapon, and the best weapon we need, is the Word of God. Your Word, Oh God, is our hope and our trust. Thank You, Oh God, that keeping, delighting in, and being obedient to Your Word brings us freedom to overcome reproaches and temptations, and prevents us from being put to shame.

CHOOSE TO MAKE TODAY AND EVERY DAY GREAT AND BLESSED NO MATTER WHAT!

#PerpetualPraise #ContinualPrayer #WorshipInSpiritAndTruth

{DAY 173}

"For God hath not given us the spirit of fear; but of power, and of love, and of a sound mind. And I say also unto thee, That thou art Peter, and upon this rock I will build my church; and the gates of hell shall not prevail against it." (2 Timothy 1:7; Matthew 16:18 KJV)

God has given us power through His Holy Spirit and all the fruit of His Holy Spirit, plus we are Christ-minded. We now have the love of God and, as God perfects our love in Him, all fear is cast out. Therefore, we have everything we need to reclaim this world for Christ, and now is the time to do it. As true believers, we are God's Church, built upon Jesus, the Rock. Hell will never be more powerful than God's Church, nor will Hell ever have the victory over God's Church. We already have the victory over death, Hell, and the grave because Christ Jesus is alive and has already won the victory for us. We are victorious! Praise Jesus!!!

CHOOSE TO MAKE TODAY AND EVERY DAY GREAT AND BLESSED NO MATTER WHAT!

#PerpetualPraise #ContinualPrayer #WorshipInSpiritAndTruth

{DAY 174}

"Let all those that seek thee rejoice and be glad in thee: and let such as love thy salvation say continually, Let God be magnified. And blessed be his glorious name for ever: and let the whole earth be filled with his glory; Amen, and Amen." (Psalm 70:4 & Psalm 72:19 KJV)

Those who seek God through praise and wholehearted worship will have joy. Those, who have been partakers of God's amazing grace and through faith have received His salvation, cannot help but share their joy of the Lord with others. They desire for others to be blessed as they have been. They desire for others to glorify God, for He is so Worthy! We are to bless God through Christ Jesus, our Redeemer. When Jesus comes again, the entire face of the earth to every far end of it will be filled with God's glory, and His Kingdom shall cover the whole earth. The knowledge of Christ will fill the whole earth, and all men will worship before Him. This is going to happen. Magnify God, for He, is big!

CHOOSE TO MAKE TODAY AND EVERY DAY GREAT AND BLESSED NO MATTER WHAT!

#PerpetualPraise #ContinualPrayer #WorshipInSpiritAndTruth

{DAY 175}

"Arise, shine; for your light has come! And the glory of the LORD is risen upon you. For behold, the darkness shall cover the earth, and deep darkness the people; but the LORD will arise over you, and His glory will be seen upon you. The Gentiles shall come to your light, and kings to the brightness of your rising." (Isaiah 60:1-3 NKJV)

God is calling us to let His glorious light shine bright in us and through us to those around us. "Arise" and "shine" are action words. God is telling us that we must take action, and do and say something. We cannot just accept and comply with the ungodliness in the world without having an active Christian response. We cannot live a totally passive life. We must have a voice for God and stand for what is right according to God's Word, no matter the cost and no matter where we are. By doing so and lifting up the Name of Jesus, He will draw men unto Him. I worship You, Jehovah-'Ori, for You are the Lord my Light. I strongly desire that the reflection of my light (Jesus, the Light Who shines within me) will remain and be seen even after I am gone.

CHOOSE TO MAKE TODAY AND EVERY DAY GREAT AND BLESSED NO MATTER WHAT!

#PerpetualPraise #ContinualPrayer #WorshipInSpiritAndTruth

{DAY 176}

"I would have lost heart, unless I had believed that I would see the goodness of the Lord in the land of the living. Wait on the Lord; be of good courage, and He shall strengthen your heart; wait, I say, on the Lord!" (Psalm 27:13-14 NKJV)

Even saints are subject to becoming overwhelmed and discouraged when their troubles become overbearing. But God is the strength of our heart! It is our faith in God that keeps us from losing confidence when we are weighed down with heavy burdens and going through the perfect storms of life. It is our faith in God that keeps us hoping, praying, and waiting on God's promises to come through. It is our faith in God that keeps our sacrifice of praise and worship alive. It is our faith in God that keeps our expectation of relief in due season intact and ever growing. It's so good to know Jesus!

CHOOSE TO MAKE TODAY AND EVERY DAY GREAT AND BLESSED NO MATTER WHAT!

#PerpetualPraise #ContinualPrayer #WorshipInSpiritAndTruth

{DAY 177}

"And they overcame him by the blood of the Lamb and by the word of their testimony," (Revelation 12:11 NKJV)

We owe our victory over the devil and sin to the blood of God's spotless Lamb, Christ Jesus. Christ Jesus Himself was victorious over Satan by His very death. Though the devil still rails accusations against us to God, those accusations have no power because the Lamb of God has already taken away the sins of the world. I believe with my heart the Gospel of Christ Jesus unto salvation, and confess it with my mouth unto righteousness. We are also victorious by the word of our testimonies. Through our testimonies, we are bearing witness to what God has done for us. We should always turn our triumphs and victories towards God. Our victories are a direct result of being dependent upon God and being obedient to God. I praise God for the blood of Jesus and the word of my testimony that have made me an Overcomer over the devil and sin! I am redeemed by the blood of Jesus! Everything we need is in the precious blood of Jesus, which still flows even now today. There is power in the blood of Jesus; power to save, power to heal, power to eternal life, power to redeem, power to set free, power to restore, power to forgive… Every single morning, I plead the blood of Jesus over me and everyone I love, in the blessed Name of Jesus! Amen, amen, and amen!

CHOOSE TO MAKE TODAY AND EVERY DAY GREAT AND BLESSED NO MATTER WHAT!

#PerpetualPraise #ContinualPrayer #WorshipInSpiritAndTruth

{DAY 178}

PRAISE TO START YOUR DAY:

"And everyone who calls on the name of the Lord will be saved." (Acts 2:21 NIV)

God sent His Only Son Christ Jesus to take away the sins of the world. Christ Jesus, through His obedience, did just that by shedding His blood and dying on the cross. Jesus did the hard part for you and for me and made it so simple for us to receive His salvation. Just call on His name with your mouth, "Jesus save me!", and believe in your heart on the Lord Jesus Christ, worship Him in spirit and in truth, follow Jesus and be obedient to Him, and you will be saved. We praise You, Jesus, for thinking we were to die for. We wholeheartedly worship You and love You, Jesus!

CHOOSE TO MAKE TODAY AND EVERY DAY GREAT AND BLESSED NO MATTER WHAT!

#PerpetualPraise #ContinualPrayer #WorshipInSpiritAndTruth

{DAY 179}

"God saved you by his grace when you believed. And you can't take credit for this; it is a gift from God. Salvation is not a reward for the good things we have done, so none of us can boast about it." (Ephesians 2:8-9 NLT)

You are saved by God's Amazing Grace through your faith in the Gospel of Christ Jesus. When you hear and believe the Gospel, and then choose to accept God's gift of salvation, you will be saved. You cannot receive this gift from God because of any good thing you have done on your own. Unless we have the righteousness of God through Christ Jesus, Scripture (Isaiah 64:6) tells us that the good things we have done are as filthy rags to God. The meaning is that we have no righteousness apart from God's righteousness, no matter how good of a person we and others may think we are. Scripture (1 Corinthians 1:29) tells us that we are not to boast or glory in God's presence. I believe the whole Gospel of Christ Jesus! I believe that Jesus is alive today! Thank You, Jesus, for saving me and giving me eternal life! All my faith is in You, Jesus! I worship You! I love You, my Jesus!

CHOOSE TO MAKE TODAY AND EVERY DAY GREAT AND BLESSED NO MATTER WHAT!

#PerpetualPraise #ContinualPrayer #WorshipInSpiritAndTruth

{DAY 180}

"Jesus wept." (John 11:35 KJV)

Though this is the shortest Scripture in the Bible, it is one of the most significant. We see in this Scripture that Jesus, being God, left Heaven to come to earth in the form of man to save man from eternal death. This Scripture shows us that Jesus though being God, like man, also had human emotions. Jesus understood our pain then, and He still does today. Scripture (Hebrews 4:15) tells us that Jesus is touched with the feeling of our infirmities. Jesus has not forgotten us since He was resurrected and went back to Heaven. Though Jesus left behind Him all the pain and suffering, He still remembers because He personally experienced all of it Himself. We praise and thank You, Jesus, for You can relate to and understand all of our physical and mental weaknesses. Thank You, Jesus, that You instruct us to sacrifice by giving them all back to You because You care (1 Peter 5:7). We worship You, Jesus, in spirit and in truth. Blessed be the Name of the Lord! We praise You, Jesus!

CHOOSE TO MAKE TODAY AND EVERY DAY GREAT AND BLESSED NO MATTER WHAT!

#PerpetualPraise #ContinualPrayer #WorshipInSpiritAndTruth

{DAY 181}

"Then Jesus said, "Come to me, all of you who are weary and carry heavy burdens, and I will give you rest. Take my yoke upon you. Let me teach you, because I am humble and gentle at heart, and you will find rest for your souls. For my yoke is easy to bear, and the burden I give you is light." (Matthew 11:28-30 NLT)

Thank You, Jesus, for this open invitation to anyone and everyone who will accept it. Do you need rest from weariness due to carrying heavy burdens for too long? Does your life seem unbearable? Do you need rest from it all? Have you tried everything you can think of to make your life manageable, but it's still not working for you? Come to Jesus. You will not be disappointed. Jesus is patiently waiting for you to accept His invitation. Allow Jesus to manage your life for you. He can and will change your life and give you rest even right now today.

CHOOSE TO MAKE TODAY AND EVERY DAY GREAT AND BLESSED NO MATTER WHAT!

#PerpetualPraise #ContinualPrayer #WorshipInSpiritAndTruth

{DAY 182}

"But blessed are your eyes, for they see: and your ears, for they hear. For verily I say unto you, that many prophets and righteous men have desired to see those things which ye see, and have not seen them; and to hear those things which ye hear, and have not heard them." (Matthew 13:16-17 KJV)

Thank You, oh God, that I am able to see the Light of Truth through Your Word. I bring my praise to You and only You, and I thank You, Jesus, for opening my spiritual eyes to see more of what You see and my spiritual ears to hear Your Word, by which my faith grows even greater and enables me to know more of what You know. I worship You in spirit and truth. I am blessed of the Lord! Blessed be the Name of the Lord!

CHOOSE TO MAKE TODAY AND EVERY DAY GREAT AND BLESSED NO MATTER WHAT!

#PerpetualPraise #ContinualPrayer #WorshipInSpiritAndTruth

{DAY 183}

"Great is the LORD, and greatly to be praised in the city of our God, in the mountain of his holiness. Beautiful for situation, the joy of the whole earth, is mount Zion, on the sides of the north, the city of the great King." (Psalm 48:1-2 KJV)

This truth is for all generations! Our God is a Great God, and He is to be praised with great praise for all He has done, for all He is doing now, and for all He shall do! Zion is the name of the referenced "city of our God". Zion was beautiful in its elevation. Located in the hidden, secure recesses on the north side (the most beautiful side) of Mount Zion, it was safe and isolated from the threat of invaders. It was God's holy place of residence, which made Mount Zion a place of great glory. The name of earthly Zion was Jehovah-Shammah, meaning the Lord is there. Zion was the city of our Jehovah God, the Great King of heaven and earth. It was the whole earth's joy. Today's Zion, in the spiritual sense, is the joy of the Kingdom of God, of the nation, of the family, and of the heart, in which God is Great and in which God is all. God is still beautiful for every situation. He still provides us with refuge and safety under the shadow of His wings, far away from the threat of danger. God still allows us to come into His presence through our praise, worship, and prayer. In the whole earth today, there is nothing more beautiful and joyful as being in the presence of the Lord. We praise and worship You, Jehovah-Shammah, for You are our ever-present God! Again I say that this truth is for all generations! Blessed be the Name of the Lord! Glory to God!

CHOOSE TO MAKE TODAY AND EVERY DAY GREAT AND BLESSED NO MATTER WHAT!

#PerpetualPraise #ContinualPrayer #WorshipInSpiritAndTruth

{DAY 184}

"Even in darkness light dawns for the upright, for those who are gracious and compassionate and righteous. Good will come to those who are generous and lend freely, who conduct their affairs with justice. Surely the righteous will never be shaken; they will be remembered forever. They will have no fear of bad news; their hearts are steadfast, trusting in the LORD. Their hearts are secure, they will have no fear; in the end they will look in triumph on their foes." (Psalm 112:4-8 NIV)

God comforts His people by providing light and joy, even in the midst of their darkest troubles. The spirits and hearts of God's righteous ones will remain settled, steady and true. Neither will they fear bad news because they trust in the Lord God Almighty to always bring good out of every bad situation, and to bring them out on top in triumph over the enemy. Lord, all my faith and trust is in You and Your promises. My heart is steadfast and secure in You. You are not a man that You would ever lie. I believe in Your Word from Genesis through Revelation.

CHOOSE TO MAKE TODAY AND EVERY DAY GREAT AND BLESSED NO MATTERWHAT!

#PerpetualPraise #ContinualPrayer #WorshipInSpiritAndTruth

{DAY 185}

"You are My witnesses," says the Lord, "and My servant whom I have chosen, that you may know and believe Me, and understand that I am He. Before Me there was no God formed, nor shall there be after Me. I, even I, am the Lord, and besides Me there is no savior. I have declared and saved, I have proclaimed, and there was no foreign god among you; therefore you are My witnesses," says the Lord, "that I am God." (Isaiah 43:10-12 NKJV)

God Himself has chosen His people to be His witnesses. God, who as Alpha and Omega knows and sees the end even before the beginning, foretold many things in Scripture, including advanced knowledge of the Messiah. Christ Jesus also foretold many things as well. Much of this foretold knowledge has already been accomplished by Almighty God. As God's witnesses, Christians are told by God to share His accomplishments and testify to unbelievers of God's truthfulness and faithfulness to keep His Words that they (like us) may also receive knowledge and understanding of God, and become fully and firmly persuaded as to the truth of God's Word. God says of Himself that He is the One and only True and Living and Eternal God. He is the first Being. He is the One and only Lord and Savior of the world, and the only Giver of Salvation. I worship You, Jehovah-Yasha, for You are the Lord my Savior! No one will ever take over or inherit Your Throne! It is Yours and Yours alone for all eternity! Glory to God!

CHOOSE TO MAKE TODAY AND EVERY DAY GREAT AND BLESSED NO MATTER WHAT!

#PerpetualPraise #ContinualPrayer#WorshipInSpiritAndTruth

{DAY 186}

PRAISE TO START YOUR DAY:

"Our help is in the name of the LORD, Who made heaven and earth. The LORD has done great things for us, and we are glad." (Psalm 124:8; Psalm 126:3 NKJV)

We worship You, Jehovah-Bara, for You are the Lord Creator of heaven and earth and everything in them. All are the works of Your great hands. You are our sure and faithful Helper. You are the Preserver of all. In You, Lord God Almighty, is our everlasting hope, strength and confidence. With much gratitude we praise You for the great things You have done for us, for the great things You are doing for us even now today, and for the great things You shall do for us in the future. We are filled with great joy! Great are You, Lord!

CHOOSE TO MAKE TODAY AND EVERY DAY GREAT AND BLESSED NO MATTER WHAT!

#PerpetualPraise #ContinualPrayer #WorshipInSpiritAndTruth

{DAY 187}

"Thus says the LORD, who makes a way in the sea and a path through the mighty waters," ""Do not remember the former things, nor consider the things of old. Behold, I will do a new thing, now it shall spring forth; shall you not know it? I will even make a road in the wilderness and rivers in the desert."" (Isaiah 43:16,18-19 NKJV)

Magnify the Lord with me! God, who has done such miraculous, great and mighty things, is telling us (in today's language), "You have heard and read about many of the great things I have done; but hey, you ain't seen nothin' yet! I have very long outstretched hands and many miracles tucked all the way up both of My sleeves! Just wait! I'm about to blow your minds with brand new epic marvels that totally defy all natural and scientific laws, which no man has ever imagined, heard of, or seen before! I'm totally going to blow your socks off!" Lord, it is exciting to know that, even after all You have done, Your best works are still yet to come in our lives!

CHOOSE TO MAKE TODAY AND EVERY DAY GREAT AND BLESSED NO MATTER WHAT!

#PerpetualPraise #ContinualPrayer #WorshipInSpiritAndTruth

{DAY 188}

"And David was greatly distressed; for the people spake of stoning him, because the soul of all the people was grieved, every man for his sons and for his daughters: but David encouraged himself in the Lord his God." (1 Samuel 30:6 KJV)

Let's just bring this down to "real". Do you have people in your life, perhaps even children or other loved ones, who are blaming you for all of their troubles and grief? Just in case you need to hear this today, you are not a failure. You are not a waste of space. You are not any of those negative thoughts you hear in your head or from other people. You are loved and wanted by God. God believes in you. You can do it! Just like David, when everyone was blaming him for their grief and ready to kill him, you can encourage yourself in the Lord through God's Word, through believing what God says about His thoughts towards you, through praising and worshiping God, through talking to God, through becoming God's trusted friend, and through GIVING Jesus all of your cares and RECEIVING His peace, love and joy, no matter how bad your situation might look or feel. Just call Him up and invite Him in even now today. It's so good to know Jesus! Blessed be the Name of the Lord!

CHOOSE TO MAKE TODAY AND EVERY DAY GREAT AND BLESSED NO MATTER WHAT!

#PerpetualPraise#ContinualPrayer #WorshipInSpiritAndTruth

{DAY 189}

"Oh, continue Your lovingkindness to those who know You, and Your righteousness to the upright in heart." (Psalm 36:10 NKJV)

Lord, I will continue to show You perpetual praise, have relationship with You with continual communication, and worship You in spirit and in truth. That day, when I am standing at Heaven's Gates of pearl, I desire to hear You say to me, "Well done, My good and faithful servant.", because You knew me and I knew You on this side of Heaven. May You say to me, "I know you! You are My friend who praises and worships Me even more than seven times every day! I will add your book of praise to My word!", in the blessed Name of Jesus! Amen, amen, and amen!

CHOOSE TO MAKE TODAY AND EVERY DAY GREAT AND BLESSED NO MATTER WHAT!

#PerpetualPraise #ContinualPrayer #WorshipInSpiritAndTruth

{DAY 190}

"Open my eyes, that I may see wondrous things from Your law. Give me understanding, and I shall keep Your law; indeed, I shall observe it with my whole heart. Make me walk in the path of Your commandments, for I delight in it." (Psalm 119:18,34-35 NKJV)

Lord, bless spiritual eyes to see that Your law is wonderful. Without it, we would never know our weaknesses and sins and the need to change and turn to You. Give us understanding and spiritual insight to see the blessings that You desire to give us as a result of our obedience to Your law. Then, as we see and understand the truth, and delight in it, make us walk in and stay on the right path of righteousness in Christ Jesus, in the blessed Name of Jesus! Amen, amen, and amen! We give You all the glory, praise, honor, power and thanksgiving! Blessed be the Name of the Lord!

CHOOSE TO MAKE TODAY AND EVERY DAY GREAT AND BLESSED NO MATTER WHAT!

#PerpetualPraise #ContinualPrayer #WorshipInSpiritAndTruth

{DAY 191}

"In the year that King Uzziah died, I saw the Lord sitting on a throne, high and lifted up, and the train of His robe filled the temple. Above it stood seraphim; each one had six wings: with two he covered his face, with two he covered his feet, and with two he flew. And one cried to another and said: "Holy, holy, holy is the Lord of hosts; the whole earth is full of His glory!"" (Isaiah 6:1-3 NKJV)

We worship You, Jehovah-Sabaoth, for You are the Lord of Hosts! During biblical times, the length of kings' robes bore great significance to their victories in wars. Each time they won a victory, a new hem was added to their robe to make it longer. Lord, please illuminate Your train in the temple that we may see all the victories You have won for us and partake of all Your glorious benefits which Your King's train holds, in the Name of Jesus! Amen, amen, and amen! Your train is full of Your Glory! Every soul won to Christ Jesus is in His train! Every victory You have won for me personally (salvation, deliverance, healing, freedom, wholeness, holiness, righteousness, joy, peace, love…) is in Your train. My soul is in Your train. I praise You, Lord, for You are my conquering King and the One who fights for me! I worship You, Lord, for You are holy, worthy, righteous, and lovely!

CHOOSE TO MAKE TODAY AND EVERY DAY GREAT AND BLESSED NO MATTER WHAT!

#PerpetualPraise #ContinualPrayer #WorshipInSpiritAndTruth

{DAY 192}

PRAISE TO START YOUR DAY:

"The name of the LORD is a strong tower; the righteous run to it and are safe." (Proverbs 18:10 NKJV)

We worship You, Jehovah-Misqabbi, for You are the Lord our High Tower! The Lord is our hiding-place where we can rest assured and be God-confident that He is our Strong Defense. As God's righteous people, we can call the Name of "JESUS!" and know He will not fail us in time of need. When we run to You for comfort, grace, mercy, truth, and lovingkindness, You take us high where our enemy cannot reach us, and You shield us from all harm. Your Love and Goodness, oh God, are more overwhelming than our troubles! Blessed be the Name of the Lord!

CHOOSE TO MAKE TODAY AND EVERY DAY GREAT AND BLESSED NO MATTER WHAT!

#PerpetualPraise #ContinualPrayer #WorshipInSpiritAndTruth

{DAY 193}

"The LORD is my rock and my fortress and my deliverer; my God, my strength, in whom I will trust; my shield and the horn of my salvation, my stronghold." (Psalm 18:2 NKJV)

I worship You, Jehovah-Sel'i, for You are the Lord my Rock. I worship You, Jehovah-Metshodhathi, for You are the Lord my Fortress. I worship You, Jehovah-Mephalti, for You are the Lord my Deliverer. I worship You, Jehovah-Eli, for You are the Lord my God. I worship You, Jehovah-Chatsahi, for You are the Lord my Strength. I worship You, Jehovah-Magen, for You are the Lord my Shield. I worship You, Jehovah-Keren-Yish'I, for You are the Horn of my Salvation. I worship You, Jehovah-Misqabbi, for You are the Lord my High Tower. The different names of the Lord are the titles by which God has made Himself known, and each title describes one of His attributes or characteristics, of which He has many. Blessed be the Name of the Lord, for He is Worthy of all worship and praise!

CHOOSE TO MAKE TODAY AND EVERY DAY GREAT AND BLESSED NO MATTER WHAT!

#PerpetualPraise #ContinualPrayer #WorshipInSpiritAndTruth

{DAY 194}

PRAISE TO START YOUR DAY:

"Trust in the Lord with all thine heart; and lean not unto thine own understanding. In all thy ways acknowledge him, and he shall direct thy paths." (Proverbs 3:5-6 KJV)

We are to wholeheartedly trust in the Lord always and rely upon His wisdom, knowledge, understanding, power, goodness, guidance, and leading for direction and help in all things. We ought always acknowledge God and consult Him in all of our works and projects, and make sure they are God-approved for His use and glory. By doing this, our faith will be great and alive, and become known to others as they see the success of our works. Then, we must point all of our successes towards God. He is a Rewarder of those who diligently seek Him. Praise God from whom all blessings flow!

CHOOSE TO MAKE TODAY AND EVERY DAY GREAT AND BLESSED NO MATTER WHAT!

#PerpetualPraise #ContinualPrayer #WorshipInSpiritAndTruth

{DAY 195}

PRAISE TO START YOUR DAY:

"Thou art worthy, O Lord, to receive glory and honour and power: for thou hast created all things, and for thy pleasure they are and were created." (Revelation 4:11 KJV)

God alone is worthy to receive all praise, worship, glory, honor and power. From nothing seen, God created all things seen, by His Will and Word. Nobody is able to truly see and understand the in-depth wonder of the universe and all that is in it, without first seeing the worthiness of God, the Creator. God created all for His own pleasure. O God, may everything I think, say and do today bring pleasure to You and glorify You, my Creator. That is my heartfelt desire not just today, but all of my days. I exist and have my being in You, my Creator. I praise and worship You, my Creator!

CHOOSE TO MAKE TODAY AND EVERY DAY GREAT AND BLESSED NO MATTER WHAT!

#PerpetualPraise #ContinualPrayer #WorshipInSpiritAndTruth

{DAY 196}

"Get wisdom! Get understanding! Do not forget, nor turn away from the words of my mouth. Do not forsake her, and she will preserve you; love her, and she will keep you. Wisdom is the principal thing; therefore get wisdom. And in all your getting, get understanding. Exalt her, and she will promote you; she will bring you honor, when you embrace her. She will place on your head an ornament of grace; a crown of glory she will deliver to you." (Proverbs 4:5-9 NKJV)

God has placed great value on His people possessing godly wisdom and understanding. God's Word says that godly wisdom is the principal thing to have and own. The fruit in the life of a Christian, as a result of having godly wisdom in its entirety, is: preservation, being kept, promotion, honor, grace and glory. God has instructed us on how to get and keep godly wisdom and understanding: (1) Do not forget or turn away from His words; (2) Do not abandon or give up godly wisdom; (3) Love godly wisdom, which only comes from loving God's words and God's law; (4) Acknowledge godly wisdom as the principal thing to get from God's words; (5) Get understanding as well; (6) Hold godly wisdom in very high regard; and (7) Welcome and accept godly wisdom, and hold on to her tightly and keep her very close to you. God's heart's desire for His people is happiness. Happiness is a result of having godly wisdom. We praise and thank You, Lord, for the godly wisdom and understanding You have given us access to receive through studying Your words and communing with You. I pray that we may all have a deep desire for godly wisdom and understanding, and may Your wisdom and understanding be greatly increased in us even now today and every day, in the blessed Name of Jesus! Amen, amen, and amen!

CHOOSE TO MAKE TODAY AND EVERY DAY GREAT AND BLESSED NO MATTER WHAT!

#PerpetualPraise #ContinualPrayer #WorshipInSpiritAndTruth

{DAY 197}

"Hear, my son, and receive my sayings, and the years of your life will be many. I have taught you in the way of wisdom; I have led you in right paths. When you walk, your steps will not be hindered, and when you run, you will not stumble. Take firm hold of instruction, do not let go; keep her, for she is your life." (Proverbs 4:10-13 NKJV)

God desires to bless His children with long life, so He has instructed us as to what we must do to receive that long life. We must hear and then be obedient to His words, by applying them to the way we live our lives. God's words are so full of His wisdom, and through His words He leads and guides us in the right paths to walk in, to keep us from stumbling and falling. Like with godly wisdom, we are to take and keep a firm hold on God's words of instruction and do not let go. Keep God's words of instruction hidden in your heart, so you will not forget them. Your long life is in God's words. O God, I love Your words because therein is where I receive Your wisdom, Your knowledge, Your instruction, Your understanding, and long life. Thank You, O God, that when You breathed into my nostrils the breath of life and made me become a living soul, I then had a mind and will and emotions. That means, from that very moment, You gave me the ability to freely make my own choices. I have chosen to hear and receive Your sayings and obey them, and to receive all You desire for me to have. I love You, Lord! Blessed be Your Holy Name, oh God!

CHOOSE TO MAKE TODAY AND EVERY DAY GREAT AND BLESSED NO MATTER WHAT!

#PerpetualPraise #ContinualPrayer #WorshipInSpiritAndTruth

{DAY 198}

PRAISE TO START YOUR DAY:

"But thou, O Lord, art a God full of compassion, and gracious, long suffering, and plenteous in mercy and truth." (Psalm 86:15 KJV)

As a mother is toward her children, God is full of compassion and mercy toward His children. God is gracious as shown through His Son Christ Jesus. God is not easily angered, but He is patient and willing to tenderly wait to bring His children to repentance, and then He saves them by His Amazing Grace. God forgives and forgets our many sins. Even when we cannot—God can and does. God's Word says it, and God's Word is true. God has plenty of mercy (undeserved favor) and truth, and always fulfills His promises. God is a Good God all the time, and all the time God is Good!

CHOOSE TO MAKE TODAY AND EVERY DAY GREAT AND BLESSED NO MATTERWHAT!

#PerpetualPraise #ContinualPrayer #WorshipInSpiritAndTruth

{DAY 199}

PRAISE TO START YOUR DAY:

"And the Lord make you to increase and abound in love one toward another, and toward all men, even as we do toward you:" (1 Thessalonians 3:12 KJV)

Thank You, Lord, for waking me up on this glorious God morning and starting me on my way! Thank You, Lord, for putting Your breath in my lungs and giving me a new day to be about our Heavenly Father's business! I am so happy to be at Your service! How will You use me today, Lord? That's it, Lord! Yes, I will show Your unconditional love towards all others, just as You have loved me! Jesus, You loved me when I was unlovable and could not even love myself, much less love others. I will be obedient to Your Word, and every day I will increase and abound in showing the love of Jesus towards others. That will please You, others, and even me. What a happier place the world would be to live in if everyone would choose to do this! I love You so much, Jesus! It's so good to know You!

CHOOSE TO MAKE TODAY AND EVERY DAY GREAT AND BLESSED NO MATTER WHAT!

#PerpetualPraise #ContinualPrayer #WorshipInSpiritAndTruth

{DAY 200}

"No weapon formed against you shall prosper, and every tongue which rises against you in judgment you shall condemn. This is the heritage of the servants of the Lord, and their righteousness is from Me," says the Lord." (Isaiah 54:17 NKJV)

This Scripture does not say that you will not have weapons formed against you because, in the world you live in, you can be sure that you will have weapons formed against you. However, these weapons will not have final success over you because the Lord is on your side, if you are on the Lord's side. No one shall be able to injure you by accusing words. If others express disapproval of you and accuse you of misrepresenting the truth, you will be able to convince them of error and convict them, by manifestation of the truth. Truth, victory, justification and vindication are the inheritance of those who serve God. It is good to know that the Lord is on our side! Praise God!

CHOOSE TO MAKE TODAY AND EVERY DAY GREAT AND BLESSED NO MATTER WHAT!

#PerpetualPraise #ContinualPrayer #WorshipInSpiritAndTruth

{DAY 201}

PRAISE TO START YOUR DAY:

"And He said, "My Presence will go with you, and I will give you rest.""
(Exodus 33:14 NKJV)

Yes, Lord, as I go through my day praising You, I will remain in Your presence. You Yourself will be with me. As I go about productively working and doing all as unto You, Jesus, I will also be resting in Your presence. Lord, I praise You for Your presence goes with me. You are my Constant Companion. You are my Personal Guide. Your presence gives me a sense of calmness and security, no matter how hard I am working or whatever I am going through. It is well with my soul. I am holy addicted to being in Your presence, Lord. As I remain in Your presence more and more, the more I desire to remain in Your presence. I worship You in spirit and in truth.

CHOOSE TO MAKE TODAY AND EVERY DAY GREAT AND BLESSED NO MATTER WHAT!

#PerpetualPraise #ContinualPrayer #WorshipInSpiritAndTruth

{DAY 202}

"For God so loved the world that He gave His only begotten Son, that whoever believes in Him should not perish but have everlasting life. For God did not send His Son into the world to condemn the world, but that the world through Him might be saved." (John 3:16-17 NKJV)

Oh God, You invested the very life of Your only begotten Son because You loved us so much, even while we were yet sinners. You did not send Your Son into the world to condemn the world, because the world was already condemned to eternal separation from God. You sent Your Son into the world to save the world through Him so that You would have an eternal and everlasting Kingdom. I am most grateful to You, Father God, for my eternal salvation through Your Son Christ Jesus, and to be a part of the Kingdom of God!

CHOOSE TO MAKE TODAY AND EVERY DAY GREAT AND BLESSED NO MATTER WHAT!

#PerpetualPraise #ContinualPrayer #WorshipInSpiritAndTruth

{DAY 203}

PRAISE TO START YOUR DAY:

"Serve the Lord with gladness; come before His presence with singing."
(Psalm 100:2 NKJV)

We are to serve the Lord with gladness in whatever ministry, or ministries, He has called us to. We are to sing praises to the Lord in His presence. Even the birds sing. If you have been redeemed, saved, delivered and set free, that is plenty of reason to rejoice in the Lord. If God woke you up this morning and breathed His breath into your lungs, that is a big reason to be glad. When we see the goodness and mercy of the Lord, that is reason to praise Him. We have great reason to praise God for His promises and all His words of comfort. All this should motivate us to sing praises unto the Lord with spiritual joy and freedom of our souls, and to serve Him with gladness. Enjoy joyful singing and serving everyone!

CHOOSE TO MAKE TODAY AND EVERY DAY GREAT AND BLESSED NO MATTER WHAT!

#PerpetualPraise #ContinualPrayer #WorshipInSpiritAndTruth

{DAY 204}

"And whatever you do, do it heartily, as to the Lord and not to men, knowing that from the Lord you will receive the reward of the inheritance; for you serve the Lord Christ." (Colossians 3:23-24 NKJV)

Just to share a tidbit of personal information, I keep a sign on the doorknob of my office which says, "Working for JESUS!" This sign was made for my office door when I was working full-time outside of my home. I now work from home, and still use this sign on my office door at home. When you have a difficult job and work long hours, it truly helps to remind yourself that you are doing your work unto Jesus, and not unto men. That reminder will cause you to do your work (no matter what your work may be) excellently as to the Lord. I used to clean homes for the elderly and vacation cabins for a living. I also cleaned the RV's and public showers/restrooms (men's and women's) in a resort park, as well as washing/drying and folding all the RV's linens (sheets, towels, etc.). It was an honest living, and I did my job in excellence as unto the Lord. Plus, I got to putter around the resort park driving a golf cart – lol! The Manager at the resort park used to tell me that the folded sheets looked like they did when they came out of the package brand new. Praise God! I boast only in God. The Lord saw the excellent work I was doing as unto Him and I know that, though I received little from my earthly masters, the Lord has an eternal inheritance and reward for me—Heaven's glory!

CHOOSE TO MAKE TODAY AND EVERY DAY GREAT AND BLESSED NO MATTER WHAT!

#PerpetualPraise #ContinualPrayer #WorshipInSpiritAndTruth

{DAY 205}

"Therefore, as the elect of God, holy and beloved, put on tender mercies, kindness, humility, meekness, longsuffering; bearing with one another, and forgiving one another, if anyone has a complaint against another; even as Christ forgave you, so you also must do." (Colossians 3:12-13 NKJV)

Forgiveness brings deliverance, freedom, and healing to the one who is being forgiven, but also to the forgiver. I remember the very moment I believed by faith that Jesus had forgiven me for all of my many ongoing sins, and at that moment I was totally arrested by God's unconditional love! I will always remember that eternal, life-saving moment! Before that moment and from the way I understood God before that time, I didn't think I stood the least chance in hell of being forgiven for all I had done in my life so far. However, from that moment, I knew and understood God in a whole new light. Of course, God already knows all of this, and that is why He commands His people to forgive one another, even as Christ forgave us. I love You so much, Jesus!

CHOOSE TO MAKE TODAY AND EVERY DAY GREAT AND BLESSED NO MATTER WHAT!

#PerpetualPraise #ContinualPrayer #WorshipInSpiritAndTruth

{DAY 206}

"God is not a man, that He should lie, nor a son of man, that He should repent. Has He said, and will He not do? Or has He spoken, and will He not make it good? Let us hold fast the confession of our hope without wavering, for He who promised is faithful." (Numbers 23:19; Hebrews 10:23 NKJV)

It is impossible for God to lie. God is without sin; therefore, He has no need to repent, or change. Jesus is the same yesterday, today, and forever. He never changes His mind. God is faithful to keep His Word and all of His promises. What God says He will do—that will He do. God makes good on all His promises! Let us cling to our hope and faith in God without wavering. Believe on God's Word and trust Him. If God said it, then it is forever established, and no man can stop it either. We praise and worship You, oh God, for You are the faithful and everlasting God!

CHOOSE TO MAKE TODAY AND EVERY DAY GREAT AND BLESSED NO MATTER WHAT!

#PerpetualPraise #ContinualPrayer #WorshipInSpiritAndTruth

{DAY 207}

"Oh, give thanks to the Lord, for He is good! For His mercy endures forever." (1 Chronicles 16:34 NKJV)

I give You thanks, Lord, for You are a good God all the time, and all the time You are good! You daily load me with benefits! Your Goodness began when You woke me up this morning with Your breath in my lungs! You are the very air I breathe! Jesus, You are my Bright and Morning Star! I worship You, Lord, for You are my Lord and my Savior! You are the Savior of the world and the Giver of salvation! You are my Redeemer! I praise You, Lord, for You are my Healer! I praise You, Lord, for You are my Deliverer! He who the Son sets free is free indeed! I praise You, Lord, for You are the Restorer of my family! I love You, Jesus, for You are my Constant Companion and my soon coming King! I praise and worship You, Jesus, for You are the Lord of Lords and the King of Kings! I thank You, Lord, for Your amazing grace and mercy! Your mercy endures forever! My soul cries out, "Hallelujah!"

CHOOSE TO MAKE TODAY AND EVERY DAY GREAT AND BLESSED NO MATTER WHAT!

#PerpetualPraise #ContinualPrayer #WorshipInSpiritAndTruth

{DAY 208}

"And God shall wipe away all tears from their eyes; and there shall be no more death, neither sorrow, nor crying, neither shall there be any more pain: for the former things are passed away." (Revelation 21:4 KJV)

Just imagine! Heaven is a place of blessed peace; a place where no tear will ever be shed; not one shall ever die—no grave shall ever be dug there—no funeral procession will ever be witnessed there; no sorrow or grief of any kind there; no crying there; and no more pain or sickness there. How different, therefore, must the blessed state of the future be from the present! How glorious! When you receive Jesus as your Lord and Savior, you will have the blessed assurance of spending eternal life in this glorious Heaven with Jesus! Thank You, Jesus, for dying on the cross for all and for loving all even while we were yet sinners so that at the end of our journey here on earth we truly can experience this glorious Heaven for all eternity with You, just as described in this Scripture! I will share this truth on Your behalf, Christ Jesus, my Lord and my Savior, to the glory of our Heavenly Father God. Blessed be the Name of the Lord!

CHOOSE TO MAKE TODAY AND EVERY DAY GREAT AND BLESSED NO MATTER WHAT!

#PerpetualPraise #ContinualPrayer #WorshipInSpiritAndTruth

{DAY 209}

PRAISE TO START YOUR DAY:

"Let brotherly love continue." (Hebrews 13:1 KJV)

Yes, Lord, I will continue to love my brothers and sisters in Christ Jesus. We are the family of God, brought together through the precious Blood of Jesus. Thank You, Jesus! Glory to our Heavenly Father God! The only thing that matters in our lives on earth is that which is Eternal. GOD IS LOVE. LOVE IS ETERNAL. Love is what moves our heart, soul and spirit. The three things I would most like to be remembered for after I have gone Home to be with Jesus are love, faith, and light.

CHOOSE TO MAKE TODAY AND EVERY DAY GREAT AND BLESSED NO MATTER WHAT!

#PerpetualPraise #ContinualPrayer #WorshipInSpiritAndTruth

{DAY 210}

"For the Scriptures say, "If you want to enjoy life and see many happy days, keep your tongue from speaking evil and your lips from telling lies. Turn away from evil and do good. Search for peace, and work to maintain it."(1 Peter 3:10-11 NLT)

Yes, Lord, I do want to enjoy life and see many happy days. Therefore, Lord, I pray You keep my mind renewed with the washing of Your Word, keep my spirit renewed through the power of Your Holy Spirit Who lives in me, and keep my heart pure and clean. Thereby, no evil word will be on the tip of my tongue ready to come out of my mouth. I will speak only according to Your words of life, love, goodness, kindness and encouragement to myself and others. I will obey Your commandment and will not tell lies. Thank You, Lord, for giving me the mind of Christ to love life and Your compassion to love others. I praise You for giving me a calm and peaceful spirit because of Your Holy Spirit Who lives in me. Yes, Lord Jesus, when men may not let me have peace when I would have peace, I will work to maintain and keep it. I desire to always have peace not only with You, Lord, and with my spirit, soul and conscience, but also with all men.

CHOOSE TO MAKE TODAY AND EVERY DAY GREAT AND BLESSED NO MATTER WHAT!

#PerpetualPraise #ContinualPrayer #WorshipInSpiritAndTruth

{DAY 211}

"Oh come, let us sing to the Lord! Let us shout joyfully to the Rock of our salvation. Let us come before His presence with thanksgiving; let us shout joyfully to Him with psalms. For the Lord is the great God, and the great King above all gods. In His hand are the deep places of the earth; the heights of the hills are His also. The sea is His, for He made it; and His hands formed the dry land. Oh come, let us worship and bow down; let us kneel before the Lord our Maker." (Psalm 95:1-6 NKJV)

We must praise God with our voice; we must speak and sing His praises out of the abundance of a heart filled with love, and joy, and thankfulness. Our praise songs should be a joyful sound to God. He is our Great God, our Heavenly Father, and our King! We must come before God and glorify Him in humble reverence and in holy awe of Him. He is the Great God and Sovereign Lord of all! Blessed be the Name of the Lord!

CHOOSE TO MAKE TODAY AND EVERY DAY GREAT AND BLESSED NO MATTER WHAT!

#PerpetualPraise #ContinualPrayer #WorshipInSpiritAndTruth

{DAY 212}

"Jesus answered him, "The first of all the commandments is: 'Hear, O Israel, the Lord our God, the Lord is one. And you shall love the Lord your God with all your heart, with all your soul, with all your mind, and with all your strength.' This is the first commandment. And the second, like it, is this: 'You shall love your neighbor (other people) as yourself.' There is no other commandment greater than these." (Mark 12:29-31 NKJV)

All of our relationships are to be marked by our love (God always first, and then our neighbors, which is referring to all other people including our enemies.) Lord, I do love You with all my heart, with all my soul, with all my mind, and with all my strength. I desire my love for You to be shown through my obedience to You and through all that I think, say and do. I know (according to Your own Word) that I cannot really love You without also loving other people. Please fill my heart with Your love as I seek to love all other people, I pray in the blessed Name of Jesus! Amen, Amen and Amen! I praise and worship You, Lord, for Your Unconditional Love! Blessed be the Name of the Lord forevermore!

CHOOSE TO MAKE TODAY AND EVERY DAY GREAT AND BLESSED NO MATTER WHAT!

#PerpetualPraise #ContinualPrayer #WorshipInSpiritAndTruth

{DAY 213}

"Because Your lovingkindness is better than life, my lips shall praise You. Thus I will bless You while I live; I will lift up my hands in Your name. My soul shall be satisfied as with marrow and fatness, and my mouth shall praise You with joyful lips." (Psalm 63:3-5 NKJV)

I praise You, Lord, for Your lovingkindness, for without it there would be no reason for me to take another breath. Apart from You and Your lovingkindness, there is no life in me. Therefore, I will bless You for Your lovingkindness as long as You are breathing Your breath into my lungs. My bones will sing praises unto You. I will show forth Your praise by the lifting up of my hands in Your Name, Jesus! Lord, because of Your lovingkindness, my soul is joy filled, comparable to the richest food with which my body can be nourished! I worship You, Lord, and I will praise You forevermore!

CHOOSE TO MAKE TODAY AND EVERY DAY GREAT AND BLESSED NO MATTER WHAT!

#PerpetualPraise #ContinualPrayer #WorshipInSpiritAndTruth

{DAY 214}

PRAISE TO START YOUR DAY:

"A happy heart makes the face cheerful, but heartache crushes the spirit. A merry heart doeth good like a medicine: but a broken spirit drieth the bones." (Proverbs 15:13 NIV; Proverbs 17:22 KJV)

Thank You, Jesus, that my face reflects the happiness in my heart, and I offer You my heartfelt gratitude for Your love towards me. Thank You, Lord, that my spirit is no longer broken, but has been restored through the power of Your Holy Spirit Who now lives in me. Thank You, O God, that being made right with You has given me a quiet, cheerful mind and a clear conscience. Thank You, Jesus, that because of Your joy in my heart, my body remains restored, preserved and strengthened, and my bones are full of moisture, no matter what my age. I love You, Jesus! God says that if you truly have a happy heart, your face will be alerted and will reflect that happiness as well.

CHOOSE TO MAKE TODAY AND EVERY DAY GREAT AND BLESSED NO MATTER WHAT!

#PerpetualPraise #ContinualPrayer #WorshipInSpiritAndTruth

{DAY 215}

"Love is patient, love is kind. It does not envy, it does not boast, it is not proud. It does not dishonor others, it is not self-seeking, it is not easily angered, it keeps no record of wrongs. Love does not delight in evil but rejoices with the truth. It always protects, always trusts, always hopes, always perseveres. Love never fails...And now these three remain: faith, hope and love. But the greatest of these is love." (1 Corinthians 13:4-8,13 NIV)

God is Love. God's people are to love as God loves—from a pure heart. This is the highest goal we should work towards achieving. Love is the greatest virtue, even superseding faith. Our love will be put through the fire to see if it keeps its value. Those of us, whose love survives the fire, will receive a reward from God. If we choose to love God's way, this Scripture is what our love will look like. We will NOT be any of the following: Envious, jealous, boastful, pride-inflated, arrogant, vain, conceited, snobbish, rude, unmannerly, self-seeking, insisting on having our own way, resentful, account keepers of evil done to us, rejoicers of unrighteousness. Lord, I choose to love Your way, and I praise You for instructing me how to do that.

CHOOSE TO MAKE TODAY AND EVERY DAY GREAT AND BLESSED NO MATTER WHAT!

#PerpetualPraise #ContinualPrayer #WorshipInSpiritAndTruth

{DAY 216}

PRAISE TO START YOUR DAY:

"As the Father loved Me, I also have loved you; abide in My love. If you keep My commandments, you will abide in My love, just as I have kept My Father's commandments and abide in His love. These things I have spoken to you, that My joy may remain in you, and that your joy may be full." (John 15:9-11 NKJV)

Thank You, Jesus, that our joy is perfected in knowing that You love us. By obeying Your commandments, we will also be accepting and following in Your love. Thank You, Jesus, for being the first partaker of obedience through Your own obedience to our Heavenly Father God. You will not instruct us to do anything that You Yourself have not already done. I love You too, Jesus, from here to Heaven and throughout all Eternity.

CHOOSE TO MAKE TODAY AND EVERY DAY GREAT AND BLESSED NO MATTER WHAT!

#PerpetualPraise #ContinualPrayer #WorshipInSpiritAndTruth

{DAY 217}

"But above all these things put on love, which is the bond of perfection."
(Colossians 3:14 NKJV)

God is Love. God's people are to be clothed with love. Love is the bond that keeps all together. Love unites and completes the whole. Love is the bond of all perfectness. Perfect love casts out all fear. Love is the highest virtue. Hope and faith are the sum of perfection on earth. Love is the sum of perfection in Heaven. We worship You, oh God, for You are Love!

CHOOSE TO MAKE TODAY AND EVERY DAY GREAT AND BLESSED NO MATTER WHAT!

#PerpetualPraise #ContinualPrayer #WorshipInSpiritAndTruth

{DAY 218}

"Now may the God of hope fill you with all joy and peace in believing, that you may abound in hope by the power of the Holy Spirit." (Romans 15:13 NKJV)

The Holy Spirit is the power Who produces in us His fruit of joy and peace as we trust and believe in the Lord's faithfulness so that we abound in large amounts of hope. God is glorified in us when we are satisfied in Him. Lord God, even though You entrust to us a portion of Your power, all power still belongs to You and You alone. You are the Omnipotent, All Powerful God! Glory to our God of Love, Joy, Peace, Hope and Power!

CHOOSE TO MAKE TODAY AND EVERY DAY GREAT AND BLESSED NO MATTER WHAT!

#PerpetualPraise #ContinualPrayer #WorshipInSpiritAndTruth

{DAY 219}

"I will give thanks to you, LORD, with all my heart; I will tell of all your wonderful deeds. I will be glad and rejoice in you; I will sing the praises of your name, O Most High." (Psalm 9:1-2 NIV)

We ought always give wholehearted praise to the Lord for all the marvelous works He had done in our lives. Our praise and worship should be directing our love and gratitude towards God with our entire being. God expects it. To God, halfhearted praise is like no praise at all. Spiritual joy comes from a life of wholehearted praise and worship, and wholehearted praise and worship is the language of spiritual joy. We are to be glad and rejoice in the Lord, Who is the Giver of all good things. All glory, praise, honor, power, and thanksgiving belong to our God! He is the Most High God! Blessed be the Name of the Lord!

CHOOSE TO MAKE TODAY AND EVERY DAY GREAT AND BLESSED NO MATTER WHAT!

#PerpetualPraise #ContinualPrayer #WorshipInSpiritAndTruth

{DAY 220}

PRAISE TO START YOUR DAY:

"Show me Your ways, O LORD; teach me Your paths. Lead me in Your truth and teach me, for You are the God of my salvation; on You I wait all the day." (Psalm 25:4-5 NKJV)

Thank You, O God, that You have already done this. God's Will is His written word—the Bible. The inheritance of God's people can be found in God's Will—the Bible, which God has already made available to whosoever desires to read it. Everything we need is in the written words of God. God wants His people to pray this Scripture's prayer to Him; however, it is also the responsibility of God's people to read and study His written word, in order to show ourselves approved unto God. God's people are to be dependent on God for everything, continually and at all times. "All Scripture is God-breathed and is useful for teaching, rebuking, correcting and training in righteousness so that the servant of God may be thoroughly equipped for every good work." (2 Timothy 3:16-17 NIV) The Bible thoroughly equips us. We praise You, Lord, for Your written Word! Thank You, Lord, for also giving us Your Holy Spirit to lead and guide us into all Truth.

CHOOSE TO MAKE TODAY AND EVERY DAY GREAT AND BLESSED NO MATTER WHAT!

#PerpetualPraise #ContinualPrayer #WorshipInSpiritAndTruth

{DAY 221}

"I can do all things through Christ who strengthens me." (Philippians 4:13 NKJV)

Amazing Scripture! It does not say that I can do a few things. It does not say that I can do most things. No, it says that I can do ALL things through Christ. That means that I can even do the impossible through Christ who gives me the strength! When Christ Jesus puts His super on your natural, you can do the supernatural and the impossible! This is a truly amazing and exciting Scripture! Just think about it. It is in the Bible, so it is a statement of truth! So, the next time you think that you cannot do something, or that something is too hard for you, just confess this Scripture out loud (and loud) and believe it and claim it for yourself! Thank You, Jesus!

CHOOSE TO MAKE TODAY AND EVERY DAY GREAT AND BLESSED NO MATTER WHAT!

#PerpetualPraise #ContinualPrayer #WorshipInSpiritAndTruth

{DAY 222}

"Love must be sincere. Hate what is evil; cling to what is good. Be devoted to one another in love. Honor one another above yourselves." (Romans 12:9-10 NIV)

Let love be sincere, without hypocrisy. When you really love others, it's not enough to just say it, you must also show it by putting some action to your words. Words are cheap when there is no corresponding action to go along with them. It is much the same as God's principle that "faith without works is dead". God's people are to hate what is evil. In this Scripture that means we are to turn away from and avoid the intention or desire to do evil, ill will, and unkindness towards others. We are to firmly attach ourselves (like being glued) to all that is good and not part from it. We are to put others before and above ourselves, thereby showing the sincere love of Jesus. We are to firmly attach ourselves to God and to Christ and to the Holy Spirit, as well as not forsaking the assembling together with the saints of God, our good brothers and sisters in Christ, and to the Good News of the Gospel of Christ, and to God's Word of truths. Thank You, Lord, for leading, guiding and teaching us! Blessed be the Name of the Lord forevermore!

CHOOSE TO MAKE TODAY AND EVERY DAY GREAT AND BLESSED NO MATTER WHAT!

#PerpetualPraise #ContinualPrayer #WorshipInSpiritAndTruth

{DAY 223}

"Also I heard the voice of the Lord, saying: "Whom shall I send, and who will go for Us?" Then I said, "Here am I! Send me." (Isaiah 6:8 NKJV)

Thank You, Lord, for waking Your servant up on this glorious God morning and starting me on my way! Thank You, Lord, for putting Your breath in my lungs and giving me a new day to be about my Father's business! I am so happy to be at Your service! How will You use me today, Lord? I am prepared, ready and willing to go do whatever You call me to do. I'm fired up and ready to go! I believe that, as I am obedient and willing to follow Your leading, You will make up the difference wherever I am lacking to get the mission accomplished for You. Lord, I have heard it said from the pulpit, many times, that You use the most unlikely people. I thank You, Jesus, from the bottom of my heart for using me. Readers, please note that the word "Us" is most probably a foreshadowing the Holy Trinity (God the Father, God the Son, God the Holy Spirit).

CHOOSE TO MAKE TODAY AND EVERY DAY GREAT AND BLESSED NO MATTER WHAT!

#PerpetualPraise #ContinualPrayer #WorshipInSpiritAndTruth

{DAY 224}

"The one who blesses others is abundantly blessed; those who help others are helped." (Proverbs 11:25 MSGB)

In living for the good of others, we shall be profited also ourselves. The path to our own happiness is to seek the good of others. In addition to glorifying God and fulfilling God's Will in our lives, we are storing up great treasures of rewards. I am fully persuaded of this because God promises it and He always keeps His promises. Lord Jesus, one of my heart's desires is to always bless, help and encourage others. I praise You and thank You for putting that good desire in my heart and for blessing me with opportunities to do that.

CHOOSE TO MAKE TODAY AND EVERY DAY GREAT AND BLESSED NO MATTER WHAT!

#PerpetualPraise #ContinualPrayer #WorshipInSpiritAndTruth

{DAY 225}

"But I fear, lest somehow, as the serpent deceived Eve by his craftiness, so your minds may be corrupted from the simplicity that is in Christ." (2 Corinthians 11:3 NKJV)

The serpent deceived Eve by adding just one or two words to what God had actually spoken to Adam and Eve. As a result, it caused confusion and doubt in Eve's mind. There is simplicity in Christ Jesus. Keep it simple. Only listen to God's voice through His Word. He will never try to deceive you. Simplicity was God's plan from the beginning, and it still is. It is God's Will that all should be saved and have eternal life; therefore, He did not make the Gospel of Christ Jesus difficult to understand for anyone. If you are a new Christian—Praise God!—get yourself a Bible in a translation you will find easier to understand. A Study Bible (with notes about the Scripture verses) is also a good idea, when starting out. I recommend beginning with the Book of John in the New Testament. Praying is also simple. It's just talking to Jesus straight from your heart like you would with your closest friend. Make Jesus your Constant Companion and begin to talk to Him as your Friend all the time. After a while as you stop to listen for His reply, You will begin to hear Him talking back to you with a still, small voice. The main thing to keep in mind is simplicity. Every Christian is God's continual work in process. We all must start at the beginning.

CHOOSE TO MAKE TODAY AND EVERY DAY GREAT AND BLESSED NO MATTER WHAT!

#PerpetualPraise #ContinualPrayer #WorshipInSpiritAndTruth

{DAY 226}

"Do not worship any other god, for the LORD, whose name is Jealous, is a jealous God." (Exodus 34:14 NIV)

The God who created the universe, the Great I Am, is jealous for you and for me! What a riveting thought! Normally, the word "jealous" brings to mind negativity. However, God carries it as far as to take it on as one of His names. The basis of God's jealousy for you and for me is Love – His Love for our well-being, safety and true joy. God's jealousy for us is pure. God wants us for Himself. God wants to protect us from false gods. Anything we put before God and spend more time doing than the time we spend with God becomes a god in our lives. We must be careful not to fill up more of our time with gods, instead of with God. A few examples of gods we make for ourselves are TV, iPhones, video games, sports, entertainment, work, etc. God knows that our true joy is only found in Him, Jesus. Thank You, O God, for being jealous for me. I worship You, Jehovah-Kanna, for You are the Lord Jealous. I am jealous for You too, Lord. Your presence and relationship is what I crave, desire and need, above all others and above all else. You are the Lover of my soul.

CHOOSE TO MAKE TODAY AND EVERY DAY GREAT AND BLESSED NO MATTER WHAT!

#PerpetualPraise #ContinualPrayer #WorshipInSpiritAndTruth

{DAY 227}

"The Lord looks down from heaven upon the children of men, to see if there are any who understand, who seek God."(Psalm 14:2 & Psalm 53:2 NKJV)

The Lord has said the same thing in two different Scriptures, in order to show us the value and importance He places on what He has said here. God desires for His children to truly know Him so that we will have a holy reverence towards Him, love and obey Him, and put our faith and trust in Him. We are being closely examined by God. One of the clearest proofs to God of our true character is whether or not we are really interested enough in getting to know and understand God's character through His Word, and desire to establish a relationship with Him, and obtain His friendship and favor. In order to have a Friend in God, we must also prove ourselves friendly to God. This is what God is looking for in His created mankind. Wow, when you really stop and think about this, the Creator of All—God Almighty Himself—is inviting and asking you and me personally to be His friend. This is deeply touching to my heart, soul and spirit, as I pray it is to yours as well. In the blessed Name of Jesus, let us all gain knowledge and grow in our understanding of God as we continually seek Him, and have a close, personal relationship and friendship with Him, and find favor with God, in the blessed Name of Jesus! Amen, amen, and amen!

CHOOSE TO MAKE TODAY AND EVERY DAY GREAT AND BLESSED NO MATTER WHAT!

#PerpetualPraise #ContinualPrayer #WorshipInSpiritAndTruth

{DAY 228}

PRAISE TO START YOUR DAY:

"A man's heart plans his way, but the LORD directs his steps."
(Proverbs 16:9 NKJV)

Man needs God's blessing to achieve his/her goals. Diligently apply yourself, but acknowledge that the outcome truly depends on God's favor, not your ability in planning your desire. When you have God's favor and follow His direction, He will give you everything you need to achieve your goals, and He will make up the difference where you may be lacking.

CHOOSE TO MAKE TODAY AND EVERY DAY GREAT AND BLESSED NO MATTER WHAT!

#PerpetualPraise #ContinualPrayer #WorshipInSpiritAndTruth

{DAY 229}

PRAISE TO START YOUR DAY:

""I, even I, am He who blots out your transgressions for My own sake; and I will not remember your sins."" (Isaiah 43:25 NKJV)

Jesus, I will never forget the day you visited and gifted me with this truth. The tremendous amount of guilt I had been carrying was totally lifted off of me. The calming and restoring of my soul and spirit was instantaneous. What true peace and joy it brought into my spirit, the likes of which I had not known! Thank You, Lord, for You are a God of forgiveness, grace and mercy, soul restoration, peace, love and joy! I love You, my Jesus! Dear reader(s), if you are carrying guilt today, I urge you to embed this Scripture deep within your heart (where the enemy cannot take it from you) and receive it in your spirit. Speak it from your mouth so you can hear yourself saying it, until it stirs up your faith, and then completely believe these words of God in your heart. God loves us one and all the same. This prayer is being prayed for you right now today, in the blessed Name of Jesus! Amen, amen, and amen!

CHOOSE TO MAKE TODAY AND EVERY DAY GREAT AND BLESSED NO MATTER WHAT!

#PerpetualPraise #ContinualPrayer #WorshipInSpiritAndTruth

{DAY 230}

PRAISE TO START YOUR DAY:

"Therefore by Him let us continually offer the sacrifice of praise to God, that is, the fruit of our lips, giving thanks to His name." (Hebrews 13:15 NKJV)

Thank You, Lord, for putting Your breath in my lungs and giving me a new day to offer You my sacrifice of perpetual praise! As believers in Christ, we are God's priests, and this is the sacrifice of praise that we are to continually offer (by speaking it aloud we are offering it from the fruit of our lips), giving thanks to God's name. His Name is JESUS! Thank You, Jesus, that I have come alive in You, that I am covered by Your precious blood, that I am blessed of the Lord, and that it is well with my soul! All glory to our Heavenly Father God through Christ Jesus!

CHOOSE TO MAKE TODAY AND EVERY DAY GREAT AND BLESSED NO MATTER WHAT!

#PerpetualPraise #ContinualPrayer #WorshipInSpiritAndTruth

{DAY 231}

PRAISE TO START YOUR DAY:

"Behold, I am the Lord, the God of all flesh. Is there anything too hard for Me?" (Jeremiah 32:27 NKJV)

The obvious and only answer to this God's prominent statement is an emphatic "NO!". There is nothing that is too hard for God to do. Nothing is impossible for God. All things, including the impossible, are possible for God! God is God all by Himself! God does not need man's help! This truth should fill all believers with a great sense of security, calmness, love, faith, trust, peace and joy. We worship You, our Lord God Almighty!

CHOOSE TO MAKE TODAY AND EVERY DAY GREAT AND BLESSED NO MATTER WHAT!

#PerpetualPraise #ContinualPrayer #WorshipInSpiritAndTruth

{DAY 232}

"I beseech you, brethren, (ye know the house of Stephanas, that it is the firstfruits of Achaia, and that they have addicted themselves to the ministry of the saints,) that ye submit yourselves unto such, and to everyone that helpeth with us, and laboureth." (1 Corinthians 16:15-16 KJV)

I, too, have holy addictions. I am holy addicted to Jesus and to the ministry of His saints, to staying in His presence, to experiencing His glory, to being a soul winner for God's Kingdom, to praising and worshiping God, to talking to God (praying) and having a relationship with God, to reading and studying God's Word, to growing in knowledge and understanding of God, just to name a few. I am always hungry and thirsty for more of Jesus. Jesus and me are connected, like glue. Jesus is my Answer to living a God-filled and godly life.

CHOOSE TO MAKE TODAY AND EVERY DAY GREAT AND BLESSED NO MATTER WHAT!

#PerpetualPraise #ContinualPrayer #WorshipInSpiritAndTruth

{DAY 233}

"Be on your guard; stand firm in the faith; be courageous; be strong. Do everything in love." (1 Corinthians 16:13-14 NIV)

As Christians, we must be expecting the soon coming return of the Lord Jesus Christ at all times, and living as though today is the day. We must always stand firm in our faith and cannot allow the enemy to cause us to retreat, or cause our faith to fail us. We must have courage when the enemy comes in like a flood and be strengthened by the Lord. We must do all in the love of Jesus and for Christ Jesus. We must love Jesus and each other. This Scripture is not just full of ideas – these are commandments from God. Therefore, if we truly love the Lord, we will obey Him.

CHOOSE TO MAKE TODAY AND EVERY DAY GREAT AND BLESSED NO MATTER WHAT!

#PerpetualPraise #ContinualPrayer #WorshipInSpiritAndTruth

{DAY 234}

"Let your conduct be without covetousness; be content with such things as you have. For He Himself has said, "I will never leave you nor forsake you." (Hebrews 13:5 NKJV)

You will not be tempted to yearn to have what others have when you are truly grateful for having God in your life, knowing that He will never leave nor forsake you. All you have ever needed is Jesus; all you need today is Jesus; all you will ever need is Jesus. God rewards you when your heart is full of true gratitude towards Him. God is your Need Supplier. When you have everything you need, then you want for nothing. I worship You, my Jehovah-Shammah, for You are my ever present God! You are right here with me all the time; You always have been and You always will be. Blessed be the Name of the Lord! Thank You, my Jesus!

CHOOSE TO MAKE TODAY AND EVERY DAY GREAT AND BLESSED NO MATTER WHAT!

#PerpetualPraise #ContinualPrayer #WorshipInSpiritAndTruth

{DAY 235}

"For My thoughts are not your thoughts, nor are your ways My ways," says the Lord. "For as the heavens are higher than the earth, so are My ways higher than your ways, and My thoughts than your thoughts." (Isaiah 55:8-9 NKJV)

There have been times when God answered my prayers and I said, "I would have never thought my prayer would have been answered in that way! I never would have even imagined God's Way of working it out!" I must say that it is so exciting and exhilarating when this happens! I learned a long time ago to stop wasting my time trying to figure out how God is going to do it. I now say to God, "I don't need to know how You're going to do it. I just know You're going to do it! I judge You "Faithful", Oh God!" In fact, the anticipation and expectation of knowing God is going to do something "mind blowing", is as thrilling to me as when He actually does it!

CHOOSE TO MAKE TODAY AND EVERY DAY GREAT AND BLESSED NO MATTER WHAT!

#PerpetualPraise #ContinualPrayer #WorshipInSpiritAndTruth

{DAY 236}

"I will praise You, for I am fearfully and wonderfully made; marvelous are Your works, and that my soul knows very well." (Psalm 139:14 NKJV)

God formed each one of us while we were still in our mother's womb. We are each God's own individually handmade design. God invested Himself in each one of us before we were even born, because we are each valuable and of great worth to God. If God had wanted all men to be the same, we could have all been manufactured in a single mold, and God would not be the Potter and us the clay. Have you ever felt like you don't fit in, or that you're different and misunderstood? Well, be encouraged and take heart because God did not create you to fit in with this world. You are in the world, but not of the world. God fearfully and wonderfully created you to stand out and be different. God sees each of us as His exceptionally good work! Thank You, Lord, for making us all unique "standouts" in Your eyes! We praise You, Lord!

CHOOSE TO MAKE TODAY AND EVERY DAY GREAT AND BLESSED NO MATTER WHAT!

#PerpetualPraise #ContinualPrayer #WorshipInSpiritAndTruth

{DAY 237}

PRAISE TO START YOUR DAY:

"O God, You are more awesome than Your holy places. The God of Israel is He who gives strength and power to His people. Blessed be God!" (Psalm 68:35 NKJV)

God is known to Himself as "I Am That I Am." God's Holiness is Perfect, as is His unfathomable Love. God calls Himself "The Holy One". There is no one to compare to God. He is unequaled, unmatched and unsurpassed. Everything concerning God is Holy. God's Holiness is more awesome than His holy places (God's Temple, Mount Zion, City of Zion, Heaven, God's Holy Throne...). If you have received Jesus Christ as your Lord and Savior, you are a born-again Believer, and you are now holy because God's Holy Spirit lives in you. Your body is a holy temple for Holy God, and He gives you strength and power. Blessed be God forevermore!

CHOOSE TO MAKE TODAY AND EVERY DAY GREAT AND BLESSED NO MATTER WHAT!

#PerpetualPraise #ContinualPrayer#WorshipInSpiritAndTruth

{DAY 238}

"I pray that your love will overflow more and more, and that you will keep on growing in knowledge and understanding. For I want you to understand what really matters, so that you may live pure and blameless lives until the day of Christ's return. May you always be filled with the fruit of your salvation—the righteous character produced in your life by Jesus Christ—for this will bring much glory and praise to God." (Philippians 1:9-11 NLT)

I am so joy filled this morning to be able to go into the house of the Lord, where I will hear and receive even more knowledge about You, Christ Jesus! You will keep me filled with the fruit of my salvation—that is, the holy and righteous character You have produced in my life. I desire to bring more glory and praise to our Heavenly Father God. I love the house of the Lord and being in Your presence where I can step right into Your Love! I love being amongst my true Livingway Church Family because we have a kindred spirit and are united as one in Christ Jesus, with the same spiritual desires, and even the more so as we see the day approaching. Blessed be the Name of the Lord!

CHOOSE TO MAKE TODAY AND EVERY DAY GREAT AND BLESSED NO MATTER WHAT!

#PerpetualPraise #ContinualPrayer #WorshipInSpiritAndTruth

{DAY 239}

PRAISE TO START YOUR DAY:

"Christ is the visible image of the invisible God. He existed before anything was created and is supreme over all creation," (Colossians 1:15 NLT) "Do you not know that you are the temple of God and that the Spirit of God dwells in you?" (1 Corinthians 3:16 NKJV)

Christians are to be like Jesus Christ. His attributes and character are to be our attributes and character (holiness, righteousness, lovingkindness, goodness, graciousness, merciful, forgiving, unchanging, faithful…). The Bible tells us that Christ is the visible image of the invisible God. Christians are to be the visible image of the unseen Christ. Jesus has given us His very own Holy Spirit Who lives in us. God lives in you and in me. We ought always to remember this and make sure that we are manifesting Jesus to the world through all we think, say and do. We praise and worship You, Lord!

CHOOSE TO MAKE TODAY AND EVERY DAY GREAT AND BLESSED NO MATTER WHAT!

#PerpetualPraise #ContinualPrayer #WorshipInSpiritAndTruth

{DAY 240}

PRAISE TO START YOUR DAY:

"When you lie down, you will not be afraid; when you lie down, your sleep will be sweet." (Proverbs 3:24 NIV)

When you lie down, you will not be afraid of the darkness because you have the light of God living on the inside of you. You need not have fear of anything evil in the night while you sleep because God is your Keeper both night and day. Your sleep will be sweet—free from disturbing thoughts, cares and imaginations. Your thoughts will be of God things. Thank You, Lord, for waking us up on this glorious God morning after giving us a night of sweet sleep! Jesus, You are the Bright and Morning Star! We love You, Jesus!

CHOOSE TO MAKE TODAY AND EVERY DAY GREAT AND BLESSED NO MATTER WHAT!

#PerpetualPraise #ContinualPrayer #WorshipInSpiritAndTruth

{DAY 241}

"When I remember You on my bed, I meditate on You in the night watches. Because You have been my help, therefore in the shadow of Your wings I will rejoice." (Psalm 63:6-7 NKJV)

If day's cares tempt us to forget God, it is well that night's quiet should lead us to remember Him. We go to our hidden, secret place in God where our memory provides us with proofs of the Lord's faithfulness in our lives, and leads us on to a growing confidence in God. We are not only safe, but happy in God, and we rejoice. Lord, thank You for waking me up on this glorious God morning, and for the special and intimate time I was blessed to spend with You through the night. Thank You, Lord, that I am rested, restored and ready to take on another day with You by my side every moment! Lord, I'm fired up and ready to go! I praise and worship You, Lord!

CHOOSE TO MAKE TODAY AND EVERY DAY GREAT AND BLESSED NO MATTER WHAT!

#PerpetualPraise #ContinualPrayer #WorshipInSpiritAndTruth

{DAY 242}

"But each day the LORD pours his unfailing love upon me, and through each night I sing his songs, praying to God who gives me life." (Psalm 42:8 NLT)

God orders and directs His lovingkindness. Each day the Lord is said to command His lovingkindness be upon us through His blessings, which causes us to sing songs of praise to God each night. Our prayers are unto God Who preserves and gives us life morning by morning. Never think the God of your life has forgotten you, if you have made His mercy, truth, and power, your refuge.

CHOOSE TO MAKE TODAY AND EVERY DAY GREAT AND BLESSED NO MATTER WHAT!

#PerpetualPraise #ContinualPrayer #WorshipInSpiritAndTruth

{DAY 243}

PRAISE TO START YOUR DAY:

"I will both lie down in peace, and sleep; for You alone, O LORD, make me dwell in safety." (Psalm 4:8 NKJV)

Divine peace that brings joy leads you to sleep. The stresses of life become less intense when we are in the presence of the Lord and He is in us. Thus, we are able to lay down in peace and sleep, and to be positioned in safety. This can only happen by being with the Lord. The man who is not with the Lord seeks peace and happiness through worldly means, or other gods, such as wealth, fame, sex, pornography, drugs and alcohol. These are man's way. Repentance, faith, trust, and belief are God's way. Thank You, Jesus, for delivering me from man's way. Man's way never worked out for me, Lord knows not from lack of trying! I used to think to myself concerning my messed up life, "I got this! I can fix it!", only to find out that I was wrong and I needed God. Lord, I pray You always have Your way in my life, in the blessed Name of Jesus! Amen, amen, and amen!

CHOOSE TO MAKE TODAY AND EVERY DAY GREAT AND BLESSED NO MATTER WHAT!

#PerpetualPraise #ContinualPrayer #WorshipInSpiritAndTruth

{DAY 244}

"You will not fear the terror of night, nor the arrow that flies by day, nor the pestilence that stalks in the darkness, nor the plague that destroys at midday." (Psalm 91:5-6 NIV)

When your love is set on God and you dwell in the shadow of the Most High, in the hidden place under His protective wings, He will protect you from all hostility. God will protect you from danger at night, as well as during the day, and also from the fear of danger. As you keep your shield of faith on, all the fiery darts of the devil will be quenched. No weapon that is formed against you will prosper. Souls who dwell in God shall live above the fear of danger and diseases. Perfect love casts out all fear. God has not given you a spirit of fear, but He has given you a spirit of power, love, and a sound mind. Put a praise on it! Rejoice and be thankful!

CHOOSE TO MAKE TODAY AND EVERY DAY GREAT AND BLESSED NO MATTER WHAT!

#PerpetualPraise #ContinualPrayer #WorshipInSpiritAndTruth

{DAY 245}

PRAISE TO START YOUR DAY:

"In the daytime also He led them with the cloud, and all the night with a light of fire." (Psalm 78:14 NKJV)

God showed the Israelites the way through the desert with a special cloud in the day and the light of a fire in the sky at night. He also provided them with food and water. They still did not obey God. Thank You, Father God, that You not only lead and guide us during the day, but also throughout the night. Thank You, Lord, that Your Holy Spirit invades our minds and hearts even as we sleep, leading and guiding us on our life journey in You, Jesus. We praise You, Lord, for also providing all our needs. We pray right now, Lord, that we show our love and gratefulness towards You through our obedience, in the blessed Name of Jesus! Amen, amen, and amen!

CHOOSE TO MAKE TODAY AND EVERY DAY GREAT AND BLESSED NO MATTER WHAT!

#PerpetualPraise #ContinualPrayer #WorshipInSpiritAndTruth

{DAY 246}

"And let us not grow weary while doing good, for in due season we shall reap if we do not lose heart." (Galatians 6:9 NKJV)

We are all very apt to tire in duty, particularly in doing good. Being a disciple and follower of Jesus Christ is literally a lifetime journey from the moment you accept Jesus as your Lord and Savior. Sadly, sometimes when a Christian grows weary of doing good, he may choose to "take a break" from going to church as often, or he may choose to step down from a church ministry, or (Heaven forbid) he may choose to backslide from God's ways for a time. There are many reasons that may cause a Christian to grow weary in well-doing. Here are just a few: Feeling tired and exhausted, or illness; life disappointments and heartaches; becoming disheartened and discouraged while waiting on the promises of God; losing faith; changes in his own circumstances; not having a true heart for the ministry due to not having a true calling from God for that ministry; ungratefulness; not doing good for the right motives and reasons. We should take special care to do good and make our Heavenly Father's business the business of our lives for Christ's sake—always for Christ's sake. He who becomes a true Christian, becomes such for eternity. He becomes committed to doing good and serving God always. By doing so without becoming disheartened, we will receive the full reward for all our self-denials and volunteering for the Lord. Father God, may You help us not to grow weary in doing good works for You. Help us to always remember the eternal rewards You have waiting for us so that we will not lose heart, in the blessed Name of Jesus! Amen, amen, and amen!

CHOOSE TO MAKE TODAY AND EVERY DAY GREAT AND BLESSED NO MATTER WHAT!

#PerpetualPraise #ContinualPrayer #WorshipInSpiritAndTruth

{DAY 247}

PRAISE TO START YOUR DAY:

"I will bless the LORD who guides me; even at night my heart instructs me. I know the LORD is always with me. I will not be shaken, for he is right beside me." (Psalm 16:7-8 NLT)

I will bless You, Lord, by offering praise to You for leading me to choose the right and happy way of life—God's way! Not only during the day, but also in the silence of the night as I turn my affections towards God, my heart meditates on holy things. I know You are always with me, Lord, as I feel Your presence. I keep You close, right by my side, so I will not be afraid and frightened, nor worried and nervous. I love You, Jesus. My very existence, my whole life, revolves around You. I love my life in You, Jesus! This is living now!

CHOOSE TO MAKE TODAY AND EVERY DAY GREAT AND BLESSED NO MATTER WHAT!

#PerpetualPraise #ContinualPrayer #WorshipInSpiritAndTruth

{DAY 248}

"For we are His workmanship, created in Christ Jesus for good works, which God prepared beforehand that we should walk in them." (Ephesians 2:10 NKJV)

Thank You, Lord, that we are Your very own work of art; Your greatest masterpieces of creation – not only as men, but also as saints (new men in Christ Jesus). Even before You formed and made us, You saw us as we would be when You re-created us in Christ Jesus. You did not see us as we were before Your re-creation of us. You knew the good works You had planned for each one of us individually, and then You hand-designed and prepared us for each of those specific good works. Lord, I pray that You will enable, strengthen and empower each Reader reading this (including myself) to walk worthy in our good works, so we will glorify You always, in the blessed Name of Jesus! Amen, amen, and amen!

CHOOSE TO MAKE TODAY AND EVERY DAY GREAT AND BLESSED NO MATTER WHAT!

#PerpetualPraise #ContinualPrayer #WorshipInSpiritAndTruth

{DAY 249}

"For he raised us from the dead along with Christ and seated us with him in the heavenly realms because we are united with Christ Jesus. So God can point to us in all future ages as examples of the incredible wealth of his grace and kindness toward us, as shown in all he has done for us who are united with Christ Jesus." (Ephesians 2:6-7 NLT)

Before being born-again in Christ Jesus, we were nothing more than dead men walking. Our spirits were dead because we had not yet been filled with God's Holy Spirit. But when we believed and confessed Jesus to be our Lord and Savior, His Holy Spirit filled us and made us alive in Jesus. We are even now seated with Jesus in holiness. I praise and worship You, Lord, in the beauty of holiness. Based upon and in light of my personal testimony shared with you in the Foreword of this book, I consider God's miraculous re-creation of me in Christ Jesus to be one of the greatest examples of His incredible wealth of grace and lovingkindness shown. I boast only of God! Oh God, where would I be today if it had not been for You?! Surely, I would either be imprisoned, in an insane asylum, or dead. I love You, Lord, for coming to my rescue!

CHOOSE TO MAKE TODAY AND EVERY DAY GREAT AND BLESSED NO MATTER WHAT!

#PerpetualPraise #ContinualPrayer #WorshipInSpiritAndTruth

{DAY 250}

"If any of you lacks wisdom, you should ask God, who gives generously to all without finding fault, and it will be given to you." (James 1:5 NIV)

In biblical times, Solomon asked God to give him a discerning heart to govern God's people and to be able to distinguish between right and wrong. Here is God's response to Solomon, as it is written in

1 Kings 3:10-14, "The Lord was pleased that Solomon had asked for this. So God said to him, "Since you have asked for this and not for long life or wealth for yourself, nor have asked for the death of your enemies but for discernment in administering justice, I will do what you have asked. I will give you a wise and discerning heart, so that there will never have been anyone like you, nor will there ever be. Moreover, I will give you what you have not asked for—both wealth and honor—so that in your lifetime you will have no equal among kings. And if you walk in obedience to me and keep my decrees and commands as David your father did, I will give you a long life."

The first thing Solomon did was to go before the presence of God and sacrifice holy offerings to Him. To this very day, King Solomon is still known as being the wisest man who has ever lived. You love to give good things to Your people! If godly wisdom may be had for the asking, it would be foolish not to ask God for it. Our God gives generously to all who sincerely desire and ask, and He always knows if your desire is sincere with a pure motive before you even ask Him. Thank You, oh God, that You are still a living and a giving God! You never change!

CHOOSE TO MAKE TODAY AND EVERY DAY GREAT AND BLESSED NO MATTER WHAT!

#PerpetualPraise #ContinualPrayer #WorshipInSpiritAndTruth

{DAY 251}

"Now to Him who is able to do exceedingly abundantly above all that we ask or think, according to the power that works in us, to Him be glory in the church by Christ Jesus to all generations, forever and ever. Amen." (Ephesians 3:20-21 NKJV)

God has no limits or boundaries. Though God is willing and able to give us more than we ask for or think, most times, we ask for too little. We put our own limits on God. The Power at work within us is the Spirit of God living in us. God instructs us through Scriptures that we have not because we ask not, and that we have not because we ask amiss. We are to very specific and exact in our prayers to God. For example, at a certain time in my life after I had been out of the public work force for years (due to becoming a stay-at-home mom until my children became school age), I began looking for work outside the home again. My children had more needs than the household income was able to provide. All I had ever done was secretarial/administrative office work. However, the times had become computerized but I had not. Therefore, my job applications were being turned down, one right after the other. So I prayed, "Lord, please give me favor with man for a job." Within a day, I had a job cleaning vacation cabins dropped right in my lap. The first thing I did was praise and thank God for hearing and answering my prayer. Though it was hard physical work, it was an honest paying job, and I cleaned those cabins excellently as unto the Lord—so excellently in fact that the other lady, who was also working there, was let go. That left me alone cleaning all those vacation cabins. It was more money for me, but it became quite a bit harder. I learned real quick the meaning of that statement, "Be careful what you ask for!" I also learned that the next time I asked God for a job, I needed to be a lot more specific. What do you have faith to ask God for today? Remember to be very specific.

CHOOSE TO MAKE TODAY AND EVERY DAY GREAT AND BLESSED NO MATTER WHAT!

#PerpetualPraise #ContinualPrayer #WorshipInSpiritAndTruth

{DAY 252}

"We then, as workers together with Him also plead with you not to receive the grace of God in vain. (2 Corinthians 6:1 NKJV) "For we are co-workers in God's service; you are God's field, God's building." (1 Corinthians 3:9 NIV)

We should always choose good over evil so that God's divine plan will be fulfilled in our lives by His grace. May it never be that we would cause His saving grace in our lives to have been in vain. We need God's help, and God requires our faithfulness, in order for His assignments to be carried out in our lives. We cannot do it alone. We are the gardens of God's planting. He puts His seed of grace in our hearts. Each of us, individually, are God's house where He lives. All of our work and service for the Lord should glorify God, and only God!

CHOOSE TO MAKE TODAY AND EVERY DAY GREAT AND BLESSED NO MATTER WHAT!

#PerpetualPraise #ContinualPrayer #WorshipInSpiritAndTruth

{DAY 253}

"Let us therefore come boldly to the throne of grace, that we may obtain mercy and find grace to help in time of need." (Hebrews 4:16 NKJV) "So let's walk right up to him and get what he is so ready to give. Take the mercy, accept the help." (Hebrews 4:16 MSGB)

The Holy Spirit continually encourages us to pray. Thanks be to the Lord Jesus Christ, there is no longer any veil to separate us and keep us away from God's Holy presence. When Jesus died on the cross, the veil was torn from top to bottom giving true believers access to God's presence whenever they want. True believers have been given a brand new approach to making our requests known to God at His Throne of Grace where He is on His Mercy Seat. When we offer our praise to God, He shows up, so praise God perpetually and first. Then make your requests known, offering more praise and thanksgiving. Believers ought to do this daily. Jesus, I most gladly receive Your grace and mercy and accept Your gracious help, and I am eternally grateful!

CHOOSE TO MAKE TODAY AND EVERY DAY GREAT AND BLESSED NO MATTER WHAT!

#PerpetualPraise #ContinualPrayer #WorshipInSpiritAndTruth

{DAY 254}

PRAISE TO START YOUR DAY:

"Save, LORD! May the King answer us when we call." (Psalm 20:9 NKJV)

Calling on the Name of Jesus is a simple prayer, yet it is still an intense prayer, showing heart sincerity. When you call out to Jesus for help, you are expressing confidence in God. He will hear and answer you. He will save, deliver and help you. We worship You, Jehovah-Hoshe'ah, for You are the Lord Who Saves! We praise You, Lord, for You do answer and save us when we call on Your Name, "JESUS!", from our innermost being.

CHOOSE TO MAKE TODAY AND EVERY DAY GREAT AND BLESSED NO MATTER WHAT!

#PerpetualPraise #ContinualPrayer #WorshipInSpiritAndTruth

{DAY 255}

"But you shall receive power when the Holy Spirit has come upon you; and you shall be witnesses to Me in Jerusalem, and in all Judea and Samaria, and to the end of the earth." (Acts 1:8 NKJV)

Christ Jesus promised the gift of His Holy Spirit, not only to His disciples but to all believers. That includes you and me even now today. The Holy Spirit is the third Person of the Holy Trinity (God the Father, God the Son, and God the Holy Spirit). God the Holy Spirit lives in all believers to, among other things, enable and empower us to live a godly Christian life. Without the Holy Spirit living in us, we cannot be witnesses, or imitators, of Jesus. After the Holy Spirit had come upon the disciples, just as Jesus had promised, they went everywhere testifying to what they had seen and heard, and very many souls were converted. If you desire for God's great gift of His Holy Spirit to come upon you, all you need to do is ask Him, and your Heavenly Father God will gladly give Him to you. God only gives good gifts!

CHOOSE TO MAKE TODAY AND EVERY DAY GREAT AND BLESSED NO MATTER WHAT!

#PerpetualPraise #ContinualPrayer #WorshipInSpiritAndTruth

{DAY 256}

"When we were utterly helpless, Christ came at just the right time and died for us sinners. Now, most people would not be willing to die for an upright person, though someone might perhaps be willing to die for a person who is especially good. But God showed his great love for us by sending Christ to die for us while we were still sinners. And since we have been made right in God's sight by the blood of Christ, he will certainly save us from God's condemnation. For since our friendship with God was restored by the death of his Son while we were still his enemies, we will certainly be saved through the life of his Son. So now we can rejoice in our wonderful new relationship with God because our Lord Jesus Christ has made us friends of God." (Romans 5:6-11 NLT)

I rejoice, because I am reconciled to God through the death and resurrection of my Lord and Savior, Christ Jesus! I now have an intimate relationship with God and can coexist in harmony with Him! It is well with my soul! Glory Hallelujah! Thank You, Jesus! There is nothing in this life better than knowing this! Blessed be the Name of the Lord!

CHOOSE TO MAKE TODAY AND EVERY DAY GREAT AND BLESSED NO MATTER WHAT!

#PerpetualPraise #ContinualPrayer #WorshipInSpiritAndTruth

{DAY 257}

"God rescued us from dead-end alleys and dark dungeons. He's set us up in the kingdom of the Son he loves so much, the Son who got us out of the pit we were in, got rid of the sins we were doomed to keep repeating." (Colossians 1:13-14 MSGB)

As much and as hard as I tried on my own, I was unsuccessful and unable to straighten out the mess I had made of my life, as a result of habitual daily sin. I tried over and over to free myself from addictions, but it was so hard that I would give up each time. I just kept repeating this insane, dead-end cycle. I finally came to myself and realized that ONLY GOD could help me and, if I didn't call on Him soon and very soon, I wouldn't need to because my life would soon be over. So I turned to God and said, "JESUS, PLEASE HELP ME!" Jesus did help me and He changed my life completely! This is why my sacrifice of offering praise and worship to God is so valuable. No man could, or would, ever do what ONLY GOD has done for me! Dear reader(s), God loves you just as much even now today as He loves me. It is so important that you know this, because it is true. God is able and willing to do the very same for you as He has done for me. If the mess my life was in is the same as yours is today, call on Jesus. He will come to you and help you, too. If Jesus could help me, believe me when I say that He can help anybody!

CHOOSE TO MAKE TODAY AND EVERY DAY GREAT AND BLESSED NO MATTER WHAT!

#PerpetualPraise #ContinualPrayer #WorshipInSpiritAndTruth

{DAY 258}

**"So now there is no condemnation for those who belong to Christ Jesus."
(Romans 8:1 NLT)**

Thank You, my Jesus, that this includes my past, present and future. My past sins are forgiven, not even remembered by You, and gone forever! You have delivered me and set me totally free. I am now free to live the rest of my days on earth praising, worshiping, and serving You! My present makes sense! My future is secured in You! I have a mansion (which You have already prepared for me Yourself) waiting for me in glorious, blissful Heaven where I will live throughout all eternity! **I am signed** in the Lamb's Book of Life, **sealed** with the Holy Spirit of promise, **and delivered** by the precious Blood of Christ Jesus! No condemnation here! I belong to God, and God belongs to me! Thanks be unto God! Praise God!

CHOOSE TO MAKE TODAY AND EVERY DAY GREAT AND BLESSED NO MATTER WHAT!

#PerpetualPraise #ContinualPrayer #WorshipInSpiritAndTruth

{DAY 259}

"But we are citizens of heaven, where the Lord Jesus Christ lives. And we are eagerly waiting for him to return as our Savior. He will take our weak mortal bodies and change them into glorious bodies like his own, using the same power with which he will bring everything under his control." (Philippians 3:20-21 NLT)

As true Christians, we are considered to be citizens of the Heavenly world, as opposed to being from a worldly community. Therefore, we are governed by the laws of Heaven, and expecting to dwell there. We believe that the Lord Jesus will return from Heaven and take us to be with Him there, and we are eagerly expecting and waiting for His return. Jesus Christ will change our bodies as it is in its present state, as subject to sickness, disease, pain and death. It is far different far from what it was when man was created, and from what it will be when in a glorified state. The body of Christ in Heaven is of the same nature as the bodies of the saints will be in the resurrection. Only God has the power to effect this great transformation in the bodies of people. What a contrast between our bodies here and our bodies as they will be in Heaven. Rejoice saints! We have Heaven to look forward to where there is nothing but happiness! If there is anyone on earth who ought to be happy, it is the Christian.

CHOOSE TO MAKE TODAY AND EVERY DAY GREAT AND BLESSED NO MATTER WHAT!

#PerpetualPraise #ContinualPrayer #WorshipInSpiritAndTruth

{DAY 260}

"For as by one man's (referring to Adam who sinned in the Garden of Eden) **disobedience many were made sinners, so also by one Man's** (referring to Christ Jesus) **obedience many will be made righteous."** **(Romans 5:19 NKJV) "For He made Him who knew no sin to be sin for us, that we might become the righteousness of God in Him."** (2 **Corinthians 5:21 NKJV)**

Through Adam's sin of disobedience to God in the Garden of Eden, mankind as a whole was placed in the position of sinners. But thanks be to God, that through Christ's obedience to God unto death, true believers in Jesus Christ's death, burial and resurrection now have the righteousness of God. If you have ever felt shame, you know it is not a good feeling, and it weighs you down. Just imagine how Jesus felt as He took upon His sinless self every sin of the world past, present and future. That is what He had to do in order to be the Perfect Sacrifice; and that is what Christ Jesus willingly and obediently did for God and for us. God made His Only Begotten Son Christ Jesus for a sin-offering for us, that we might be reconciled to God and become the righteousness of God in Christ Jesus. Glory to the Most High God!

CHOOSE TO MAKE TODAY AND EVERY DAY GREAT AND BLESSED NO MATTER WHAT!

#PerpetualPraise #ContinualPrayer #WorshipInSpiritAndTruth

{DAY 261}

"Our lives are a Christ-like fragrance rising up to God..." (2 Corinthians 2:15 NLT)

Our lives in Christ are a sweet Christ-like fragrance rising up to God, as well as to those around us. Christ has connected us with God and dedicated us to God for a divine purpose. Our works and service for God are now acceptable to Him. We are Christ's own offering to God, which He has appointed, devoted and made holy unto God. We are the offering which Christ Jesus is continually making to God. Let us live lives that continually praise and glorify the Lord. We bless You, Lord! Praise the Lord!

CHOOSE TO MAKE TODAY AND EVERY DAY GREAT AND BLESSED NO MATTER WHAT!

#PerpetualPraise #ContinualPrayer #WorshipInSpiritAndTruth

{DAY 262}

"He is so rich in kindness and grace that he purchased our freedom with the blood of his Son and forgave our sins." (Ephesians 1:7 NLT) "Let the redeemed of the LORD say so, whom He has redeemed from the hand of the enemy," (Psalm 107:2 NKJV)

Lovingkindness, grace, mercy, forgiveness, salvation, redemption, deliverance and freedom from sinful living are some of our Heavenly Father God's richest spiritual blessings. The Lord has redeemed us (who must pass through this dangerous world often ready to faint through troubles, fears, and temptations) from the bondage and power of Satan. He redeemed us from the evil one with the precious Blood of His Only Begotten Son and forgave us. Those who hunger and thirst after God and His righteousness, and who have relationship with Jesus, will be filled with the goodness, grace and glory of His house. If you have been redeemed, you ought to say so. I AM REDEEMED! GLORY TO GOD!

CHOOSE TO MAKE TODAY AND EVERY DAY GREAT AND BLESSED NO MATTER WHAT!

#PerpetualPraise #ContinualPrayer #WorshipInSpiritAndTruth

{DAY 263}

"But we understand these things, for we have the mind of Christ." (1 Corinthians 2:16 NLT)

Praise God! We, who have the Holy Spirit living in us, have the mind of Christ. We are influenced by His Holy Spirit as to Christ's views, feelings and temper (our state of mind as far as being angry or calm). For the Holy Spirit, who teaches us, knows the mind of Jesus and reveals it to us. God reveals true wisdom and understanding to us by His Holy Spirit. No one can know the things of God, but His Holy Spirit, Who is one with the Father and the Son. Carnal man, who follows his worldly passions and appetites, does not understand the things of God. God gives knowledge and understanding of His Will only to the spiritual man. We praise You, Lord, for giving us the mind of Christ!

CHOOSE TO MAKE TODAY AND EVERY DAY GREAT AND BLESSED NO MATTER WHAT!

#PerpetualPraise #ContinualPrayer #WorshipInSpiritAndTruth

{DAY 264}

"And the LORD will make you the head and not the tail; you shall be above only, and not be beneath, if you heed the commandments of the LORD your God, which I command you today, and are careful to observe them." (Deuteronomy 28:13 NKJV)

What a blessed promise! God will not allow His people who trust in Him to be failures in life's difficulties. He will cause your enemies to see that His blessing rests upon you. God works on your behalf giving you acknowledged excellence, making you the uppermost rather than the lowermost—the one more honorable. The condition on which all this blessed promise depends is your obedience to God's commandments. As saints of the Most High God, we are to be the ruling force in this world today and keep the Lord Jesus in the forefront—not in the background! Thank You, Lord, for Your blessed promise!

CHOOSE TO MAKE TODAY AND EVERY DAY GREAT AND BLESSED NO MATTER WHAT!

#PerpetualPraise #ContinualPrayer #WorshipInSpiritAndTruth

{DAY 265}

"By his divine power, God has given us everything we need for living a godly life. We have received all of this by coming to know him, the one who called us to himself by means of his marvelous glory and excellence. And because of his glory and excellence, he has given us great and precious promises. These are the promises that enable you to share his divine nature and escape the world's corruption caused by human desires." (2 Peter 1:3-4 NLT)

If you are a born-again Christian who knows Jesus as your Lord and Savior, God has given you everything you need to enable you to live a godly through the power of His Holy Spirit living in you. By His own glorious power He has freely given you exceeding great and invaluable promises. The objective of all God's promises is to bring you back to the image of God, which was lost due to sin and being a partaker of the world's nature, rather than being a partaker of God's Divine nature. Thanks be to God, who is the Waymaker, He has made a way for you where there was no way. Glory to God!

CHOOSE TO MAKE TODAY AND EVERY DAY GREAT AND BLESSED NO MATTER WHAT!

#PerpetualPraise #ContinualPrayer #WorshipInSpiritAndTruth

{DAY 266}

"I will praise the name of God with a song, and will magnify Him with thanksgiving." (Psalm 69:30 NKJV)

As the result of my deliverance and being set totally free, I composed a psalm (a sacred worship poem) to God, which expressed my feelings of worship, praise and thanksgiving. Everyone's personal experience with God is different; however, composing a song or psalm, or a written testimony, serves as a memorial of the greatness of God in your life. When you magnify God, you make Him seem even bigger and greater, and you spread this good news with as many as will listen. Jesus, I have a worshiping, praising, grateful and thankful heart towards You, and I love showing and telling You and others about it! Dear reader(s), you will find "Psalm from JoAnn Koening to God" on the page following Day 365.

CHOOSE TO MAKE TODAY AND EVERY DAY GREAT AND BLESSED NO MATTER WHAT!

#PerpetualPraise #ContinualPrayer #WorshipInSpiritAndTruth

{DAY 267}

"Oh, give thanks to the LORD, for He is good! For His mercy endures forever. Oh, give thanks to the God of gods! For His mercy endures forever. Oh, give thanks to the Lord of lords! For His mercy endures forever:" (Psalm 136:1-3 NKJV)

The meaning of God's mercy is undeserved favor. One of God's attributes is that He is Merciful. We ought always give thanks to the Lord, for He is a Good God all the time, and all the time God is Good. God is the One and Only True and Living God. There is no other god like unto God and no other god above God. God reigns Sovereign and Supreme. He is the Lord of lords, and His Name is Jesus. Oh, give thanks to the Lord for His mercy endures forever! We praise You, Lord, for Your enduring mercy!

CHOOSE TO MAKE TODAY AND EVERY DAY GREAT AND BLESSED NO MATTER WHAT!

#PerpetualPraise #ContinualPrayer #WorshipInSpiritAndTruth

{DAY 268}

"Everyone will share the story of your wonderful goodness; they will sing with joy about your righteousness." (Psalm 145:7 NLT)

When you experience the salvation of the Lord and become a born-again Christian, the excitement, and joy in your spirit is uncontainable! The unconditional love of God is incomparable to any love you have ever known before! The new-found faith you have discovered gives you a wholehearted trust in God! You cannot help but share all of this with as many people as you can, and you want others to experience the very same thing you have! You want to share your excitement and joy! When you have been newly clothed in the garments of praise, joy, holiness and righteousness in the Lord, it makes you want to shout and sing for joy, and you want all to see the totally new you! It's like if you were blessed with a brand new wardrobe of the most beautiful clothes you had ever seen, you would want to be seen in them and let others see your blessing. When we share God's wonderful goodness and what He has done in our lives, we are glorifying God. Spread the truth of God's great goodness and be joy filled while singing of His righteousness! I love You, Lord!

CHOOSE TO MAKE TODAY AND EVERY DAY GREAT AND BLESSED NO MATTER WHAT!

#PerpetualPraise #ContinualPrayer #WorshipInSpiritAndTruth

{DAY 269}

"That I may proclaim with the voice of thanksgiving, and tell of all Your wondrous works." (Psalm 26:7 NKJV)

We can only be complete in Christ Jesus. When a man walks in honesty and moral uprightness, and having strong moral principles, yet trusting wholly in the grace of God, that man is accepted by God. As an expression of his gratitude to God, he is inspired to win others also to God's worship and praise, and to God's service; and to tell others of God's wondrous works of creation, salvation.... With voices of thanksgiving, let us tell of God's wonderful deeds and works so others may know what we know; thereby, winning many souls to God and glorifying Him!

CHOOSE TO MAKE TODAY AND EVERY DAY GREAT AND BLESSED NO MATTER WHAT!

#PerpetualPraise #ContinualPrayer #WorshipInSpiritAndTruth

275

{DAY 270}

PRAISE TO START YOUR DAY:

"I will give You thanks in the great assembly; I will praise You among many people." (Psalm 35:18 NKJV)

Lord, You have miraculously delivered me. I am not ashamed of my testimony because my testimony is now Your testimony used to increase Your Kingdom and glorify You, oh God! It is the Power of God to save, deliver, and set totally free! Therefore, I am not ashamed to praise and worship, bless and thank You in the midst of the congregation and in public places. I delight in blessing You, Lord, and I trust and believe that I will join the great assembly in Heaven, singing praises to God and to the Lamb for all eternity.

CHOOSE TO MAKE TODAY AND EVERY DAY GREAT AND BLESSED NO MATTER WHAT!

#PerpetualPraise #ContinualPrayer #WorshipInSpiritAndTruth

{DAY 271}

PRAISE TO START YOUR DAY:

"Whoever offers praise glorifies Me; and to him who orders his conduct aright I will show the salvation of God." (Psalm 50:23 NKJV)

God is glorified through our praise and worship. The way we praise and worship is very important to God. God views our outward praise and worship is a true indicator of our heart. Those whose praise and worship, godly living, conduct, and conversation are pure is evidence to God of their true reverence, holiness and devotion towards Him; and they will enjoy God's presence, favor and salvation. Lord, may our sacrifice of praise always be glorifying to You, in the blessed Name of Jesus! Amen, amen, and amen!

CHOOSE TO MAKE TODAY AND EVERY DAY GREAT AND BLESSED NO MATTER WHAT!

#PerpetualPraise #ContinualPrayer #WorshipInSpiritAndTruth

{DAY 272}

PRAISE TO START YOUR DAY:

"Arise, bless the Lord your God forever and ever! O may Your glorious name be blessed and exalted above all blessing and praise! You alone are the Lord. You have made the heavens, the heaven of heavens with all their host, the earth and all that is on it, the seas and all that is in them. You give life to all of them, and the heavenly host bows down before You." (Nehemiah 9:5-6 NASB)

We are to stand up and show our reverence and spirit of devotion to the God Most High through your praise. We are blessed to have the freedom to praise and worship the Creator of All, Lord of All, Giver of Life, and Giver of Salvation. God is God all by Himself! Even when we have praised and worshiped God with all our strength and might, we can never outshine our God. As often as we breathe, we are to breathe out the praises of God and make our breath like the perfumed smoke of the tabernacle from the burning of incense in biblical times.

CHOOSE TO MAKE TODAY AND EVERY DAY GREAT AND BLESSED NO MATTER WHAT!

#PerpetualPraise #ContinualPrayer #WorshipInSpiritAndTruth

{DAY 273}

PRAISE TO START YOUR DAY:

"Make a joyful shout to the LORD, all you lands! Serve the LORD with gladness; come before His presence with singing. Know that the LORD, He is God; it is He who has made us, and not we ourselves; we are His people and the sheep of His pasture. Enter into His gates with thanksgiving, and into His courts with praise. Be thankful to Him, and bless His name. For the LORD is good; His mercy is everlasting, and His truth endures to all generations." (Psalm 100 NKJV)

Our happy God should be worshiped by a happy people. A joyful spirit comes together with the gratitude which we should express for His great mercies. In every nation God's goodness is seen; therefore, in every nation, God should be joyfully praised. The world will not be in the perfect condition God intended for it to be in until He is adored and praised with one unanimous and joyful shout. Let the whole world know that Jesus is Lord! He is our gracious Lord; therefore, He is to be served with great joy. We should come into His presence with joyful praise through singing. God loves that! God delights in the praise by a congregation of His saints, plus it reflects our anticipation and expectation of the continuous worship in Heaven. We ought to know the God we worship and why we worship Him. As long as we are receivers of God's mercy, we must be givers of thanks. Our praise and worship in God's own house belong to the Lord of the house—JESUS! For the Lord is good. He who does not praise the Lord for His goodness is not good himself. Our heart leaps for joy as we praise the One who has never broken His word or changed His purpose.

CHOOSE TO MAKE TODAY AND EVERY DAY GREAT AND BLESSED NO MATTER WHAT!

#PerpetualPraise #ContinualPrayer #WorshipInSpiritAndTruth

{DAY 274}

"Yours, O LORD, is the greatness, the power and the glory, the victory and the majesty; for all that is in heaven and in earth is Yours; Yours is the kingdom, O LORD, and You are exalted as head over all. Both riches and honor come from You, and You reign over all. In Your hand is power and might; in Your hand, it is to make great and to give strength to all. Now, therefore, our God, we thank You, and praise Your glorious name." (1 Chronicles 29:11-13 NKJV)

Magnificence belongs to You, oh Lord; for You created the world by Your great power. All things that are in Heaven and earth are the work of Your hands, and You are Ruler over and Sustainer of all that is in the heavens and on the earth. Yours, oh Lord, is the Kingdom. You are exalted above the Heavenly angels, and over all the rulers of the earth. All riches and honor come from You. You give strength to all; even to those who are the weakest, who You can make strong; and to the strongest, who are weak without Your help. Therefore we thank, praise and worship You, oh God! Blessed be the Name of the Lord our God!

CHOOSE TO MAKE TODAY AND EVERY DAY GREAT AND BLESSED NO MATTER WHAT!

#PerpetualPraise #ContinualPrayer #WorshipInSpiritAndTruth

{DAY 275}

PRAISE TO START YOUR DAY:

"How great is the goodness you have stored up for those who fear you. You lavish it on those who come to you for protection, blessing them before the watching world." (Psalm 31:19 NLT)

God's goodness is limitless and impossible to measure. There is more than enough for everyone. God's goodness is stored up for those who have a holy reverence for Him. God has already prepared His goodness for those whose trust is in the Lord, for those who boldly confess God to the world, for those who take refuge in the Lord. It is to those who God will bestow His extravagant blessings on, in the public's eye. We praise and worship You, Lord, for Your goodness!

CHOOSE TO MAKE TODAY AND EVERY DAY GREAT AND BLESSED NO MATTER WHAT!

#PerpetualPraise #ContinualPrayer #WorshipInSpiritAndTruth

{DAY 276}

PRAISE TO START YOUR DAY:

"Rejoice in the LORD, you righteous, and give thanks at the remembrance of His holy name." (Psalm 97:12 NKJV)

May all who are godly be happy in the LORD and praise His Holy Name! Jesus sacrificed His very life for use that we could take on His righteousness. For true Christians, that alone is more than enough to cause us to be joyful and praise God! Give thanks to God at the remembrance of His Holiness. Blessed be the Name of the Lord forever!

CHOOSE TO MAKE TODAY AND EVERY DAY GREAT AND BLESSED NO MATTER WHAT!

#PerpetualPraise #ContinualPrayer #WorshipInSpiritAndTruth

{DAY 277}

"You who love the LORD, hate evil! He preserves the souls of His saints; He delivers them out of the hand of the wicked. Light is sown for the righteous, and gladness for the upright in heart." (Psalm 97:10-11 NKJV)

If you really love the Lord, then hate evil. Have no toleration for it or acceptance of it; certainly no place in your life. God is the Soul Preserver of His saints. He preserves the mind, will, and emotions of His saints, and delivers them out of the hand of the wicked. As we live in You, we will have Your Light to direct our steps, and our hearts will always be glad! We love You, Jesus, and we praise You!

CHOOSE TO MAKE TODAY AND EVERY DAY GREAT AND BLESSED NO MATTER WHAT!

#PerpetualPraise #ContinualPrayer #WorshipInSpiritAndTruth

{DAY 278}

PRAISE TO START YOUR DAY:

"Oh, give thanks to the LORD! Call upon His name; make known His deeds among the peoples! Sing to Him, sing psalms to Him; talk of all His wondrous works!" (Psalm 105:1-2 NKJV)

God is the Giver of Benefits to all His people; therefore, let Him have all our gratitude and thanksgiving. Declare His titles publicly and fill the world with His reputation and fame by sharing His wondrous works. Let the worldly people hear of our God, that they may abandon their gods and learn to worship God. Make sweet sounds to God's ears through singing praise songs directly to Him.

CHOOSE TO MAKE TODAY AND EVERY DAY GREAT AND BLESSED NO MATTER WHAT!

#PerpetualPraise #ContinualPrayer #WorshipInSpiritAndTruth

{DAY 279}

PRAISE TO START YOUR DAY:

"We thank you, God, we thank you—your Name is our favorite word; your mighty works are all we talk about." (Psalm 75:1 MSGB)

We thank You, oh God, we thank You! (Please Note: Repetition of words in the Bible shows wholehearted emphasis on what is being said. For example, when Jesus begins a statement with, "Verily, Verily…", or "Truly, Truly…", He is placing special emphasis on what He is about to say, and wants you to pay very close attention to it.) This Scripture denotes a special call for giving thanksgiving to God for all the mighty works He has done. We thank You, Jesus, we thank You, for You alone have saved us and done marvelous and miraculous works in our lives! JESUS, JESUS, JESUS, the most precious Name we know!

CHOOSE TO MAKE TODAY AND EVERY DAY GREAT AND BLESSED NO MATTER WHAT!

#PerpetualPraise #ContinualPrayer #WorshipInSpiritAndTruth

{DAY 280}

"You say, "I'm calling this meeting to order, I'm ready to set things right. When the earth goes topsy-turvy and nobody knows which end is up, I nail it all down, I put everything in place again. I say to the smart alecks, 'That's enough,' to the bullies, 'Not so fast.'" Don't raise your fist against High God. Don't raise your voice against Rock of Ages. He's the One from east to west; from desert to mountains, he's the One. God rules: he brings this one down to his knees, pulls that one up on her feet. And I'm telling the story of God Eternal, singing the praises of Jacob's God." (Psalm 75:2-6,7,9 MSGB)

God has His own appointed time at which His power will flash forth into action. Until that moment arrives, evil is permitted to run its course on earth. As true believers of God's Word can see, all things are rushing to ruin in the world today. Those who are enemies of God, the godless ones, have provoked His warning. God will be just in His dealings with all people upon the face of the earth—the godless and the godly. The godless must deal with the wrath of God. God's people, the godly ones, will receive all of God's eternal promised blessings. Lord God, as true believers, we worship You for You reign sovereign and supreme for all eternity! We praise You for You are longsuffering in Your lovingkindness, grace, and mercy! We praise You, Lord, that we are on Your side!

CHOOSE TO MAKE TODAY AND EVERY DAY GREAT AND BLESSED NO MATTER WHAT!

#PerpetualPraise #ContinualPrayer #WorshipInSpiritAndTruth

{DAY 281}

"Be anxious for nothing, but in everything by prayer and supplication, with thanksgiving, let your requests be made known to God." (Philippians 4:6 NKJV)

Thank You, Lord, that Your people do not need to worry, or be anxious, about anything. We just need to come directly to You with a sincere heart and humbly pray. Then we must have faith and believe that You have already taken care of it (whatever "it" is) for us. We must always give thanks to You for all You have already done in our lives, and for what we now have in Christ Jesus. We must keep praying and trusting You. In everything, we must trust that You are in control because You are. Blessed be Your Names "Trustworthy" and "Faithful"!

CHOOSE TO MAKE TODAY AND EVERY DAY GREAT AND BLESSED NO MATTER WHAT!

#PerpetualPraise #ContinualPrayer #WorshipInSpiritAndTruth

{DAY 282}

"In this manner, therefore, pray: Our Father in heaven, Hallowed be Your name. Your kingdom come. Your will be done on earth as it is in heaven. Give us this day our daily bread. And forgive us our debts, as we forgive our debtors. And do not lead us into temptation, but deliver us from the evil one. For Yours is the kingdom and the power and the glory forever. Amen." (Matthew 6:9-13 NKJV)

This is the prayer taught to us by Jesus Christ Himself. When we pray the "Lord's Prayer" with a spirit of true devotion, it will profit our souls. When we pray "Our Father", rather than "My Father", we are including our brethren in Christ in the prayer. In this way, we are praying from a brotherly heart and desiring the same for all other Christians, who we are unified within Christ Jesus. We are praying to God Himself who is in Heaven, and whose Name is Holy. We are praying that God's Kingdom may "come" into its fullness, when all created beings may bring their wills into harmony with God's Will. We are praying that the Lord will supply us with our daily needs. We are praying for God's forgiveness, and acknowledging that we must also forgive others in order to receive God's forgiveness. We are requesting God to keep us on His path of righteousness, so we will not fall into temptation. We are praying for deliverance from the evil one. We are acknowledging that God is King over all and that God has all power and glory forever. Lord Jesus, thank You for teaching us this prayer model, known as the "Lord's Prayer".

CHOOSE TO MAKE TODAY AND EVERY DAY GREAT AND BLESSED NO MATTER WHAT!

#PerpetualPraise #ContinualPrayer #WorshipInSpiritAndTruth

{DAY 283}

"Be still, and know that I am God. I will be exalted among the nations, I will be exalted in the earth!" (Psalm 46:10 ESV)

The Hebrew definition of "be still" is to stop striving, to let go, surrender. The Greek definition of "be still" is "Hush!". God is commanding us to silently and quietly wait upon Him without fear; knowing Him to be God, and God alone. Sometimes this is the hardest thing for us to do. Of course, God already knows that; therefore, that is the reason for this command to us from God. After we have given our cares over to God, we must stop talking about it and just know that God is more than able to take care of things. God is always in control. When we take back those concerns we have already given to God and start trying to help God fix it, not only are we being disobedient to God's command; but we will also mess things up and delay God's fixing it His way. God ways are altogether different from our ways. God is God all by Himself, and He does NOT need man's help. God is saying of Himself that He will be exalted in all the nations and in all the earth. Thank You, Lord, that I have learned from personal experience it is always best to "let go and let God". That enables my spirit to rest in You, and enables me to be able to say, "It is well with my soul."

CHOOSE TO MAKE TODAY AND EVERY DAY GREAT AND BLESSED NO MATTER WHAT!

#PerpetualPraise #ContinualPrayer #WorshipInSpiritAndTruth

{DAY 284}

"Forever, O Lord, Your word is settled in heaven." (Psalm 119:89 NKJV)

God's word stands as firmly as the Heaven in which it dwells, and it will remain so forever and ever. Every age provides fresh proofs of the truth of God's word. Unlike the changes that take place on the earth, the truth of God's word is forever established in Heaven. It cannot and will not ever be changed because it is already established by God Himself as God's truth. Thank You, oh God, that Your word is forever established and settled! End of story!

CHOOSE TO MAKE TODAY AND EVERY DAY GREAT AND BLESSED NO MATTER WHAT!

#PerpetualPraise #ContinualPrayer #WorshipInSpiritAndTruth

{DAY 285}

"Oh, how I love your law! I meditate on it all day long. Your commands are always with me and make me wiser than my enemies. How sweet are your words to my taste, sweeter than honey to my mouth! I gain understanding from your precepts; therefore I hate every wrong path." (Psalm 119:97-98,103-104 NIV)

Loving God's law and commandments is one of the strongest indicators of a gracious and devout heart, formed in the nature and character of obedience towards God. He delights in God's commandments, and this delight is shown by him making God's commandments the frequent subject of his meditation. Obedience to God's commandments makes us wiser and more knowledgeable than our enemies. Lord, thank You for giving me a spiritual taste for Your words and thank You that Your words are sweet to my spirit. Thank You for the saving knowledge that You have given me through Your words. Therefore, I hate everything that is contrary to Your Word and Your righteous path for me. I love You, Lord.

CHOOSE TO MAKE TODAY AND EVERY DAY GREAT AND BLESSED NO MATTER WHAT!

#PerpetualPraise #ContinualPrayer #WorshipInSpiritAndTruth

{DAY 286}

"Oh, taste and see that the LORD is good; blessed is the man who trusts in Him! Oh, fear the LORD, you His saints! There is no want to those who fear Him. The young lions lack and suffer hunger; but those who seek the LORD shall not lack any good thing." (Psalm 34:8-10 NKJV)

Don't wait until you have tried everything else in this world to satisfy you and make you happy. Instead, choose Jesus even now today. God's Word, Jesus, is more satisfying than anything you have ever tried before. Jesus will take you higher than you have ever been before. You may be saying, "What!" I say, "Yes, that's just what I meant—higher than you have ever been before!" When you trust in Jesus, you will be so blessed, beginning with the true joy of salvation and knowing you are Heaven bound and right with God. You will no longer be lacking in any good thing. Jesus will satisfy the hunger and thirst you have in your soul and spirit. You will experience the delightful taste of His goodness and His endless, unconditional love. He really does care about you and He loves you. Choose Jesus, and you will see.

CHOOSE TO MAKE TODAY AND EVERY DAY GREAT AND BLESSED NO MATTER WHAT!

#PerpetualPraise #ContinualPrayer #WorshipInSpiritAndTruth

{DAY 287}

"Now He who establishes us with you in Christ and has anointed us is God, who also has sealed us and given us the Spirit in our hearts as a guarantee." (2 Corinthians 1:21-22 NKJV)

We are established (made an integral part in Christ); anointed by God for His special purpose, and we now have joy, authority, and power in the Holy Ghost, thereby giving us strength to do His will and be employed in His holy service; and sealed by God (God has marked us as His own property.). I like to confess, "I am signed (in the Lamb's Book of Life), sealed (with God's Holy Spirit), and delivered (God delivers on all of His promises) for my eternal hereafter with Christ Jesus!" God has done it all! Praise God from whom all blessings flow!

CHOOSE TO MAKE TODAY AND EVERY DAY GREAT AND BLESSED NO MATTER WHAT!

#PerpetualPraise #ContinualPrayer #WorshipInSpiritAndTruth

{DAY 288}

PRAISE TO START YOUR DAY:

"What then shall we say to these things? If God is for us, who can be against us?" (Romans 8:31 NKJV)

God is for us—His own people! God is for us because He has foreordained us for His divine purpose, called us, justified us, and made us holy and righteous through Christ Jesus. God has foreordained us to be conformed to the image of His own Son. So, who can be against us? The obvious answer is, "No one—nowhere—no how—no way!" HALLELUJAH! All things obey God; Heaven adores Him; Hell trembles at Him; no creature can resist Him. Belief in this kind of security leads to a stable and productive Christian life, just as God purposes for all His people. We should confess this Scripture daily to keep ourselves reminded of it. What joy, peace and security we have in knowing this truth! We praise You, oh God, for You are for us!

CHOOSE TO MAKE TODAY AND EVERY DAY GREAT AND BLESSED NO MATTER WHAT!

#PerpetualPraise #ContinualPrayer #WorshipInSpiritAndTruth

{DAY 289}

"Can anything ever separate us from Christ's love? Does it mean he no longer loves us if we have trouble or calamity, or are persecuted, or hungry, or destitute, or in danger, or threatened with death? No, despite all these things, overwhelming victory is ours through Christ, who loved us. And I am convinced that nothing can ever separate us from God's love. Neither death nor life, neither angels nor demons, neither our fears for today nor our worries about tomorrow—not even the powers of hell can separate us from God's love. No power in the sky above or in the earth below—indeed, nothing in all creation will ever be able to separate us from the love of God that is revealed in Christ Jesus our Lord." (Romans 8:35,37-39 NLT)

God's love for us is not lessened or ended by our failures, shortcomings, or sins because God chose us before the foundation of the world. There are evil powers and enemies that will try to separate us from the love of Christ, but God's love for us is not threatened. God's love for us in Christ Jesus our Lord enables us to be more than conquerors through every trial for His sake. God's love always triumphs! I praise and worship You, oh God, for I can never be separated from Your love! I choose to never allow anything, or anyone, to separate You from my love either.

CHOOSE TO MAKE TODAY AND EVERY DAY GREAT AND BLESSED NO MATTER WHAT!

#PerpetualPraise #ContinualPrayer #WorshipInSpiritAndTruth

{DAY 290}

PRAISE TO START YOUR DAY:

"So we are Christ's ambassadors; God is making his appeal through us. We speak for Christ when we plead, "Come back to God!" (2 Corinthians 5:20 NLT)

Lord, You have given us as believers in Christ Jesus a great and royal responsibility to speak on behalf of Christ for the sake of the Kingdom of God. Believers are to make Christ's request to "Come back to God!" known to lost souls with urgency and by showing great intensity of spirit, feeling, and enthusiasm. We have been given the honor of being Christ's ambassadors. Along with this honor, comes a great and exciting responsibility. God is depending on us. Are you fired up and ready?! Hallelujah! We are Christ's ambassadors!

 CHOOSE TO MAKE TODAY AND EVERY DAY GREAT AND BLESSED NO MATTER WHAT!

#PerpetualPraise #ContinualPrayer #WorshipInSpiritAndTruth

{DAY 291}

"Yet now he has reconciled you to himself through the death of Christ in his physical body. As a result, he has brought you into his own presence, and you are holy and blameless as you stand before him without a single fault." (Colossians 1:22 NLT)

It pleased God to restore friendly relations between fallen man with Himself. He did that through the sacrifice and death of His Son Christ Jesus. As a result, we are now holy and blameless as we stand before God, without a single fault, because God now sees us through His Son Christ Jesus. Seeing this, what should we do now for God? Perpetually praise God; pray continually; worship God in spirit and in truth; increase in our holy service to God; die to sin, and live no more to yourselves, but live to Christ. Christ died for us. Precious, Jesus, thank You for reconciling me to God through Your death in my place. I rejoice in the hope set before me. I owe You my life, and I give You my life.

CHOOSE TO MAKE TODAY AND EVERY DAY GREAT AND BLESSED NO MATTER WHAT!

#PerpetualPraise #ContinualPrayer #WorshipInSpiritAndTruth

{DAY 292}

"No longer do I call you servants, for a servant does not know what his master is doing; but I have called you friends, for all things that I heard from My Father I have made known to you." (John 15:15 NKJV)

Though Jesus is the Lord of Lords and the King of Kings, and Whose Name is above every name known in Heaven and earth, He calls true believers His friends. How humbling is that on the part of Jesus, considering how inferior man is! What an honor! Because Jesus calls us His friends, as far as God is concerned Jesus and us are on the same list as being heirs, and joint-heirs with Christ, of God's eternal inheritance! Because Jesus calls us His friends, He has entrusted to us everything He has heard from His Father—our Heavenly Father God! We are friends of God! Jesus has called us friends! That alone makes my day! Thank You, Jesus, for being my Constant Companion! My spirit is totally humbled. I love You, Jesus!

CHOOSE TO MAKE TODAY AND EVERY DAY GREAT AND BLESSED NO MATTER WHAT!

#PerpetualPraise #ContinualPrayer #WorshipInSpiritAndTruth

{DAY 293}

"The Spirit Himself bears witness with our spirit that we are children of God, and if children, then heirs—heirs of God and joint-heirs with Christ, if indeed we suffer with Him, that we may also be glorified together." (Romans 8:16 NKJV)

God the Holy Spirit Himself testifies together with our own spirit assuring us that we are, in truth, children of God; He speaks to us deep in our hearts and tells us that we are, in truth, children of God; He declares His support of our firmly held belief that we are, in truth, children of God; He is constantly bearing joint-testimony with our human spirit that we are, in truth, children of God. Therefore, this truth also makes us heirs, and joint-heirs with Christ Jesus, of God's inheritance. This means that Christ Jesus is not only our Lord and Savior, but Christ Jesus is also our Brother. A believer may come to the point of doubting his salvation because his or her growth in holiness has proceeded so slowly and so defectively. God knows believers need support in regards to the assurance of their salvation, and He makes abundant provision for our need through His Holy Spirit. The Holy Spirit does bear witness with our spirit that we are children of God, but it is not based on our progress, or the lack of progress, in our Christian walk. Remember that the Holy Spirit is Holy and lives in all true believers, even though their steps in holy and righteous growth may come with difficulty from time to time. However, there will always be some evidence of a supernatural change in a genuine believer's behavior. Dear reader(s), if any one of you is questioning and/or doubting your salvation, I pray this helps you, in the blessed Name of our Lord and Savior Christ Jesus! Amen, amen, and amen!

CHOOSE TO MAKE TODAY AND EVERY DAY GREAT AND BLESSED NO MATTER WHAT!

#PerpetualPraise #ContinualPrayer #WorshipInSpiritAndTruth

{DAY 294}

"'For I will restore health to you and heal you of your wounds,' says the LORD, 'Because they called you an outcast saying: "This is Zion; no one seeks her."'" (Jeremiah 30:17 NKJV)

I worship You, Jehovah-Rophe, for You are the Lord my Healer! You have healed me on a physical and spiritual level. Have any of you reading this ever had a family member who you love, or perhaps a friend, give up on you and dismiss you as an outcast and hopeless? If your answer to that question is "yes", it is difficult to forget how that made you feel, even though you have forgiven that person in your heart (and it is vitally important that you forgive). You may also lose connection with family members or friends because of your love for Jesus, and for putting Him first in your life. But God can and will restore all of you from the inside to the outside, just as He has restored me. God can and will restore relationships between you and your loved ones and/or friends. Jesus loves you so much that He died for you. You are that precious to Him. JESUS SAVES AND SO MUCH MORE!

CHOOSE TO MAKE TODAY AND EVERY DAY GREAT AND BLESSED NO MATTER WHAT!

#PerpetualPraise #ContinualPrayer #WorshipInSpiritAndTruth

{DAY 295}

"My sheep hear My voice, and I know them, and they follow Me." (John 10:27 NKJV)

Happy are they whose Good Shepherd is Christ Jesus, for they prove themselves to be the chosen of God, and they are eternally secure. I worship You, my Jehovah-Rohi, for You are my Good Shepherd. I praise You, Lord, that I am able to recognize and distinguish Your voice above all other voices. I hear Your voice and listen to Your voice. We know each other personally because of the daily relationship we have together. I will continue to follow close behind You all the days of my life.

CHOOSE TO MAKE TODAY AND EVERY DAY GREAT AND BLESSED NO MATTER WHAT!

#PerpetualPraise #ContinualPrayer #WorshipInSpiritAndTruth

{DAY 296}

PRAISE TO START YOUR DAY:

"As for me, I will call upon God, and the LORD shall save me. Evening and morning and at noon I will pray, and cry aloud, and He shall hear my voice." (Psalm 55:16-17 NKJV)

As often as the evil one is plotting against you and seeking your ill, you should seek good from God. I praise You, Lord, that not only do I know Your voice, but You know and hear my voice as well, because we communicate with each other every day, as I do not wait until trouble, storms, and disaster strike before calling upon You. Our voices are very familiar to each other. I am certain that my prayers come up before You; and I not only expect, but also see the blessings. I praise You for that and I love You, Jesus!

CHOOSE TO MAKE TODAY AND EVERY DAY GREAT AND BLESSED NO MATTER WHAT!

#PerpetualPraise #ContinualPrayer #WorshipInSpiritAndTruth

{DAY 297}

PRAISE TO START YOUR DAY:

**"Seven times a day I praise You, because of Your righteous judgments."
(Psalm 119:164 NKJV)**

King David (in biblical times) could not get enough of praising God; he did it often, he did it often and consistently—seven times a day—and if King David praised God seven times a day because of God's righteous judgments, how much more should we do it because of God's abounding grace! Ah! Now there's a special cause for giving thanks to God! Lord Jesus, I offer perpetual praise to You every day because You are Worthy, and because I desire to live in Your presence for as long as I am still on the earth. I am holy addicted to praising You and being in Your presence, Lord Jesus. I am unable to be without You, Jesus, without incurring adverse effects.

CHOOSE TO MAKE TODAY AND EVERY DAY GREAT AND BLESSED NO MATTER WHAT!

#PerpetualPraise #ContinualPrayer #WorshipInSpiritAndTruth

{DAY 298}

"Great peace have those who love Your law, and nothing causes them to stumble." (Psalm 119:165 NKJV)

Those who love God's commandments strive wholeheartedly to walk in obedience to them, and they have great peace. They believe they have been reconciled back to God through the shed Blood of Christ Jesus; they have felt the power and the comfort of the Holy Spirit, and they stand before Father God as men accepted; and they have felt the Lord's great peace, which passes all understanding. They have many troubles, yet they have a deep calm and peace too great for the world to break. Thank You, Lord, for Your commandments that I love!

CHOOSE TO MAKE TODAY AND EVERY DAY GREAT AND BLESSED NO MATTER WHAT!

#PerpetualPraise #ContinualPrayer #WorshipInSpiritAndTruth

{DAY 299}

**"LORD, I hope for Your salvation, and I do Your commandments."
(Psalm 119:166 NKJV)**

This is the attitude all of God's people should desire to have—hoping in His mercy, and obeying His commands. It is our hope of salvation and mercy which motivates us to holiness. In times of trouble, there are two things which should be done; the first is to hope in God, and the second is to do what is right according to God's commands. A good hope of salvation will draw the heart to desire doing the commandments. Our love for the word of God must conquer our lusts and carnal desires. Our hearts must be involved. We must keep the commandments of God by being obedient to them, and His promises by relying on them. God's eye is on us at all times; this should make us very careful to keep His commandments.

CHOOSE TO MAKE TODAY AND EVERY DAY GREAT AND BLESSED NO MATTER WHAT!

#PerpetualPraise #ContinualPrayer #WorshipInSpiritAndTruth

{DAY 300}

"There is one body and one Spirit, just as you were called in one hope of your calling; one Lord, one faith, one baptism; one God and Father of all, who is above all, and through all, and in you all." (Ephesians 4:4-6 NKJV)

"But he who is joined to the Lord is one spirit with Him." (1 Corinthians 6:17 NKJV)

The union between you and Christ Jesus is a spiritual one. As a believer, your body has been set apart and declared holy and righteous by your union with Christ's body. You are now united to the Lord and one spirit with Him. In the true Church of Jesus Christ, there is "one God and Father of all, who is above all, and through all, and in you all". The repetition of "one" brings out the emphasis on unity. The church is one. Every sincere Christian is a brother or sister in that church and has an equal right with all others to its privileges. There is one body. Christ is the head and the Church is the body. The hope of our calling is the appearing of the glory of our great God and Savior, Christ Jesus. The hope of our calling is also our Heaven-bound destination and includes all that awaits the saints at the return of the Lord Jesus. We who are joined to the Lord are one spirit with Him. We come to think and feel as Jesus does. Glory to God!

CHOOSE TO MAKE TODAY AND EVERY DAY GREAT AND BLESSED NO MATTER WHAT!

#PerpetualPraise #ContinualPrayer #WorshipInSpiritAndTruth

{DAY 301}

"Now you are the body of Christ, and members individually." (1 Corinthians 12:27 NKJV)

Believers are the body of Christ, with Christ being the Head of the body. Believers are individual, God-designated members of the body of Christ. We are all important to the body of Christ as a whole. The Lord has placed His trust in us, and we must be united in the common faith of Christ, and faithful and diligent in working together in unity doing the work of the Lord, each in our God-designated ministries. There are no "nobodies" in the body of Christ! We are all "important somebodies" to Jesus and to His Ministry on earth! Praise God! Thank You, Jesus!

CHOOSE TO MAKE TODAY AND EVERY DAY GREAT AND BLESSED NO MATTER WHAT!

#PerpetualPraise #ContinualPrayer #WorshipInSpiritAndTruth

{DAY 302}

"He treated us as equals, and so made us equals. Through him we both share the same Spirit and have equal access to the Father." (Ephesians 2:18 MSGB)

The sacrifice Jesus made now makes it possible for us as believers to be at peace with our Heavenly Father. Just as Jesus (when He walked on the earth) went directly to Father God through prayer, man now has that same direct and equal access to the Father. We are permitted to approach God through Christ, or "in the Name of Jesus". We are allowed to draw near to our Heavenly Father God and are brought with acceptance into His presence with our praise and worship and services, through His Holy Spirit, as one with the Father and the Son. Christ purchased our accepted access to God, and His Holy Spirit gives us a heart to come, and strength to come, and then grace to serve God acceptably. Thank You, Father God! Thank You, Jesus! Thank You, Holy Spirit!

CHOOSE TO MAKE TODAY AND EVERY DAY GREAT AND BLESSED NO MATTER WHAT!

#PerpetualPraise #ContinualPrayer #WorshipInSpiritAndTruth

{DAY 303}

"Do not be wise in your own eyes; fear the LORD and depart from evil. It will be health to your flesh, and strength to your bones. (Proverbs 3:7-8 NKJV)

These instructions from the Lord, when taken and done, are like physical vitamins for believers. Desire more of God's wisdom. Do not rely on man's wisdom. Do not be conceited in your own wisdom, thinking you do not need God's direction and assistance. There is no greater enemy to the fear of the Lord in the heart than self-conceit of our own wisdom. Reverence God's wisdom, and despise your own. Have a holy and reverent respect for God and be dependent on Him. This healthy fear of God is not only necessary for our soul salvation, but it also promotes the health of the body and bones. It prevents those diseases which come upon us as a result of our sinful lusts and passions. Therefore, hate sin, but love all that which is good and right according to God. It will be nourishment to your body and strength to your bones, and a great preserver and prolonger of your life. Our bones sing praises to You, oh God, for if we abide by and obey Your instructions and teachings, You will keep us healthy physically and spiritually, and preserve and prolong our lives!

CHOOSE TO MAKE TODAY AND EVERY DAY GREAT AND BLESSED NO MATTER WHAT!

#PerpetualPraise #ContinualPrayer #WorshipInSpiritAndTruth

{DAY 304}

"You never saw him, yet you love him. You still don't see him, yet you trust him—with laughter and singing. Because you kept on believing, you'll get what you're looking forward to: total salvation." (1 Peter 1:8-9 MSG)

Notice that the "laughter and singing" is found in the middle of this Scripture. That is because faith declares the outcome even in the middle of adversity. You see the victorious end of the challenge you are facing. When you are really a Bible-believing Christian, there must be some rejoicing, even in the middle of whatever difficulty you are going through. You must let it out somehow through laughing (laughing until you're crying and your mascara is running down your face), shouting, leaping, running, or dancing for joy. These are demonstrations of the power of God through His Holy Spirit, and they are all connected to faith. This kind of joy is full of glory. Some people would have great faith, but they are too concerned about looking "prim and proper" or cool and sophisticated, and pretty all the time. Everyone needs faith. The spirit of faith may often cause a person to look foolish to men. Don't be ashamed to get "ugly' for Jesus! Jesus got plenty "ugly" for us as He was nailed to the cross, bleeding, and dying a gruesome death! He did it all for the joy that was set before Him—a Holy and Righteous Kingdom for God! Glory be to God! Blessed be the Name of the Lord Jesus Christ forevermore!

CHOOSE TO MAKE TODAY AND EVERY DAY GREAT AND BLESSED NO MATTER WHAT!

#PerpetualPraise #ContinualPrayer #WorshipInSpiritAndTruth

{DAY 305}

"But now I come to You, and these things I speak in the world, that they may have My joy fulfilled in themselves." (John 17:13 NKJV)

This is a wonderful prayer that Jesus is praying to Father God, as Mediator between God and man. Our Divine Lord seems to think nothing about His own sufferings, but all His thoughts are on that which concerns His people. All His prayers are for us, that we may be made holy so that God may be glorified in us. Thank You, Jesus, for giving us access to Your measure of joy! Your joy will be fulfilled in us as we completely surrender all of ourselves to You, as we give You our sacrifices of praise in all things, as we serve You and the Kingdom of God, and as we do Your Will and stay in right standing with our Heavenly Father God. Joyful, joyful, we adore You, Jesus!

CHOOSE TO MAKE TODAY AND EVERY DAY GREAT AND BLESSED NO MATTER WHAT!

#PerpetualPraise #ContinualPrayer #WorshipInSpiritAndTruth

{DAY 306}

"For you died to this life, and your real life is hidden with Christ in God. And when Christ, who is your life, is revealed to the whole world, you will share in all his glory." (Colossians 3:3-4 NLT)

If you are a true born-again Christian, your old life before Christ is now dead. Your new life, which is now your real life, is hidden with Christ in God. You are now "living in the heavenlies", seeking and thinking on the things above. You have died to the world's beliefs, through your faith and intimate union with Christ in His death and resurrection. You have died to yourself and are now living to God. Your new and real life, which is now hidden with Christ in God, will be glorified with Christ in Heaven. Thank You, Jesus, that we have a brand new life in You. You are now our life. We pray that our new life in You, Jesus, will be such a blessing and encouragement to others and so glorifying to God, and will reflect to men that we have been with You, in the blessed Name of Jesus! Amen, amen, and amen!

CHOOSE TO MAKE TODAY AND EVERY DAY GREAT AND BLESSED NO MATTER WHAT!

#PerpetualPraise #ContinualPrayer #WorshipInSpiritAndTruth

{DAY 307}

"The jailer got a torch and ran inside. Badly shaken, he collapsed in front of Paul and Silas. He led them out of the jail and asked, "Sirs, what do I have to do to be saved, to really live?" They said, "Put your entire trust in the Master Jesus. Then you'll live as you were meant to live - and everyone in your house included!" They went on to spell out in detail the story of the Master - the entire family got in on this part. They never did get to bed that night. The jailer made them feel at home, dressed their wounds, and then - he couldn't wait till morning! - was baptized, he and everyone in his family. There in his home, he had food set out for a festive meal. It was a night to remember: He and his entire family had put their trust in God; everyone in the house was in on the celebration." (Acts 16:29-34 MSG)

Put all your trust in the Lord, and you and your entire family will be saved! This is God's Word and God's Blessed Promise! Lord Jesus, I believe in You and have put all my faith and trust in You. I judge You Faithful to perform that which You have promised concerning me and my entire family. I know You will bring it to pass. My joy is fulfilled in You and Your promises, Lord Jesus! As I wait patiently on You, Lord, I will continue living a godly life, praising and worshiping you, praying, glorifying You, and serving You with gladness!

CHOOSE TO MAKE TODAY AND EVERY DAY GREAT AND BLESSED NO MATTER WHAT!

#PerpetualPraise #ContinualPrayer #WorshipInSpiritAndTruth

{DAY 308}

"We who are strong must be considerate of those who are sensitive about things like this. We must not just please ourselves. We should help others do what is right and build them up in the Lord. For even Christ didn't live to please himself. As the Scriptures say, "The insults of those who insult you, O God, have fallen on me." (Romans 15:1-3 NLT)

Those who have been made strong in the Lord by the renewing of their minds through God's Word and His Holy Spirit should demonstrate this by their godly conduct. Those who have been totally set free from a lifestyle of sin should not use their liberty in a way that would offend or hinder others who have just begun their walk with Christ with little Bible knowledge and understanding in the things of God; but rather should bear with them in their weaknesses and failings, and not condemn or despise them. Those who are strong should be helping, encouraging, and building up those who have not yet reached the same level of spiritual maturity, and provoking them to good works by not only demonstrating godly conduct, but also by godly speech and godly works. After all, we all begin our spiritual walk with Jesus as infants, and grow as we continue gaining knowledge and understanding of God, God's love, and the things of God; also by watching, listening to, and asking questions of the stronger and more mature saints, who have gained godly wisdom.

For example, as I began growing in the Lord, I asked one of my sisters in the Lord, Sister Gloria Nichols, if I would go to Hell for smoking cigarettes. Obviously, I had not yet been set totally free from that particular addiction, or I wouldn't have felt the need to ask that question. Sister Gloria's reply to my question was, "Well, you might not go to Hell; but do you really want to go to Heaven smelling like a cigarette?" That was a great answer! She did not judge nor condemn me; however, her reply definitely provoked me to good works. Shortly after that, Jesus set me totally free! Praise God! The stronger saints are to take the infants and younger saints "under their wings" to spiritually mother, or spiritually father, them. When you help and do good to others, you receive the joy of the Lord. Happy helping, everyone!

CHOOSE TO MAKE TODAY AND EVERY DAY GREAT AND BLESSED NO MATTER WHAT!

#PerpetualPraise #ContinualPrayer #WorshipInSpiritAndTruth

{DAY 309}

"In that day you will sing: "I will praise you, O Lord! You were angry with me, but not anymore. Now you comfort me. See, God has come to save me. I will trust in him and not be afraid. The Lord God is my strength and my song; he has given me victory." With joy, you will drink deeply from the fountain of salvation!" (Isaiah 12:1-3 NLT)

This means there is something for us to do. We must drink deeply and show exceeding great joy for what the Lord has done for us! God does not meet our needs as we sit inactively doing nothing other than waiting on God to drop blessings into our lap. We must reach out and draw forth what He has provided. Because it is all of the Lord, we draw from the wells of salvation with joy. There should be no "gloom and doom" faces at the Lord's well of salvation. He has saved us! He is on our side, and we are now on the Lord's side! God has turned our mourning into joy! Everything about us should reflect exceeding great joy. We draw water and drink deeply with joy! Hallelujah!

CHOOSE TO MAKE TODAY AND EVERY DAY GREAT AND BLESSED NO MATTER WHAT!

#PerpetualPraise #ContinualPrayer #WorshipInSpiritAndTruth

{DAY 310}

"Blessed are the people who know the joyful sound! They walk, O Lord, in the light of Your countenance. In Your name they rejoice all day long, and in Your righteousness they are exalted. (Psalm 89:15-16 NKJV)

Happy are those who know the joyful sound of the Gospel, the Message of Salvation, and obey it; who experience its power upon their hearts and produce the fruit of it in their lives. They walk in the light of the Lord's presence. True believers rejoice always in their Lord and Savior and find their happiness in His righteousness. The effect of the knowledge of Christ's righteousness elevates believers in moral character, in happiness, in respect and regard towards others, and in true prosperity. There is no reason why the people of God should not be constantly happy, whose God never changes His mind on His promises.

CHOOSE TO MAKE TODAY AND EVERY DAY GREAT AND BLESSED NO MATTER WHAT!

#PerpetualPraise #ContinualPrayer #WorshipInSpiritAndTruth

{DAY 311}

PRAISE TO START YOUR DAY:

"For His anger is but for a moment, His favor is for life; weeping may endure for a night, but joy comes in the morning." (Psalm 30:5 NKJV)

Thank You, Lord, that You do not stay angry with us when we miss the mark. You are the Bright and Morning Star! You are the One Who puts a smile on our faces every morning! Thank You, Lord, that though we sometimes make You angry for a moment, we still have Your favor for a lifetime. We praise You, oh God, that You are faithful to forgive us and to cleanse us from all unrighteousness. Our weeping may last for a night, but in the morning You enable us to shout for joy! Every morning You gift us with is the first day of the rest of our lives in You, Jesus! We are so blessed to have You in our lives, Lord Jesus! Glory to our Heavenly Father God!

CHOOSE TO MAKE TODAY AND EVERY DAY GREAT AND BLESSED NO MATTER WHAT!

#PerpetualPraise #ContinualPrayer #WorshipInSpiritAndTruth

{DAY 312}

"For the LORD has chosen Zion; He has desired it for His dwelling place: "This is My resting place forever; here I will dwell, for I have desired it...And her saints shall shout aloud for joy." (Psalm 132:13-14,16 NKJV)

God chose Mount Zion for His Holy Hill, and He delighted in it. God chose Mount Zion for the home of His Ark of the Covenant and said, "This is My resting place forever". Zion, located on Mount Zion, was the city of David; chosen by King David for the royal city because God had chosen it for the Holy City. God gives abundant joy to His people. God always provides for His people and sends His blessing with it. God always gives good measure, pressed down, and running over. Often, we have not because we ask not, or because we ask amiss. If you ask great things of God, He will give you even greater things for He is "able to do exceeding abundantly above all that we ask or think." Glory to God!

CHOOSE TO MAKE TODAY AND EVERY DAY GREAT AND BLESSED NO MATTER WHAT!

#PerpetualPraise #ContinualPrayer #WorshipInSpiritAndTruth

{DAY 313}

"Everything of God gets expressed in him, so you can see and hear him clearly. You don't need a telescope, a microscope, or a horoscope to realize the fullness of Christ, and the emptiness of the universe without him. When you come to him, that fullness comes together for you, too. His power extends over everything." (Colossians 2:9-10 MSG)

Everything about God is revealed through Christ Jesus so that we may see and hear Him clearly. Christ Jesus is the expressed image of the invisible God. In Christ, we are filled with the knowledge of God and God's Will. There is no defect in the truths and teachings of God's Word. God alone is able to save us. God alone is able to meet all our wants and needs. There is no necessity, therefore, that we should look to the aid of philosophy or science. When united to the Lord Jesus Christ, you are filled up with His fullness and are made complete in Him. In Christ, you enter into the fullness and completeness of life both materially and spiritually. In Christ, there is nothing left wanting. We are complete in Christ, Who is the head of all principality and power.

CHOOSE TO MAKE TODAY AND EVERY DAY GREAT AND BLESSED NO MATTER WHAT!

#PerpetualPraise #ContinualPrayer #WorshipInSpiritAndTruth

{DAY 314}

"When a woman gives birth, she has a hard time, there's no getting around it. But when the baby is born, there is joy in the birth. This new life in the world wipes out memory of the pain. The sadness you have right now is similar to that pain, but the coming joy is also similar. When I see you again, you'll be full of joy, and it will be a joy no one can rob from you. You'll no longer be so full of questions. "This is what I want you to do: Ask the Father for whatever is in keeping with the things I've revealed to you. Ask in my name, according to my will, and he'll most certainly give it to you. Your joy will be a river overflowing its banks!""" (John 16:21-24 MSG)

I am always pregnant with the expectancy of Your return, Lord Jesus, when I will see You face to face, and have a joy that no one can ever take from me! Thank You, Jesus, for Your instructions on praying. I have learned from You to always begin and end my prayers with, "In the blessed Name of Jesus! Amen, amen, and amen!" Also, Lord, I pray according to Your good and perfect will. I praise You, Lord, that the Sovereign Creator of all hears and answers my prayers! My cup runs over with joy!

CHOOSE TO MAKE TODAY AND EVERY DAY GREAT AND BLESSED NO MATTER WHAT!

#PerpetualPraise #ContinualPrayer #WorshipInSpiritAndTruth

{DAY 315}

"Because of Christ and our faith in him, we can now come boldly and confidently into God's presence." (Ephesians 3:12 NLT)

Though God holds the greatest and highest office as Sovereign over all, He has removed every obstacle which might keep us from entering into His presence. Thank You, Jesus, because of our faith in You and that You have reconciled us to God, we may now approach God with boldness, freedom, and confidence, without having to go through man. Our Christian boldness is wasted unless we use it in coming nearer to God. We see God as our Father waiting to be gracious, and our prayer should be as the glad request of His child. True Christians have a longing for the presence of God, not because they want something but, just to be with Him, to feel His power, and to know by personal experience that He is beside us. I am holy addicted to being in the presence of God, just to be with Him.

CHOOSE TO MAKE TODAY AND EVERY DAY GREAT AND BLESSED NO MATTER WHAT!

#PerpetualPraise #ContinualPrayer #WorshipInSpiritAndTruth

{DAY 316}

"You are coming to Christ, who is the living cornerstone of God's temple. He was rejected by people, but he was chosen by God for great honor. And you are living stones that God is building into his spiritual temple. What's more, you are his holy priests. Through the mediation of Jesus Christ, you offer spiritual sacrifices that please God." (1 Peter 2:4-5 NLT)

It is Christ Jesus Himself on Whom we, the Church, is built. We are God's living stones, being built up in Christ as God's spiritual house. Christ is the living Chief Cornerstone. Jesus is the One Foundation, and all humble believers are the living stones built upon Him. We who are in Christ should continually make the effort to come nearer to Christ Jesus. Christ was and still is rejected by the world, but He, Who is precious to God as God's only begotten Son, was chosen by God to be the Lord and Savior of the world. To those who believe in Christ Jesus; by the incorruptible (everlasting) blood and the incorruptible seed, He has brought us into a heavenly priesthood, and we are to offer up spiritual sacrifices of love, prayer, praise and worship, acceptable to God by Jesus Christ. These are sacrifices with which God is well pleased. Praise God!

CHOOSE TO MAKE TODAY AND EVERY DAY GREAT AND BLESSED NO MATTER WHAT!

#PerpetualPraise #ContinualPrayer #WorshipInSpiritAndTruth

{DAY 317}

"As you therefore have received Christ Jesus the Lord, so walk in Him, rooted and built up in Him and established in the faith, as you have been taught, abounding in it with thanksgiving." (Colossians 2:6-7 NKJV)

When you receive Jesus Christ as your Lord and Savior, your guilt is gone and you are at peace with God and with yourself. He gives you His joy and the hope of eternal life. You are a brand new creation in Christ and it feels wonderful, kind of like falling in love. Due to life's troubles and disappointments, you must work at making those initial wonderful feelings last. You must strengthen that love so that it grows deeper and stronger over a lifetime, much like a marriage. You must work at keeping it alive for a lifetime. As you walk closely and daily with Christ, and continue progressing towards being transformed into His image, you are being built up in Him and established in the faith. You are overflowing with gratitude and thanksgiving. When you genuinely trust in Christ, God roots you in Him.

In order to get more deeply rooted, you must spend time alone with God, seeking Him in His Word and in prayer (talking to God). You learn to trust and obey Him in all matters, whether big or small. You judge yourself, getting rid of your natural lusts and appetites and replacing them with spiritual appetites, and replacing your grumbling with gratitude. You speak good over yourself. You speak kindly to others, even when they are mean towards you. You are gradually being built up in Him. You are being established in the faith as you grow in the knowledge and understanding of God and the truths of God's Word. You should be overflowing with gratitude to God for His abundant grace towards you and for your salvation. Make Jesus your First Love and your Eternal Love. If you have not yet received Jesus as your Lord and Savior, why not do that right now? The "Prayer of Salvation" is included within the Foreword pages at the beginning of this book. Jesus still makes house calls, and He is ready and available to come to your house even now today. He is patiently and lovingly waiting for your personal invitation.

CHOOSE TO MAKE TODAY AND EVERY DAY GREAT AND BLESSED NO MATTER WHAT!

#PerpetualPraise #ContinualPrayer #WorshipInSpiritAndTruth

{DAY 318}

"And we know that the Son of God has come and has given us an understanding, that we may know Him who is true; and we are in Him who is true, in His Son Jesus Christ. This is the true God and eternal life." (1 John 5:20 NKJV)

Every true Christian should, not just think it but, know this truth. Christ Jesus, the Son of God, has already come and instructed use that we understand the great truths of God, and know the One and Only True and Living God. We are united to Him Who is true; we belong to Him; we are His friends. Jesus is the Source and "Fountain of Life" to the soul. Praise God, for we are born of God! Praise God from whom all blessings flow! Praise the Father, praise the Son, and praise the Holy Ghost!

CHOOSE TO MAKE TODAY AND EVERY DAY GREAT AND BLESSED NO MATTER WHAT!

#PerpetualPraise #ContinualPrayer #WorshipInSpiritAndTruth

{DAY 319}

"How blessed is God! And what a blessing he is! He's the Father of our Master, Jesus Christ, and takes us to the high places of blessing in him. Long before he laid down earth's foundations, he had us in mind, had settled on us as the focus of his love, to be made whole and holy by his love. Long, long ago he decided to adopt us into his family through Jesus Christ. (What pleasure he took in planning this!) He wanted us to enter into the celebration of his lavish gift-giving by the hand of his beloved Son." (Ephesians 1:3-6 MSG)

Our Heavenly Father God is to be praised for His Master Plan of eternal salvation and for all His plans. God has blessed each Christian individually with all spiritual blessings (including redemption, salvation, adoption, peace, the Holy Spirit, and the list goes on) in Christ in regard to things pertaining to Heaven, to prepare us for Heaven. These blessings are bestowed upon Christians in accordance with God's eternal purpose. God's eternal purpose is to have His Own holy people, which God chose in Christ before the foundation of the world. God knows the individuals who He has chosen. God's choice in accordance with His eternal purpose was not just to bring a certain number of people to Heaven, or to use any means of saving them. It was God's eternal purpose that they should be saved by His only begotten Son Christ Jesus. God's eternal plan and purpose has been in the mind of God always, even before earth's foundations, and God took great pleasure in His planning of it. It is not a new, or changed, plan. His plan is to make His people holy before God in love. It is all due to the love of God. What higher love could God show us than to give us eternal life? What a blessing our God is to us! We should spend every waking moment of our lives blessing Him in return! No one else would have, or could have, done this for us!

CHOOSE TO MAKE TODAY AND EVERY DAY GREAT AND BLESSED NO MATTER WHAT!

#PerpetualPraise #ContinualPrayer #WorshipInSpiritAndTruth

{DAY 320}

"Indeed, let no one who waits on You be ashamed..." (Psalm 25:3 NKJV)

No one who waits on God by a believing hope and faith will be ashamed of it. No one who lifts up his soul to God in worship will be ashamed. When God pardons our sin, He also forgets it. The prayer in the hearts of godly believers is that they may never be put to shame; that they may never be overcome by sin; that they may never fall under the power of temptation; and that they may not fail to have eternal salvation. I praise and thank You, Lord, for Your mercy which has taken away all my guilt and shame. The precious Blood of Jesus has washed away every stain of my past. There is such power in the Blood of Jesus! Thank You, Jesus, for Your precious blood You shed for me! There's nothing like the Blood of Jesus!

CHOOSE TO MAKE TODAY AND EVERY DAY GREAT AND BLESSED NO MATTER WHAT!

#PerpetualPraise #ContinualPrayer #WorshipInSpiritAndTruth

{DAY 321}

"For God gives wisdom and knowledge and joy to a man who is good in His sight;" (Ecclesiastes 2:26 NKJV)

Men are only really good, who are good in the sight of God, who sees the heart, and knows what is in man. They are those who are made good by God's grace. They are those whose hearts have been made clean, and who have had new and right spirits created in them by God. They are those who have God's Holy Spirit living in them, in whose hearts Christ dwells by faith. They are those who love God's Word and have it hidden in their hearts, so they might not sin against God. They are those who are born-again Christians, and who live by faith in Jesus Christ. They are those who are clothed in Christ's righteousness; and who do all in faith, without which it is impossible to please God. To such men, God gives wisdom and knowledge and joy. Glory to God!

CHOOSE TO MAKE TODAY AND EVERY DAY GREAT AND BLESSED NO MATTER WHAT!

#PerpetualPraise #ContinualPrayer #WorshipInSpiritAndTruth

{DAY 322}

"But know that the LORD has set apart for Himself him who is godly; the LORD will hear when I call to Him." (Psalm 4:3 NKJV)

You cannot hurt him, for God has surrounded him with His protection. You may say what you please against him, but God loves him, and will take care of him. Now if God has set us apart as His people to be His own, He will defend us. He will guard us against every enemy. We shall not be destroyed. What security we have in God! Brothers and sisters in Christ, God's mercy-seat is always open to us! God hears us when we call to Him! The sweet assurance that prayer will prevail is one of the best comforts we have in the dark days of trouble. We praise You, oh God, and we love You!

CHOOSE TO MAKE TODAY AND EVERY DAY GREAT AND BLESSED NO MATTER WHAT!

#PerpetualPraise #ContinualPrayer #WorshipInSpiritAndTruth

{DAY 323}

"O LORD, our Lord, how excellent is Your name in all the earth, Who have set Your glory above the heavens! When I consider Your heavens, the work of Your fingers, the moon and the stars, which You have ordained, what is man that You are mindful of him, and the son of man that You visit him? O LORD, our Lord, how excellent is Your name in all the earth! (Psalm 8:1,3-4,9 NKJV)

How well known, respected, and admired is the name of Jesus throughout all the world! His incarnation (Jesus was the embodiment of God in the flesh), birth, humble life, preaching, miracles, passion, death, resurrection, and ascension, are celebrated throughout the whole world. The gifts of His Holy Spirit, His people—Christians, and His Gospel are spoken of everywhere. No name is so universal, no power and influence so generally felt, as those of Christ Jesus—the Lord and Savior of mankind. Amen. The heavens (sun, moon and stars) are the most glorious of all the works of God which the eye of man can reach; but the glory of God is infinitely above even these. When we consider all of God's glorious and wondrous works, and then consider that we are but mere clay, molded by a divine hand, we must be moved to most humbly ask God, "what is man that You are mindful of him, the son of man (any descendant of man) that You visit Him?" Why should God, who is so huge, limitless and glorious, and Who has all the starry worlds to claim His attention—why should He turn His thoughts on man? "O Lord, our Lord, how excellent is Your name in all the earth! We praise and worship You forevermore!

CHOOSE TO MAKE TODAY AND EVERY DAY GREAT AND BLESSED NO MATTER WHAT! #PerpetualPraise

#ContinualPrayer #WorshipInSpiritAndTruth

{DAY 324}

"Since you were precious in My sight, you have been honored, and I have loved you;…" (Isaiah 43:4 NKJV)

God has a kind feeling of approval and support towards His people. God will defend and deliver His people because He loves His people. God honors His people by giving us His precious truths. It is God Who makes us honorable by the favors He bestows on us; not that we are honorable due to our own personal character and worth. Dear Lord, Your favor and goodwill towards Your people brings great comfort to all believers. I praise and worship You, oh God, for I am one of Your people! You have always shown Your love towards me! I love You too, Lord!

CHOOSE TO MAKE TODAY AND EVERY DAY GREAT AND BLESSED NO MATTER WHAT!

#PerpetualPraise #ContinualPrayer #WorshipInSpiritAndTruth

{DAY 325}

"The Lord is your keeper;…The LORD shall preserve you from all evil; He shall preserve your soul. The LORD shall preserve your going out and your coming in from this time forth, and even forevermore." (Psalm 121:5,7-8 NKJV)

For those who trust in God, the Lord is your Keeper, your Preserver and Defender. God will keep you from the dominion and damning power of sin, and He will keep you from a final and total falling away from Him through sin. God will keep you from giving into the world's lusts and temptations, and from perishing by them. God will keep you unto salvation by preserving your soul. God will preserve you in going out and coming in; in going from home and coming back; that is, everywhere, and at all times. God provides safety for His people, those who trust in Him. Therefore, our confidence must be in God only. We must turn to God for all our help; from Him we must expect it, in His own way and time. We must comfort ourselves in the Lord, when difficulties and dangers are greatest in our lives. We do this through God's Word and by talking to Him. God is our Protector through this life and forevermore. In Heaven there will be no sin, and consequently no need of discipline. Glory to our Most High God! We bless You, Lord!

CHOOSE TO MAKE TODAY AND EVERY DAY GREAT AND BLESSED NO MATTER WHAT!

#PerpetualPraise #ContinualPrayer #WorshipInSpiritAndTruth

{DAY 326}

"I will be your God throughout your lifetime—until your hair is white with age. I made you, and I will care for you. I will carry you along and save you." (Isaiah 46:4 NLT)

God's love, care and nurturing of His sons and daughters is ageless and extends even through old age. His care and lovingkindness towards us lasts from our beginning to our end and forevermore. He even carries us along when we become old and gray; more than the most tender parent is able to do! God will not leave His people in the decline of life, when infirmities may be upon them, and they stand in as much need as ever of being supported and carried. Thank You, oh God, for Your ageless care. You will not cast Your sons and daughters aside even when they are old and gray. You are a lifetime Protector, Deliverer and Savior from our childhood through old age. We praise You, worship You, and glorify You!

CHOOSE TO MAKE TODAY AND EVERY DAY GREAT AND BLESSED NO MATTER WHAT!

#PerpetualPraise #ContinualPrayer #WorshipInSpiritAndTruth

{DAY 327}

"When God made his promise to Abraham, he backed it to the hilt, putting his own reputation on the line. He said, "I promise that I'll bless you with everything I have—bless and bless and bless!" Abraham stuck it out and got everything that had been promised to him. When people make promises, they guarantee them by appeal to some authority above them so that if there is any question that they'll make good on the promise, the authority will back them up. When God wanted to guarantee his promises, he gave his word, a rock-solid guarantee—God can't break his word. And because his word cannot change, the promise is likewise unchangeable. We who have run for our very lives to God have every reason to grab the promised hope with both hands and never let go. It's an unbreakable spiritual lifeline, reaching past all appearances right to the very presence of God where Jesus, running on ahead of us, has taken up his permanent post as high priest for us, in the order of Melchizedek." (Hebrews 6:13-20 MSG)

Have you ever known anyone whose promises usually turned out to be empty words. That person may have wanted to come through on his promises, but then either did not or could not. Regarding every one of God's promises, He has already sworn by Himself to uphold as unchanging. God is more than able and willing to fulfill every promise He has made. God's promises never change, just as God never changes. God's only begotten Son Christ Jesus is now our Great High Priest, and is ever in the presence of God interceding on our behalf. Oh God, You still give us Your Word and stand by it even now today; therefore, we can stand on Your rock-solid Word which never changes. I praise You, oh God, for You are the Anchor of my soul!

CHOOSE TO MAKE TODAY AND EVERY DAY GREAT AND BLESSED NO MATTER WHAT!

#PerpetualPraise #ContinualPrayer #WorshipInSpiritAndTruth

{DAY 328}

"Oh, satisfy us early with Your mercy, that we may rejoice and be glad all our days!" (Psalm 90:14 NKJV)

Good men know how to turn their darkest trials into arguments at God's Throne of Grace. He who has the heart to pray and make his request made known to God in an urgent and emotional manner, with fervency, will be satisfied with God's favor. When the Lord refreshes us with His presence, our joy is such that no man can take it from us. Nothing is able to distress those who enjoy the present favor of God, those who leave their future in His loving hands. I praise You, my Jesus, and come to You with my whole heart full of thanksgiving because every morning You show me Your mercy (undeserved favor). Your mercy refreshes my soul and lets me know that I am in right standing with You, no matter what I may be going through. Your presence and favor consoles my heart and comforts me. Thank You, my Jesus! I love You, too!

CHOOSE TO MAKE TODAY AND EVERY DAY GREAT AND BLESSED NO MATTER WHAT!

#PerpetualPraise #ContinualPrayer #WorshipInSpiritAndTruth

{DAY 329}

"Blessed is the man You choose, and cause to approach You, that he may dwell in Your courts. We shall be satisfied with the goodness of Your house, of Your holy temple." (Psalm 65:4 NKJV)

We are chosen by God for Christ's sake, according to the good pleasure of His Will, and this alone is blessedness. In Christ Jesus, we are received by God, as being accepted in God's Son; and, therefore, in Christ are we blessed. He is our blessing. God works graciously in us, and attracts us powerfully. He conquers our unwillingness by His transforming grace. Happy is the one who is "at home" with God, that he may dwell in the house of the Lord forever. He will be like a child at home. He will experience and be satisfied with spiritual joys. He will be so filled that he will have nothing to want for or look for outside. Lord, I am so grateful that You drew me close to You by Your grace. I praise You and thank You for permitting me to approach You. I praise You that Your Holy Spirit leads me to worship You. All I want and all I need is found in You, Lord, and in Your house! I have an insatiable appetite and thirst that cannot be quenched for being in Your house. I am holy addicted to being in Your house and in Your presence, Lord.

CHOOSE TO MAKE TODAY AND EVERY DAY GREAT AND BLESSED NO MATTER WHAT!

#PerpetualPraise #ContinualPrayer #WorshipInSpiritAndTruth

{DAY 330}

"I will be glad and rejoice in Your mercy, for You have considered my trouble; You have known my soul in adversities," (Psalm 31:7 NKJV)

Thank You, Lord, for Your mercy and lovingkindness! When all lost hope in me (including myself) and there was nobody who would help me, and when the devil thought he had me; then You found me and drew me close to You. Then I found You, and You became my Forever Constant Companion. You know the troubles and heavy burdens I have had, most of which I brought on myself. You did not throw me away when You found me. You were my Deliverer then, and You are my Deliverer even now today. It is comforting to know that, in good times as well as in times of trouble, my thoughts and feelings are known and understood by You. I praise and worship You forevermore! There is none like You, Jesus, none like You!

CHOOSE TO MAKE TODAY AND EVERY DAY GREAT AND BLESSED NO MATTER WHAT!

#PerpetualPraise #ContinualPrayer #WorshipInSpiritAndTruth

{DAY 331}

PRAISE TO START YOUR DAY:

"In You, O LORD, I put my trust; let me never be ashamed; deliver me in Your righteousness. Bow down Your ear to me, deliver me speedily; be my rock of refuge, a fortress of defense to save me. For You are my rock and my fortress; therefore, for Your name's sake, lead me and guide me." (Psalm 31:1-3 NKJV)

Yes, Lord, all my faith, and trust is in You and You alone. I praise You because You took all my guilt and shame upon Yourself on the cross at Calvary. You saved me, delivered me, set me totally free, and gave me Your righteousness. You hid me in You and became my Defender. I worship You, Jehovah-Ganan, for You are the Lord Our Defense! May Your Holy Spirit continue to lead and guide me all the days of my life for Your Name's sake, in the blessed Name of Jesus! Amen, amen, and amen!

CHOOSE TO MAKE TODAY AND EVERY DAY GREAT AND BLESSED NO MATTER WHAT!

#PerpetualPraise #ContinualPrayer #WorshipInSpiritAndTruth

{DAY 332}

"Pull me out of the net which they have secretly laid for me, for You are my strength. Into Your hand I commit my spirit; You have redeemed me, O Lord God of truth." (Psalm 31:4-5 NKJV)

The devil tries to get God's people caught up in sin—anything that is against God and the things of God. The devil will use anybody who will let him entangle you whenever and wherever and however he can. When this happens, the true believer knows that he can only be delivered through God's power. Like Jesus, we ought to continually commit our spirit into our great Father's hands, for there is no other place that can be so safe and blessed as between the strong, almighty, never-failing hands of the eternal God. Thank You, Lord, for You keep me from falling into the net that the devil (and those the devil uses) lays for me when and where and how I least suspect it. But, if I do fall, You are right there to pull me out quickly. My hope of defense is in You and You alone. I worship You, Jehovah-'Uzam, for You are my Lord Strength in Trouble! I commit my spirit into Your hands always, my Lord! Glory to our Heavenly Father God!

CHOOSE TO MAKE TODAY AND EVERY DAY GREAT AND BLESSED NO MATTER WHAT!

#PerpetualPraise #ContinualPrayer #WorshipInSpiritAndTruth

{DAY 333}

PRAISE TO START YOUR DAY:

"Good people, cheer GOD! Right-living people sound best when praising. Use guitars to reinforce your Hallelujahs! Play his praise on a grand piano! Invent your own new song to him; give him a trumpet fanfare." (Psalm 33:1-3 MSG)

God's righteous people are strongly encouraged to praise Him because of the excellency of His character and His majestic creation. God views a sacred praise as holiness. The praises of the upright are the Lord's delight. Singing praises unto God is the sweetest and best of music to His ears. All notes are His, and all music belongs to Him. All songs of praise should be sung unto God. We should put life, soul and heart into every song, since we have new mercies every day. God deserves the most excellent that we have. Oh yes, Lord! You delight in Your godly people's reverent and thankful praise when You hear our songs. The joy of the Lord shines brightly through our praise. I am holy addicted to praising You, Lord! Praise gives me holy joy! I praise You for Your creative power. May Your Own creation be creative for You and show forth Your rightful praise, in the manner that is most pleasing and glorifying to You, and that You delight in hearing!

CHOOSE TO MAKE TODAY AND EVERY DAY GREAT AND BLESSED NO MATTER WHAT!

#PerpetualPraise #ContinualPrayer #WorshipInSpiritAndTruth

{DAY 334}

"For GOD's Word is solid to the core; everything he makes is sound inside and out. He loves it when everything fits, when his world is in plumb-line true. Earth is drenched in GOD's affectionate satisfaction." (Psalm 33:4-5 MSG)

God's creative work & governing work are faithful. God has faithfully been ruling, controlling and caring for His creation as a Faithful Creator. God loves righteousness and justice. Everything God does is right, just and good. The earth is filled with the goodness of God. God's goodness is displayed even in the little details of life on earth; through the sunrise with birds chirping, and through the rain that nourishes the ground, plants, and animals. Oh God, Your Word is righteous and true, and Your people are right only when they agree with Your Word. All of Your works are done in faithfulness to Your promises. The earth is full of Your Goodness! Try as I do to imagine, I cannot fathom what You have waiting for Your righteous people in Heaven!

CHOOSE TO MAKE TODAY AND EVERY DAY GREAT AND BLESSED NO MATTER WHAT!

#PerpetualPraise #ContinualPrayer #WorshipInSpiritAndTruth

{DAY 335}

"But thanks be to God, who gives us the victory through our Lord Jesus Christ." (1 Corinthians 15:57 NKJV)

God has given us the victory over sin, Satan, death, Hell and the grave, through our Lord and Savior Christ Jesus, Who has given us the hope of a glorious resurrection. God formed the plan; He executed it in the gift of His Son, and He gives it to us personally when we come to die. Christ Jesus obtained this victory for true believers through His own death on the cross in our place, through His burial, and through His glorious resurrection. The law could not do this because it could not forgive or excuse sinners. Only Christ Jesus could do this! I praise You, Jesus, for giving me the victory! I choose not to allow anything to get to me because I know that victory is mine already! That is why I can say, "It is well with my soul!" I praise and worship You, Jesus, to the glory of our Heavenly Father God!

CHOOSE TO MAKE TODAY AND EVERY DAY GREAT AND BLESSED NO MATTER WHAT!

#PerpetualPraise #ContinualPrayer #WorshipInSpiritAndTruth

{DAY 336}

"They are abundantly satisfied with the fullness of Your house, and You give them drink from the river of Your pleasures." (Psalm 36:8 NKJV)

Those who put their trust in God and live by faith in nearness to the Lord will receive His rich river of blessings (love, grace, mercy, salvation, peace, joy, faith, hope, provision, healing, miracles, protection, deliverance, freedom, strength…). Those who are satisfied in the fullness of the Lord's house find that their sacred worship is the richest spiritual food, and nothing can so completely fill the soul as the Gospel of Christ Jesus. God not only brings us to the river of His everlasting love but makes us drink. The happiness given to the faithful is that same happiness of God Himself. JESUS SAVES AND SO MUCH MORE!!! We praise and worship You, oh God, for You alone are Worthy!

CHOOSE TO MAKE TODAY AND EVERY DAY GREAT AND BLESSED NO MATTER WHAT!

#PerpetualPraise #ContinualPrayer #WorshipInSpiritAndTruth

{DAY 337}

"For with You is the fountain of life; in Your light we see light." (Psalm 36:9 NASB)

No counsel or sympathy from man can truly comfort or help us. Anything becomes an idol when it keeps us from turning to God for every spiritual need. We are like the prodigal son when we forget the Father's house. God is the Fountain of Eternal Life. The best position for a Christian is living wholly and directly on God's grace. We are complete in Him. When we get thirsty enough, we are sure to eagerly turn to the Fountain of Life. Jesus, when we see You face to face, then will we see the Light of Life; pure light, glory, all knowledge (no questions necessary), holiness, complete joy, and wholeness. We worship You, oh God, for You are the True Source of Life and Light.

CHOOSE TO MAKE TODAY AND EVERY DAY GREAT AND BLESSED NO MATTER WHAT!

#PerpetualPraise #ContinualPrayer #WorshipInSpiritAndTruth

{DAY 338}

"When a man's ways please the LORD, He makes even his enemies to be at peace with him." (Proverbs 16:7 NKJV)

All men make great efforts to please; some to please themselves, some to please other men, and some to please the Lord. We should seek to walk as to please God. For He is our Master, Father, and King. There is one great benefit attached to pleasing the Lord. God is the Holder of everyone's heart, and He can give even your enemies the inclination to be kind to you and make them be at peace with you, even if it lasts just long enough for you to find favor for a victory in a certain situation involving them. God is the Guardian and Defender of all who fear and love Him; and it is truly amazing to see how wonderfully God works on their behalf, raising friends up for them, and turning their enemies into friends. God does this for those with whom He is pleased. We praise You, oh God, for Your favor, and we humbly request that You enable us to always please You, in the blessed Name of Jesus! Amen, amen, and amen!

CHOOSE TO MAKE TODAY AND EVERY DAY GREAT AND BLESSED NO MATTER WHAT!

#PerpetualPraise #ContinualPrayer #WorshipInSpiritAndTruth

{DAY 339}

"Peace I leave with you, My peace I give to you; not as the world gives do I give to you. Let not your heart be troubled, neither let it be afraid." (John 14:27 NKJV)

The blessed legacy which our Lord left us with is His peace. Thank You, Jesus, for Your personal gift of peace that You left with us until we see You come again—not just any peace, but Your Own peace. Yours is a peace that is far beyond what the world can understand. Your peace leaves no room in us for a troubled heart, or for fear. This is also the peace which exists among the people of God toward one another. There is a peace of God which reigns in our hearts through Jesus Christ, by which we are bound in unity to every other child of God. Thank You, Lord Jesus, for the blessed legacy of Your peace! Blessed be the Name of the Lord forevermore!

CHOOSE TO MAKE TODAY AND EVERY DAY GREAT AND BLESSED NO MATTER WHAT!

#PerpetualPraise #ContinualPrayer #WorshipInSpiritAndTruth

{DAY 340}

"Jesus answered them, "Do you finally believe? In fact, you're about to make a run for it—saving your own skins and abandoning me. But I'm not abandoned. The Father is with me. I've told you all this so that trusting me, you will be unshakable and assured, deeply at peace. In this godless world you will continue to experience difficulties. But take heart! I've conquered the world." (John 16:31-33 MSG)

Just as our Heavenly Father God was with Christ Jesus, He is also with every true believer who is living in Christ Jesus. Even the most difficult of times cannot disturb the peace of Christ Jesus, which is always "in-house" within you; so long as you remain "up close and personal" with Christ Jesus and in Him, by remaining faithful to the truth of God's Word, by allowing God to keep your head lifted up, by not allowing the spirit of fear to come in, and by standing up for Jesus in boldness and being courageous through the power of His Holy Spirit living in you. Christ has already overcome the world. We who are in Him will overcome the world too, through the same power which dwelt in Him. He has put His life into His people; He has given His Holy Spirit to live in His people, and we are more than conquerors through Christ Jesus! Praise God! Thank You, Jesus!

CHOOSE TO MAKE TODAY AND EVERY DAY GREAT AND BLESSED NO MATTER WHAT!

#PerpetualPraise #ContinualPrayer #WorshipInSpiritAndTruth

{DAY 341}

"And let the peace of God rule in your hearts, to which also you were called in one body; and be thankful." (Colossians 3:15 NKJV)

We are called to the peace of God in one body, and Christ Jesus is the Head and Ruler over every member of His body. Therefore, since our Head has perfectly overcome, it may truly be said that every member will follow to do the same. We can and will overcome the corruption in our hearts and allow the peace of God to rule in our hearts instead, by the power of God's Holy Spirit Who lives in us. As members of Christ's body, we have been given the mind of Christ, which He rules over. Every one of our actions begins with a thought. Therefore, by allowing Jesus to rule our thoughts and in our hearts, our actions and words following will be godly. We praise You, oh God, who enables us to be at peace with You, with each other, and with all men. We know this is Your Good and Perfect Will. We bless you, Lord!

CHOOSE TO MAKE TODAY AND EVERY DAY GREAT AND BLESSED NO MATTER WHAT!

#PerpetualPraise #ContinualPrayer #WorshipInSpiritAndTruth

{DAY 342}

"But the fruit of the Spirit is love, joy, peace, longsuffering, kindness, goodness, faithfulness, gentleness, self-control. Against such there is no law." (Galatians 5:22-23 NKJV)

It is God's Holy Spirit living in us to lead and guide us in living God's way. As a result of our obedience, God brings us the fruitful gifts of His Own Love (affection for others), joy (full of energy, excitement about life, excessive spiritual growing), peace (serenity), longsuffering (compassion in our hearts for others), self-control (abstinence, moderation, self-restraint), and more. There is no divine nor human law against these things. If these things are not found in us, then we do not have God's Holy Spirit living in us. If these things are found in us, then we do have God's Holy Spirit living in us, and we should boast the fruit of the Spirit for others to see, and thereby be glorifying God! JESUS SAVES AND SO MUCH MORE!!!

CHOOSE TO MAKE TODAY AND EVERY DAY GREAT AND BLESSED NO MATTER WHAT!

#PerpetualPraise #ContinualPrayer #WorshipInSpiritAndTruth

{DAY 343}

"The LORD will give strength to His people; the LORD will bless His people with peace." (Psalm 29:11 NKJV)

The Lord's power is promised to be the strength of His chosen people. He gives His redeemed the wings of eagles; He will terrify the enemies of His saints, and give His children peace. God perfects strength in His people's weakness. For the sake of righteousness, God equips His people for every good work. The work of righteousness is peace. Why are we weak when we have divine strength to flee to? Why are we troubled when the Lord's own peace is ours? Jesus, the Mighty God is our peace—what a blessing this is today!

CHOOSE TO MAKE TODAY AND EVERY DAY GREAT AND BLESSED NO MATTER WHAT!

#PerpetualPraise #ContinualPrayer #WorshipInSpiritAndTruth

{DAY 344}

"Therefore the LORD will wait, that He may be gracious to you; and therefore He will be exalted, that He may have mercy on you. For the LORD is a God of justice; blessed are all those who wait for Him." **(Isaiah 30:18 NKJV)**

God sometimes delays in answering prayers. There are several instances of this in God's Word. Jacob had to wrestle for his blessing with the Lord's angel all night long and did not get his blessing from the angel until close to dawn. Paul requested three times that the Lord would remove from him the thorn in his flesh. Instead, Paul received a promise from God that His grace should be sufficient for him. Perhaps you have requested something from God, but have not yet received your requested blessing. I know I have as well. Our Heavenly Father God has reasons known only to Himself for keeping us waiting. Sometimes it is to show His Power and His Sovereignty, but usually, the delay is for our own spiritual good and profit. God knows that delay will increase our desire and cause us to seek Him more and pray with more fervency; that His mercy will have more meaning to us when we see our prayer answered; delay gives God opportunity to remove anything wrong from within us such as self-reliance, rather than trusting simply and entirely in our Lord Jesus; or that He may show you the riches of His grace, when your waiting is over. The prayers of God's saints are all filed in Heaven and are certainly not forgotten. We must not despair but must continue praying, even the more so and with more passion. In God's Way and in His perfect timing, our prayers will be fulfilled to our great joy! I worship You, oh God, for You are the God of Justice, Patience, Righteousness, Faithfulness, Grace, Mercy, and Truth! Lord Jesus, just as You patiently waited so very long for me, I will wait for You.

CHOOSE TO MAKE TODAY AND EVERY DAY GREAT AND BLESSED NO MATTER WHAT!

#PerpetualPraise #ContinualPrayer #WorshipInSpiritAndTruth

{DAY 345}

"God is faithful, by whom you were called into the fellowship of His Son, Jesus Christ our Lord." (1 Corinthians 1:9 NKJV)

God Himself calls you. You may be one who has read some of the Bible before, but your heart was not truly touched. Perhaps God has called you before, but you turned a deaf ear to His call. That was me for a very long time. I was a sinner who had no peace with God, with myself, or with others. I was mad at God and ran as far from Him as I could. However, one unforgettable evening at home, God totally arrested me with His Unconditional Love. I will never, ever forget! Thank You, God! I immediately stopped ignoring and fighting God, and yielded to God's call. I was totally drawn into the fellowship of Christ Jesus, and I knew without a doubt that it was due to the finger of God. I worship You, oh God, for You are Loving and Faithful and True! Now that Jesus is my Lord and Savior, through Him I DO have peace with God, with myself, and with others. Dear Jesus, I know You will keep me until You come again and forevermore. Dear precious reader(s), with heartfelt tears, I am praying this will be your testimony as well even now today, in the blessed Name of Jesus! Amen, amen, and amen!

CHOOSE TO MAKE TODAY AND EVERY DAY GREAT AND BLESSED NO MATTER WHAT!

#PerpetualPraise #ContinualPrayer #WorshipInSpiritAndTruth

{DAY 346}

PRAISE TO START YOUR DAY:

"...but whoever listens to me will live in safety and be at ease, without fear of harm." (Proverbs 1:33 NIV)

Great peace and security come to those who listen to God's wise instructions and then obey Him in love. Fear of evil will be replaced with tranquility. God takes special care of His people's security. God's people are safe. Come what may, true believers will be secure as in the calmest hour of rest. If God cannot save His people under Heaven, He will save them in Heaven. If the world becomes too hot to hold them, then they will be received in Heaven where they will be safe forevermore. Therefore, have no fear when you hear of wars and rumors of wars. Come what may upon the earth, KNOW that you will be secure. Stand upon God's promise and rest in His Faithfulness. As one of God's Own (and I pray you are), your only concern should be to show forth to the world the blessedness of listening to and obeying God's voice of wisdom. All my faith and trust is in You, Lord, and in You alone. Thank You for Your great peace and security!

CHOOSE TO MAKE TODAY AND EVERY DAY GREAT AND BLESSED NO MATTER WHAT!

#PerpetualPraise #ContinualPrayer #WorshipInSpiritAndTruth

{DAY 347}

PRAISE TO START YOUR DAY:

"But what does it say? "The word is near you, in your mouth and in your heart" (that is, the word of faith which we preach): that if you confess with your mouth the Lord Jesus and believe in your heart that God has raised Him from the dead, you will be saved. For with the heart, one believes unto righteousness, and with the mouth confession is made unto salvation." (Romans 10:8-10 NKJV)

It is with your heart that you believe and are made right with God. When you confess with your mouth that Jesus is Lord, you are making a profession of your faith and are saved. This will come to pass in your life if you believe it in your heart by faith, and then speak out loud the "Prayer of Salvation" directly to Jesus. You will be made righteous in Christ Jesus today, no matter what you are doing, or where you are in your life, even right now today. Jesus loves you, and He is with you now.

CHOOSE TO MAKE TODAY AND EVERY DAY GREAT AND BLESSED NO MATTER WHAT!

#PerpetualPraise #ContinualPrayer #WorshipInSpiritAndTruth

{DAY 348}

"The LORD will guide you continually, and satisfy your soul in drought, and strengthen your bones; you shall be like a watered garden, and like a spring of water, whose waters do not fail." (Isaiah 58:11 NKJV)

Thank You, Lord, that You promise to continually show me where I should go and what I should do and say, and You will keep me in a state of spiritual thriving and growing in You. You are my Soul Satisfier. You will sustain, preserve and strengthen my bones when I get frail and weary from age. I praise You for You are such an amazing, loving and caring God! I can't make it without You in my life, nor would I ever want to. You, oh God, are my Eternal Lifeline! I worship You!

CHOOSE TO MAKE TODAY AND EVERY DAY GREAT AND BLESSED NO MATTER WHAT!

#PerpetualPraise #ContinualPrayer #WorshipInSpiritAndTruth

{DAY 349}

"Or do you not know that your body is the temple of the Holy Spirit who is in you, whom you have from God, and you are not your own? For you were bought at a price; therefore glorify God in your body and in your spirit, which are God's." (1 Corinthians 6:19-20 NKJV)

When you believe by faith that you have been redeemed by the precious Blood of Christ Jesus, and invite Jesus into your heart, and confess Him as your very own personal Lord and Savior; then His Holy Spirit comes and lives inside of you in your spirit and in your heart, and you and Jesus become united as one. When our Heavenly Father sees you, He sees you as holy and righteous through the Blood of Christ Jesus. You are now a brand new creation from the inside to the outside. God has made all things about you new. Let your body reflect the brand new you through new godly living, new godly speech, new holy habits, new godly thoughts, and even through new modest dress attire. Let God plant you in a true word and worship church, and allow God to use you, with all the gifts and fruit you now have, to serve Him, His Kingdom and His saints. Now that you have a brand new spirit, with all the fruit of His Holy Spirit living in you and empowering you, be a living illustration of godliness. Everything about you should make others around you think of Jesus. Do this and you will be a great glorifier of God. This will bring you true joy—unspeakable joy—joy full of the glory of the Lord!

CHOOSE TO MAKE TODAY AND EVERY DAY GREAT AND BLESSED NO MATTER WHAT!

#PerpetualPraise #ContinualPrayer #WorshipInSpiritAndTruth

{DAY 350}

**"Obviously, I'm not trying to win the approval of people, but of God. If pleasing people were my goal, I would not be Christ's servant."
(Galatians 1:10 NLT)**

I do not seek popularity with people. I seek to please God because I love Him. Everyone must choose to please and serve God, or man. It is impossible to do both. By not choosing, you have still chosen. As one of God's servants, I seek to share God's truth, God's whole truth, and nothing but God's truth always (without sugar-coating it or watering it down), because God's truth is what lost souls need to be able to receive the faith necessary to be saved and made right with God by His Amazing Grace. Faith comes by hearing, and by hearing the Truth of the Word of God. I will never bow to man, nor apologize to man, for choosing God over man. I belong to God, and God belongs to me. I am on the Lord's side, and the Lord is on my side. I am the Lord's constant companion, and the Lord is my Constant Companion. I boast ONLY in the Lord, never of myself.

CHOOSE TO MAKE TODAY AND EVERY DAY GREAT AND BLESSED NO MATTER WHAT!

#PerpetualPraise #ContinualPrayer #WorshipInSpiritAndTruth

{DAY 351}

"The LORD shall reign forever—your God, O Zion, to all generations. Praise the LORD!" (Psalm 146:10 NKJV)

This is a call to all to unite in praising God. His Kingdom shall continue throughout all eternity. Knowing that God is all Sovereign should bring great delight to His people. Knowing that God reigns forever on His Throne should make His people shout their "Hallelujah's" with all their heart, with all their strength, and with all their might. This truth should make us glorify God and give thanks to Jesus—always praising and worshiping God, always trusting in God, always blessing and pleasing God with our faith in Him! Praise the Lord! HALLELUJAH!

CHOOSE TO MAKE TODAY AND EVERY DAY GREAT AND BLESSED NO MATTER WHAT!

#PerpetualPraise #ContinualPrayer #WorshipInSpiritAndTruth

{DAY 352}

"But be doers of the word, and not hearers only, deceiving yourselves. For if anyone is a hearer of the word and not a doer, he is like a man observing his natural face in a mirror; for he observes himself, goes away, and immediately forgets what kind of man he was. But he who looks into the perfect law of liberty and continues in it, and is not a forgetful hearer but a doer of the work, this one will be blessed in what he does." (James 1:22-25 NKJV)

Just as we use a mirror to observe our natural makeup, we must use God's Word to observe our spiritual makeup. We see imperfections in our natural makeup and, with the help of a lighted mirror and to the best of our ability, we do all we can do to correct and improve on those imperfections, until we are pleased with what we see and feel confident that we can now present our natural selves to the public in an approving manner. God's Word is our spiritual mirror, which shows us our spiritual imperfections and guides us as to how to correct and improve on those imperfections. We must use our spiritual eyes and ears to hear what the truth and light of God's Word is showing and telling us. Then, we must remember and be obedient, and DO what God's Word has said so that we will be received by God and accepted as holy and righteous through Christ Jesus. Glory to God!

CHOOSE TO MAKE TODAY AND EVERY DAY GREAT AND BLESSED NO MATTER WHAT!

#PerpetualPraise #ContinualPrayer #WorshipInSpiritAndTruth

{DAY 353}

"The LORD shall reign for ever and ever." (Exodus 15:18 KJV)

This Scripture is very simplistic, yet contains great truth and force. It expresses faith in God's Everlasting Kingdom. The reign of the Lord Jesus Christ began in eternity. He reigned throughout the whole Old Testament dispensation and was acknowledged as well as prophesied of as a King. In His state of humiliation He had a Kingdom, though not of this world, and upon His ascension to Heaven, He was made and declared Lord and Christ. Since His ascension to Heaven, He has ruled by His Holy Spirit and grace in the hearts of many men. Time itself shall not put a period to the reign of our Lord Jesus Christ which, like Himself, is Eternal. Oh God, You are glorified and honored today and every day!

CHOOSE TO MAKE TODAY AND EVERY DAY GREAT AND BLESSED NO MATTER WHAT!

#PerpetualPraise #ContinualPrayer #WorshipInSpiritAndTruth

{DAY 354}

"But joyful are those who have the God of Israel as their helper, whose hope is in the LORD their God. He made heaven and earth, the sea, and everything in them. He keeps every promise forever." (Psalm 146:5-6 NLT)

Joyful are those who turn to God and depend on Him for help, those whose hope is in the Lord their God. Those who trust in God are happy, for they will never be ashamed. The Lord never dies, nor His thoughts. His mercy, like Himself, endures throughout all generations. He who made the earth can preserve us while we are on earth, and help us to make good use of it. He who made the sea and all its mysteries can lead and guide us across the deeps of a troubled life, and make a way, where there is no way, for His redeemed to pass over. He who still keeps the world in existence is more than able to keep us, His people, to His Eternal Kingdom and Glory. Oh, how blessed it is to know that God is our present help and our eternal hope! My spirit remains joy filled! Hallelujah!

CHOOSE TO MAKE TODAY AND EVERY DAY GREAT AND BLESSED NO MATTER WHAT!

#PerpetualPraise #ContinualPrayer #WorshipInSpiritAndTruth

{DAY 355}

"Let us be glad and rejoice and give Him glory, for the marriage of the Lamb has come, and His wife has made herself ready." And to her it was granted to be arrayed in fine linen, clean and bright, for the fine linen is the righteous acts of the saints. Then he said to me, "Write: 'Blessed are those who are called to the marriage supper of the Lamb!'" And he said to me, "These are the true sayings of God.'" (Revelation 19:7-9 NKJV)

In the Old Testament, God likened His relationship to Israel as a husband and wife. In the New Testament, the church is declared to be the bride of Christ. In this Scripture, an announcement is made that the time has come for the marriage of the Lamb and that His wife has made herself ready. It was granted that she should be clothed in fine linen, clean and white. We are told that the fine linen is the righteousness of the saints, which is accounted to them by God because of their faith in Christ Jesus. The words in this Scripture are true sayings of God Himself! How happy they will be who are invited to the marriage supper of the Lamb! Have you ever thought of where you will be when all of this is taking place? You will be in one of three places: You might be in Hell; you might be on earth having survived all of the hell on earth during the tribulation period, after all, the true Christians have already been removed and taken to safety in glorious Heaven; or you will be among those standing in Heaven clothed in the righteousness of Christ, hearing these glorious announcements concerning the marriage of the Lamb and the invitation to the marriage feast. My heart's desire is to be in Heaven among those who are invited to the marriage supper of the Lamb. I am sure that is your heart's desire, too. That is why I am serving God in a true word and worship church, and because I truly and wholeheartedly believe every one of God's written words. Glory to the Lamb of God!

CHOOSE TO MAKE TODAY AND EVERY DAY GREAT AND BLESSED NO MATTER WHAT!

#PerpetualPraise #ContinualPrayer #WorshipInSpiritAndTruth

{DAY 356}

"Keep me as the apple of Your eye; hide me under the shadow of Your wings," (Psalm 17:8 NKJV)

You are the apple of God's eye! God guards, protects, and treats you with the utmost of His care, just as the natural man does with the pupil of his natural eye because the pupil is the most vulnerable part of the natural eye. No part of the body is more precious, more tender, and more carefully guarded than the eye; and of the eye, no portion is to be more protected than the central apple, or the pupil. The all-wise Creator has placed the eye in a very well-protected position. The eye is surrounded by projecting bones like Jerusalem encircled by mountains. God, the Creator, has also surrounded the eye with inward coverings, in addition to the eyebrows, the eyelids, and the eyelashes. No member of the body is more faithfully cared for and guarded than the organ of sight. The pupil is the little opening in the middle of the eye through which the rays of light pass to form an image, and it also controls the amount of light that passes through. God sees your reflection in His pupil! Just as the Creator placed the eye in a very well-protected position, God also shields His sons and daughters from evil by covering them with His wings, because our Heavenly Father's love for us is perfect. We are so blessed! We adore You, Father God!

CHOOSE TO MAKE TODAY AND EVERY DAY GREAT AND BLESSED NO MATTER WHAT!

#PerpetualPraise #ContinualPrayer #WorshipInSpiritAndTruth

{DAY 357}

"Keep my commands and you will live; guard my teachings as the apple of your eye." (Proverbs 7:2 NIV)

The first part of this Scripture is a promise from God in the form of a command. In the last part, we are instructed by God to guard and keep His teachings with all possible care and diligence, as men guard the eye. The eye is most necessary, and therefore is a most valued and treasured part of the body; and the apple of the eye, or the pupil, is the most honorable, beautiful, and useful part of the eye. The pupil is the most tender part, most easily hurt or destroyed, and therefore needs to be diligently watched and guarded. So, in effect, God is comparing the vital importance of guarding His teachings to being the same value and degree of importance as a man guarding the apple, or pupil, of his eye. We praise and thank You, Lord, for all Your commandments, instructions, and teachings. We understand they are all for our best interest because You love us.

CHOOSE TO MAKE TODAY AND EVERY DAY GREAT AND BLESSED NO MATTER WHAT!

#PerpetualPraise #ContinualPrayer #WorshipInSpiritAndTruth

{DAY 358}

"Now after Jesus was born in Bethlehem of Judea in the days of Herod the king, behold, wise men from the East came to Jerusalem, saying, "Where is He who has been born King of the Jews? For we have seen His star in the East and have come to worship Him...and behold, the star which they had seen in the East went before them, till it came and stood over where the young Child was. When they saw the star, they rejoiced with exceedingly great joy. And when they had come into the house, they saw the young Child with Mary His mother, and fell down and worshiped Him. And when they had opened their treasures, they presented gifts to Him: gold, frankincense, and myrrh." (Matthew 2:1-2,9-11 NKJV)

Just as His bright star guided the wise men to the exact place where Jesus was, He draws and guides us to Him even now today. In the Bible, gold represents the Divinity and Kingship of Christ Jesus; frankincense represents the prayers of the saints, flowing up to God as a pleasing aroma; and myrrh represents Christ's death and resurrection. If we walk in the Light, as God is in the Light, and have fellowship with Him; then we, too, shall shine as God's light-bearers, and our whole life shall be as the star which guided the wise men to Christ—influencing men for God. We bow down and worship You, Lord, and acknowledge You as our Sovereign and Divine Lord of Lords and King of Kings! We praise and worship You, Christ Jesus, for sacrificing Your very life for us when You died on the cross for one and all! We acknowledge and confess that You are no longer that Baby Jesus laying in the manger, nor are You still on the cross at Calvary, but YOU, JESUS ARE ALIVE TODAY! YOU ARE THE ONE AND ONLY TRUE AND LIVING GOD! HALLELUJAH!

CHOOSE TO MAKE TODAY AND EVERY DAY GREAT AND BLESSED NO MATTER WHAT!

#PerpetualPraise #ContinualPrayer #WorshipInSpiritAndTruth

{DAY 359}

"God reigns over the nations; God sits on His holy throne." (Psalm 47:8 NKJV)

Our Sovereign God has universal dominion over all the nations. God also reigns over the heathen (or unbelievers) when, by the preaching of the Gospel, they are brought into Christ's church. He is a holy God; He declares with strong emphasis the importance of holiness. God's laws are holy, He requires holiness, and His genuine people are all holy. The throne of His holiness is Heaven and in the hearts of the faithful. Our Lord God reigns! Let's sing praises to our Lord, and worship Him forevermore, for He alone is Worthy of all glory, praise, honor, power and thanksgiving!

CHOOSE TO MAKE TODAY AND EVERY DAY GREAT AND BLESSED NO MATTER WHAT!

#PerpetualPraise #ContinualPrayer #WorshipInSpiritAndTruth

{DAY 360}

"For the LORD is good. His unfailing love continues forever, and his faithfulness continues to each generation." (Psalm 100:5 NLT)

We should praise the Lord for He is a good God! He is not a being of mere power, and He is not merely the Creator; but God is good, well-meaning, and rich in lovingkindness, and is, therefore, worthy of universal praise. Our God is a God Whose love softens His power; a God Whose power magnifies His love. God is worthy of praise and honor and true worship. We could not love, praise, or truly worship a being of mere power. A being whose power was united with an intense ill will could only be the object of hatred and terror; but a being whose power is united with goodness, well-meaning, and love ought to be loved, praised and worshiped. Our God is the God of goodness, mercy, unfailing and all-conquering love, truth and faithfulness, Who shows Himself to be faithful to His promises to all generations. Open your hearts to see that the only God Whom men can love is God in Christ. We worship You, oh God, in spirit and in truth, for You are Worthy!

CHOOSE TO MAKE TODAY AND EVERY DAY GREAT AND BLESSED NO MATTER WHAT!

#PerpetualPraise #ContinualPrayer #WorshipInSpiritAndTruth

{DAY 361}

"Now to the King eternal, immortal, invisible, to God who alone is wise, be honor and glory forever and ever. Amen." (1 Timothy 1:17 NKJV)

We serve the one and only infinite, limitless, boundless, never-ending Great God! He is the King of the Ages. He alone has all wisdom; the only wise God; and the Giver of wisdom! God alone is worthy of all honor and glory forevermore! When we think of the goodness of the Lord and all He has done for us, and how far He has brought us from where He found us, we cannot hold our praise in, but must give Him a holy outburst of praise! As true Christians, may we have a continual warmth of thankfulness in our hearts, and may our lives always be filled with outbursts of praise unto our Lord, in the blessed Name of Jesus! Amen, amen, and amen!

CHOOSE TO MAKE TODAY AND EVERY DAY GREAT AND BLESSED NO MATTER WHAT!

#PerpetualPraise #ContinualPrayer #WorshipInSpiritAndTruth

{DAY 362}

"Keep a cool head. Stay alert. The Devil is poised to pounce, and would like nothing better than to catch you napping. Keep your guard up. You're not the only ones plunged into these hard times. It's the same with Christians all over the world. So keep a firm grip on the faith. The suffering won't last forever. It won't be long before this generous God who has great plans for us in Christ—eternal and glorious plans they are!—will have you put together and on your feet for good. He gets the last word; yes, he does." (1 Peter 5:10-11 MSG)

Don't get slack; stay alert! Satan knows full well that his time is very short now on the earth, and he is taking every opportunity he is given, and entering everywhere there is a crack in the door, in order to steal, kill, and destroy as much and as many lives as he can now. Keep fighting the Good Fight for your faith, holding on to it tight as you can, and keep standing on your faith. Jesus is coming back soon and very soon for us, if we don't quit. We know who wins anyway. God has already won, so we have already won! Don't give in, or faint, right at the finish line! God gets the last word—His Word—and God has already established that!!!

CHOOSE TO MAKE TODAY AND EVERY DAY GREAT AND BLESSED NO MATTER WHAT!

#PerpetualPraise #ContinualPrayer #WorshipInSpiritAndTruth

{DAY 363}

"When Moses came down from Mount Sinai with the two tablets of the covenant law in his hands, he was not aware that his face was radiant because he had spoken with the LORD." (Exodus 34:29 NIV)

God allowed Moses to witness eternal glory to the extent that the skin of his face shined radiantly. God had seen Moses' inward holiness. The brilliance of the glory of Christ Jesus far exceeds the glory which was seen on the face of Moses. What honor God may put upon any one of us, if we really put honor upon God! If you are made holy unto God as Moses was, He can give you an influence which you may be unaware of, but which others will be forced to recognize. The heavenly light of divine grace will rest upon you! All glory to God, the Giver of glory!

CHOOSE TO MAKE TODAY AND EVERY DAY GREAT AND BLESSED NO MATTER WHAT!

#PerpetualPraise #ContinualPrayer #WorshipInSpiritAndTruth

{DAY 364}

"And He Himself gave some to be apostles, some prophets, some evangelists, and some pastors and teachers, for the equipping of the saints for the work of ministry, for the edifying of the body of Christ, till we all come to the unity of the faith and of the knowledge of the Son of God, to a perfect man, to the measure of the stature of the fullness of Christ; that we should no longer be children, tossed to and fro and carried about with every wind of doctrine, by the trickery of men, in the cunning craftiness of deceitful plotting, but, speaking the truth in love, may grow up in all things into Him who is the head—Christ—from whom the whole body, joined and knit together by what every joint supplies, according to the effective working by which every part does its share, causes growth of the body for the edifying of itself in love."
(Ephesians 4:11-16 NKJV)

God's callings and giftings on His people as individuals are not all alike, and not all equals. God's people are not all called and gifted to do the same work. Jesus Christ gave a variety of different gifts. Therefore, whatever spiritual gifts we have been given, they are not our own to use as we please; they are only entrusted to us that we may use them to help our fellow-Christians. As brothers and sisters in Christ, we are one with Christ, and we are one with each other. Therefore, an important question every Christian should be asking is, "How can I best use my God-given calling and gifts for the benefit of the rest of the members of the Church?" The Word of God contains much spiritual nourishment. Those who are as infants, new in Christ's family, need to be nurtured by receiving spiritual milk; those who are already strong in the Lord and in understanding of God's Word desire the strong meat of His Word; but all need to be fed. Every part of the human body has its own special function. With certainty, God has created no part of our body in vain. It is the same in the body of Christ, every Christian has his own calling and gifting—his own ministry—something he can do that nobody else can do; and our great objective should be to find out what that ministry is, and to give our whole strength to it in love, for the nourishing and edification of the entire body of Christ.

CHOOSE TO MAKE TODAY AND EVERY DAY GREAT AND BLESSED NO MATTER WHAT!

#PerpetualPraise #ContinualPrayer #WorshipInSpiritAndTruth

{DAY 365}

PRAISE TO START YOUR DAY:

"May the grace of the Lord Jesus Christ, the love of God, and the fellowship of the Holy Spirit be with you all." (2 Corinthians 13:14 NLT)

May the grace of the Lord Jesus Christ (the free and unmerited favor of God, as manifested in the salvation of sinners and the bestowal of blessings) be with you all; may the love of God (that love which brings salvation, imparts comfort, pardons sin, sanctifies the soul, and fills the heart with joy and peace) be shown towards you all and be manifested in each of your lives; and may the fellowship of the Holy Spirit (by Whom the Father and Son communicate their love and grace to the saints) be with you all. I pray that God will bestow these blessings upon each and every dear reader of this book, in the blessed Name of Jesus! Amen, amen, and amen! Jesus loves each and every one of you, as do I!

CHOOSE TO MAKE TODAY AND EVERY DAY GREAT AND BLESSED NO MATTER WHAT!

#PerpetualPraise #ContinualPrayer #WorshipInSpiritAndTruth

Oh Lord my God, how I do praise and worship Thee! Verily, verily, my Jesus, I say unto Thee, 'There is none like You, there is none like You'.

On the 26th of November in the year 2000, led by Your Holy Spirit, came I to the altar. Face down, knees bowed, wearing my heart on my sleeve, my salvation was secured in Thee. Glory to God! My Jesus set me free! Finally, at long last, free from the condemnation of my past! I was filled up with Your Holy Spirit and then baptized in water in the Name of Jesus, Name above all names!

Oh Lord, I know it took me longer than most and repeated visits from Your Holy Ghost. All those years I could only see the devil winning. Only You could see the end from the beginning. Oh Lord, only You knew the true desires of my heart. Oh Lord, only You saw a soul worth saving, from the very start. Verily, verily, my Jesus, I say unto Thee, 'There is none like You, there is none like You'.

Through faith, I finally understand and have fully received the cleansing power of Your precious blood; that only You shed for a wretch like me on Calvary because of Your Amazing Grace and Unconditional Love. No longer have I a past; now I am living! I'm a new creation in You, Lord, with a brand new beginning. Old things have passed away and all things are brand new. A past I have no longer; I'm now a living sacrifice in Christ and growing every stronger. Oh my Jesus, verily, verily, I say unto Thee, 'There is none like You, there is none like You'.

Since that glorious day, Oh Lord, You have taken me from faith to faith, glory to glory, and victory to sweet victory. I will praise and worship Thee for all eternity. My Jesus, only You are my All In All. Only in You can I stand so tall and never have to fall. Oh Lord, only in You I know my worth and, with the keys You have given me, I am in Heavenly places right here on earth! Jesus, You truly are the Lover of My Soul! I owe You my life for not letting me go! Jesus, verily, verily, I say unto Thee, 'There is none like You, there is none like You'.

In You, my Jesus, I can only go higher and higher as I lift You up; letting the world know how awesomely faithful to me You have been, and how to them You will be, as well; until in the clouds You come again!

Only in You, Oh Lord my God, have I true joy and pleasure and only in You have I treasure without measure. Only in You, my precious Jesus, only in You. Verily, verily, I say unto Thee, 'There is none like You, there is none like You'.

Oh Lord, how I desire to be more like You, in everything I think, say, and do. So, day by day, in Your Word will I stay. For Your Word is Truth and Light and Life; so on Your Word shall I meditate both day and night. Lord, I will keep Your Word hidden in my heart. Oh Lord, like David my father before me, I, too, desire a heart after Your own heart. Thank You, my Lord, all my praise and worship to You do I impart! Oh Lord, my God! How I thank Thee for creating me for Your own pleasure; for by my praise and worship to You, my joy is complete, even without measure! Verily, verily, I say unto Thee, 'There is none like You, there is none like You'.

Oh Lord my God, unto You is given all the Glory for the greatest, age-old Gospel story and all Your Power that is in it to bring lost sinners to true repentance. Experiencing God and Heaven has only just begun! To quote my Pastor Steve Fender, "The best is yet to come!" My precious Jesus, verily, verily, I say unto Thee, 'There is none like You, there is none like You'.

SPECIAL ACKNOWLEDGEMENTS

My Spiritual Father, Bishop Steve Fender, who has generously shared and instilled tremendous insight into God's Word and whose two-fold agenda for his congregation of saints is eternal life and living life more abundantly. Through his preaching of God's Word, Bishop Steve has taken me from being a spiritual infant, to being a spiritual child of God, to now being a spiritual adult and daughter of the Most High God. You have been a refresher of my soul and taught me how to grow my faith. Thank you so much, Bishop Steve. You are the most unwavering Christian Pastor I know. I love you and praise God for you always! God has used you mightily in my life-transformation, and I praise and worship Him and give God all the glory!

My Spiritual Mother and Living Praise Choir Director/ Chenaniah, Senior Pastor Becky Fender, who has taught me according to God's Word and by her own life's example: (1) what it truly means to be a Woman of God; (2) what it truly means to be a Disciple and Follower of Christ Jesus; (3) what it truly means to be like Jesus; (4) how to be a praiser and a worshiper; (5) that obedience is better than sacrifice; (6) that everything in life is a choice—including the thoughts you choose to think, the actions you choose to take, the things you choose to do, the words you choose to say, the places you choose to go, the people you choose to be with, the clothes you choose to wear—literally everything; (7) what it truly means to be a Proverbs 31 Woman; and (8) what it truly means to be a godly Christian wife, mother and grandmother. The list could go on and on. When I first came to Livingway Church in 1998, I could not get past your awesome singing voice. Then I began to hear you preach to the Lively Ladies and then to the No Matter What Women. I thought, "Wow! This Christian Woman of God does everything with awesomeness!" Pastor Becky, I love and admire you so much! I praise God for you always! God has used you mightily in my life-transformation, and I praise and worship Him and give God all the glory!

My Pastor, Pastor Brandon Fender, who is a powerfully anointed Pastor and who has instructed me on how to become, not a mere disciple of Christ Jesus but, an apostle with the knowledge and understanding to know the difference. Thank you for increasing and enlightening my knowledge and understanding about praise, through your sermon on the seven different types of praise. When I first became a member of Livingway Church, you were a youth at that time. God has graced me with the blessing of seeing you grow into the powerfully anointed Pastor you are today, as well as a wonderful Christian husband and father. Your preaching encourages me to go even deeper and higher in Christ and to do even greater works! Thank you so much, Pastor

Brandon. I am most grateful that you answered the call of God to Pastor. I love you and praise God for you always!

My Pastor, Pastor Amanda Fender, who is an anointed, gifted, loving, and faith-filled Pastor and author. Pastor Mandy, you exemplify the Love of God and your personal love for God through your preaching and leading of the EmpowHer Ministry, through your authoring, and in all you do and say. I praise God that you answered the call of God to preach and minister to Christian women of God, both from the pulpit and through your anointed gift of Christian writing. Years ago, God planted the seed in me to become an author and you watered that seed when you chose me to author my personal testimony in your book "Ridiculous Redemption". In addition, your Defier Series books, so rich and full of faith-filled Scriptures, took me to a deeper and higher dimension in God and again watered the authoring seed God had already planted in me. God planted the seed in me, Pastor/Author Mandy Fender watered it, and God made it grow and is giving the increase (*1 Corinthians 3:6*). You have been God's instrument in the fulfillment of my destiny. I love you and thank you so much! I praise God for you always! I praise and worship God and give Him all the glory!

My Pastor, Associate Pastor Sean Fender, who loves God and His people and who answered God's call and has given his life to full-time ministry at Livingway Church. Since coming to Livingway Church in 1998, God has graced me with hearing you preach from time to time. You have preached some of the most profound and memorable sermons I have been blessed to hear and receive at Livingway Church. Though your full-time ministry is not directly in the pulpit, it is certainly no less valuable to Livingway Church and to God's Kingdom. Thank you so much, Pastor Sean. I love you and praise God for you always! You are such a blessing! I praise and worship God and give Him all the glory!

My Livingway Church Family, who has shown me the Love of Jesus from my very first visit. There is no place I would rather be than in the presence of God in His house united with my Livingway Church Family, as we praise and worship and fellowship together with God and each other. We are the apple of God's eye, and you all are the apple of my eye. I love you all from here to Heaven and throughout all eternity, and I praise God for you always! I praise and worship God and give Him all the glory!

While writing this book, I received four individual confirmations from God through four of my Livingway Church Family Members, as follows: (1) **Sister Rachel Becerra** on Sunday, October 16, 2016; (2) **Brother Chris**

Vara on Tuesday, October 18, 2016; (3) **Sister Carol Foster** on Wednesday, October 19, 2016; and (4) **Bishop Steve Fender** (from the pulpit) on Wednesday, October 26, 2016. Whether any of you were aware, or not, God used you and I am eternally grateful.

About the Author

JoAnn Koening is a Christian who loves God and the Kingdom of God. She has built her temporal home on earth, as well as her eternal home in Heaven, in Jesus. She lives in His presence through perpetual praise, continual prayer, and worshiping Him in spirit and in truth.

She was born in Houston, Texas, and currently lives in San Antonio, Texas, with her beloved Christian husband Mark Koening. Mark and JoAnn have been married over 18 years. JoAnn has one grown son, two grown daughters, and two grandchildren; Stacy Davis, Jack Davis, Jr., Jeanna Davis Freeman, Tarry Hewitt, and Trista Hewitt.

JoAnn has faithfully served in Living Praise Choir for 18 years at Livingway Church in San Antonio, Texas, and participates in other ministries.

JoAnn is an Ambassador for Christ Jesus and represents Praise and Worship. She has a willing heart to obey God and a strong desire to always please God; is wholeheartedly committed to glorifying God; and a compassion to encourage and help others and give others hope in God, who are walking where she once walked and struggling as she once struggled.

CONNECT WITH JOANN

Facebook: https://www.facebook.com/joannkoening/

Twitter: https://twitter.com/JoAnnKoening

Instagram: https://www.instagram.com/joannkoening/

Pinterest: https://www.pinterest.com/15c9mh4o5n0yo6j/

Goodreads: https://www.goodreads.com/author/show/16265286.JoAnn_Koening

Google+: https://plus.google.com/u/0/+JoAnnKoening

Linkedin: https://www.linkedin.com/groups/12025488

Website: joannkoening.com

www.ingramcontent.com/pod-product-compliance
Lightning Source LLC
Chambersburg PA
CBHW071403090426
42737CB00011B/1332